C000055910

HARMONIOUS ALLIANCE

Harmonious Alliance

A HISTORY OF THE
PERFORMING RIGHT SOCIETY

CYRIL EHRLICH

Oxford   New York
OXFORD UNIVERSITY PRESS
1989

Oxford University Press, Walton Street, Oxford OX2 6DP
Oxford New York Toronto
Delhi Bombay Calcutta Madras Karachi
Petaling Jaya Singapore Hong Kong Tokyo
Nairobi Dar es Salaam Cape Town
Melbourne Auckland
and associated companies in
Berlin Ibadan

Oxford is a trade mark of Oxford University Press

Published in the United States
by Oxford University Press, New York

© The Performing Right Society 1989

All rights reserved. No part of this publication may be reproduced,
stored in a retrieval system, or transmitted, in any form or by any means,
electronic, mechanical, photocopying, recording, or otherwise, without
the prior permission of Oxford University Press

British Library Cataloguing in Publication Data
Ehrlich, Cyril
Harmonious alliance: a history of The Performing Right Society.
1. Great Britain. Music. Performing
rights. Organisations. Performing Right
Society
I. Title
344. 1064'82
ISBN 0–19–311924–2

Library of Congress Cataloging-in-Publication Data
Ehrlich, Cyril.
Harmonious alliance: a history of the Performing Right Society /
Cyril Ehrlich.
p.cm.
Bibliography: p.
Includes index.
1. Performing Right Society—History. 2. Copyright—Performing
rights—Great Britain—History. 3. Copyright—Music—Great Britian-
-History.   I Title.
ML27. G7P443 1989   88–15612
780'.6'041—dc19
ISBN 0–19–311924–2:

Set by Pentacor Limited, High Wycombe, Bucks
Printed in Great Britain
at the University Printing House, Oxford
by David Stanford
Printer to the University

For Joshua

PREFACE

An official history is not usually of much concern to the general reader. Occasioned by the pious requirements of an anniversary, or a desire for publicity, it can fall into the category of 'vanity publishing'. The style of such compilations is familiar. Proclaiming relentless significance and unblemished virtue; parading drab groups of hitherto anonymous individuals whose lives, if worthy, remain unremarkable; exhibiting photographs better left in boardrooms and family albums: the commemorative volume may please its sponsors, but will be easily rejected by the public. There are occasions, however, when an institution deserves wider attention, because it has involved interesting people, or because its activities have had extensive influence. On both grounds the Performing Right Society qualifies for such attention. For seventy-five years it has occupied a central, though rarely a prominent, place in the cultural upheaval of our times; and its membership list provides the roll call for a parade of British music.

During the twentieth century music became ubiquitous and inescapable, the product of a vast industry, with few political, social, or economic barriers. The PRS was not directly responsible for this upheaval, of course, but its role was strategic. It is a commonplace that new technologies—gramophone, radio, television and, above all, tape recording,—have initiated a complete realignment of our musical life, and of music itself. Less familiar, but equally significant, is the fact that these technologies have also disrupted, endangered, and transformed the composer's livelihood. In the nineteenth century there were two ways for him to earn a living, more often a pittance: from the sale or hire of sheet music, or by exacting a fee for performance. The latter alternative was pioneered in France, with appropriate legislation and elaborate, but effective, administrative procedures. It was then adopted in other countries, along with a Gallic legal vocabulary. Frequently it was administered at first by representatives of the French *Société des Auteurs, Compositeurs, et Editeurs de Musique* (SACEM), and later by the formation of indigenous societies. The collection of *grands droits* for big theatre works, was comparatively easy to organize because only prominent locations had to be monitored. The administration of *petits droits*, which entailed collecting fees from a multitude of locations, was potentially more remunerative. But it was also far more complex, expensive, and problematical. As technology took command of the market, sales of sheet music began to fall away, and eventually they dwindled into insignificance. Slowly, but inexorably the effective administration of *petits droits* became an essential precondition for the survival of the composer and of live music. This book attempts to explain how the PRS perceived and attempted to meet that challenge, providing indispensable service as a link between consumers and producers of music.

If the Society's story merits attention, its members and staff also deserve more than a passing glance. They were once described by the historian, Lord Briggs, as a 'glorious coalition' bringing together 'the different forces within the world of music'.[1] Like most successful coalitions it represents a compromise between an eclectic diversity of interests; an alliance, sometimes uneasy, often incongruous, but in the last analysis necessary and benign. Incongruity becomes apparent in the juxtaposition of members' names, past and present. Many are instantly recognizable, from Edward Elgar, Gustav Holst, and Michael Tippett, to Vivian Ellis, Eric Coates, and the Beatles. Others may no longer be so familiar, though their music was once part of everyday life, and may even re-emerge from time to time in new guise, as 'themes' or 'background' for film or television. To take but one case, F. J. Ricketts, once musical director of the Royal Marines, wrote many marches under the name of 'Kenneth Alford'. In 1916 he published 'Colonel Bogey', which became, in a sense, *the* military march for a generation and two world wars. Then, fifty years after its composition, it was worked into Malcolm Arnold's brilliant score for *The Bridge on the River Kwai*, recorded, whistled, sung, and played all over the world. It is the PRS which ensures that such composers, or their successors, are recompensed for their original input of creative talent. The most anonymous members of the alliance, rarely mentioned in history books and musical dictionaries, are the publishers, administrators, and staff. Some, like Leslie Boosey, have exerted a crucial, if largely unacknowledged, influence in shaping the music of our century. Many have provided devoted service, without which the whole immensely complex organization would long ago have fallen apart, wreaking havoc upon music in this country.

C. E.

---

[1] *Performing Right*, May 1975, 5.

ACKNOWLEDGEMENTS

No one can write the history of a large, complex, and vital institution without continuous assistance from the people who make it work. My principal indebtedness, therefore, is to the PRS management and staff who answered my queries and patiently explained the intricacies of their jobs. I hope that those not specifically mentioned below will realize how grateful I am to them. But first I must thank Peter Dadswell for allowing me to see some records of the Music Publishers' Association, and Andrew Roberts for general stimulus and advice. My PRS tutorials began with David Vidgen, who provided tactful guidance on my first visits to Berners Street. Gordon Jones brought a lifetime of experience to his shrewd, amusing, and highly informative reminiscences. George Neighbour, immensely knowledgeable about all kinds of music and musicians, was a constant source of stimulus and understanding. Michael Hudson explained licensing, past and present, with infectious enthusiasm. Tony Ghilchik prepared and elucidated statistics, and advised on their presentation. Nicholas Lowe was not only sympathetic to a layman's bewilderment, attempting to educate me in appropriate branches of the law, but maintained a steady, morale-boosting interest in the project. Ruth Beltram, similarly, provided legal expertise and generous support. Jonathan Hodgetts took the brunt of my incessant requests for files, reports, and papers, unearthing, and occasionally dusting, hidden treasure from Hays Wharf. Celia Smith provided access to the beautifully preserved board and committee minutes, and John Logan to thousands of members' application forms, never failing to produce the relevant document on demand. Peter Stroud explained such arcane mysteries as the system of music classification, and Andy Walsh provided a much-needed crash course in pop. Lesley Bray deserves special mention, for without her the work would never have progressed. Tireless in arranging interviews, organizing comfortable working facilities, charming away difficulties, and concealing my incompetence and tactlessness, her ability to cope with 'the professor' was a virtuoso demonstration of public relations. Several of her colleagues shared these burdens with comparable skill, notably Eileen Stow, and, particularly, Wendy Brooks, who devotedly undertook numerous chores in the final stages, before going to press.

Two retired pillars of the Society, who figure prominently in the following pages, were immensely helpful. Denis de Freitas reduced a plethora of detail so lucidly as to suggest that analysis and appraisal was a simple task. Royce Whale was too ill to see me, but left copious notes for a projected history, with many pointers to research. Several members of the Society assisted in various ways, but I must particularly place on record my indebtedess to Christopher Morris, and to Hero de Rance, whose recollections of an extraordinary life in the music business provided one of the most memorable and enjoyable hours spent in researching this book. Three distinguished and very busy men took a close and fruitful interest in the book's progress. Vivian Ellis was, unsurprisingly and in equal measure, charming, funny, informative, and stimulating. I treasure several idiosyncratic letters from him, and an inscribed copy of his memoirs. Ron White was more austere, but no less supportive. Donald Mitchell, formidably qualified in three relevant skills, music, writing, and publishing, gave me more time than I had any right to expect, and was generous in drawing my attention to some Britten letters. Finally, I cannot adequately express my indebtedness to Michael Freegard. No one matches his profound experience and encyclopaedic knowledge of the subject, in all its international ramifications, balanced by a unique ability to see the wood for the trees. Indeed, it requires what can only be described as chutzpah for a novice to write on these matters and submit the result to Freegard for comment. Unfailingly generous, despite an overloaded timetable, he answered queries, corrected numerous errors, challenged interpretations, but never attempted to manipulate ultimate judgements. His forbearance in these circumstances has been quite remarkable; but, of course, neither he, nor any of the people mentioned above can be held responsible for any inadequacies in the present volume. That responsibility is mine.

CONTENTS

ILLUSTRATIONS

The signatures featured in the jacket illustration are those of Gustav Holst, Vivian Ellis, Arthur Bliss, John Lennon, Paul McCartney, and Benjamin Britten

I

BEGINNING

The Performing Right Society was launched in 1914. Its début was late, long after the equivalent event in France (where SACEM, established in 1851, became the prototype for all such organizations), and later than Italy (1882), Austria (1897), Spain (1901), and Germany (1903). Among countries with a music industry of comparable size, only the United States was equally tardy. Why was there so long a delay? Surely British composers and publishers were aware of this potential source of income, particularly after 1886, when Britain acceded to the Berne Convention for the Protection of Literary and Artistic Works. The French Society then began to employ agents in London and the provinces to collect fees for performances of foreign, but not British, music. It seems inevitable that such preferential treatment would have incurred resentment and stimulated organization. In fact, there were a few desultory discussions about possible initiatives, but such was the balance of power within the industry, and the prevailing climate of opinion among producers and users of music, that nothing came of these aspirations. Therefore, when the Society was eventually launched it represented so great a break with the past, and appeared to be so precarious, disunited, and, as fate decreed, ill timed, that its mere survival remained uncertain for at least another decade. Eventually it succeeded, to such effect that performing right could be acknowledged, by an eminent publisher with a lifetime of experience, as doing 'more than anything else to change the economic status of composers'.[1] It is impossible to appreciate the scale of this extraordinary achievement without first understanding how uncertainly and tentatively it all began.

The pioneers' task was daunting. First, they had to recognize and come to terms with a fundamental technological, economic and cultural revolution which was beginning to transform society's use of music, and, therefore, the opportunities and risks for everyone working in the industry. The shape of things to come could be discerned before 1914, but only by men of unusual vision. To assimilate this knowledge and adapt to the new conditions required unusual flexibility and adroitness. It entailed reappraising, perhaps reversing, long-established procedures. It necessitated a constant and

[1] Ernst Roth, *The Business of Music* (1969), 32.

sustained attack on deeply ingrained attitudes, preconceptions, and behaviour, not only among the general public, who had to be persuaded to pay for new forms of consumption, but even within the music industry itself, where hostility to performing right was common among those who could ultimately benefit from it. This instinctive antipathy would continue to beset the Society for many years after its foundation. Among consumers it was a natural, if unacceptable, desire for free goods at others' expense. Among producers it was often a rational and articulate antagonism, based upon objective, if increasingly obsolescent, perceptions of self-interest. For people on all sides the persistence of antagonism stemmed from a collective memory of one man's unscrupulous manipulation of performing right, which soured public opinion for a generation, and perpetuated opposition to its future use, however restrained and scrupulous. The individual whose once notorious activities, thus, became ineluctably connected in the public mind with the malevolent exercise of performing right, whose name was an unfailing guarantee of antagonism, was Harry Wall.[2]

In 1875 Wall set up an impressively named 'Copyright and Performing Right Protection Office' to exploit the current law, which required £2 damages and full costs for infringements of performing right. Cheaply and quietly, for secrecy was essential to his way of business, Wall would pick up old copyrights which were generally assumed to have expired, and roam the country in search of illegal, but unintended, infringements. These were generally to be found at 'penny readings', charity concerts, and similarly modest entertainments. Victims were presented by Wall with a demand for £2, and an implied threat of court action against singer, accompanist, and concert organizer. A typical printed 'Notice' has survived in the PRS archives. Couched in language similar to the Victorian 'penny frighteners', which were still being used by unscrupulous hire-purchase dealers, it is a deliberately intimidating document.[3] Citing the appropriate laws, it reminds potential offenders that they are liable for 'an amount *not less than 40s.* . .together with Costs.', that ignorance of the law is no excuse,and that there is no amnesty for

---

[2] Several writers, including McFarlane, describe him as Thomas Wall, but a contemporary document (see n. 3 below) lists the Secretary of the Copyright and Performing Right Protection Office as 'Harry Wall, 8 Colebrook Row, Islington, London, N.', and is overstamped 'H. Wall'.

[3] This rare and important document is headed 'Copyright and Performing Right Protection Office. (Established 1875).' It also carries an advertisement for a 'Book of Words' for Benedict's opera, *The Lily of Killarney*, as published by the Copyright Protection Office. Attached to the PRS copy is a note from someone at Chappell's (M. E. Ricketts?), dated 7 May, 1930, saying 'Looking through old file—you might like to put away in your files for future reference'. On 'penny frighteners' see Cyril Ehrlich, *The Piano: A History* (1976), 103–4.

amateur or unpaid performers. It then lists examples of cases successfully brought to court, *pour encourager les autres*. Offering advice upon and management of any copyright business, it concludes by anticipating a possible line of defence: a complete list of protected works is impracticable, but proposed programmes can be scrutinized. A fee of 2s.6d. is required 'owing to the excessive amount of labour (beyond all anticipation) incurred by this self-imposed burden, a gratuitous continuance of which is found to be insupportable'.

Doubtless, Wall was not alone in these practices of extortion, but he was by far their most notorious exponent, and legislators made repeated attempts to bring him to heel. He was exposed in evidence before a commission of inquiry which was followed by legislation in 1882 'to protect the public from vexatious proceedings for the recovery of penalties for. . .unauthorised performance'.[4] When this proved insufficient to curb him, another Act was passed in 1888, abolishing the minimum £2 penalty for breach of performing right, and leaving the assessment of damages and costs to the court's discretion. This legislation did not prevent the existing legitimate activity of SACEM, in collecting fees for performance and taking legal action against infringements; but it did shift the balance against any new initiative to establish an indigenous organization for *petits droits*.

Thus, Wall can be held responsible for the erection of formidable legal and psychological barriers to the development of performing right in Britain; but that does not mean that his activities were the principal reason for the time lag between SACEM and the PRS.[5] Less still does it support the more common explanation that delay in launching the PRS was primarily due to deficiences in the legal system.[6] Such interpretations of history give undue weight to intricacies of law, a common tendency in this field of study, and pay scant regard to economic realities. In practice, legislation has always tended to limp behind changes in economy and society, rather than to anticipate them, particularly in volatile times: the repeated attempt of copyright law to catch up with technology is a familar modern example. Similarly, bad public relations are often damaging but rarely abortive; a challenge to business initiative, rather than its strait-jacket, provided there are sufficient market opportunities to encourage action. In the light of these truths one looks elsewhere for a convincing explanation of the Society's late birth, to the idiosyncrasies of English music publishing, and its market. It was an industry of small family businesses, where contractual relationships between

[4] Gavin McFarlane, *Copyright: The Development and Exercise of the Performing Right* (1980), 86.
[5] As suggested by McFarlane, op. cit., 88.
[6] C. F. James, *The Story of the Performing Right Society* (1951), 16–17.

publishers and composers were rarely congenial; the latter notoriously lacking in *esprit de corps*, and usually in a weak bargaining position.

It is a commonplace that composers have usually been miserably rewarded for their labour, but the economic context is usually glossed over. As Ernst Roth remarks, music publishers have commonly been represented as 'hard boiled businessmen living off their unworldly victims'. In other trades shrewdness is esteemed, but a successful music publisher is 'suspect to everybody, contemptible to many. His wealth has an air of illegitimacy and it will be whispered that the degree of his comfort varies according to the degree of discomfort of his composers.'[7] Such indictments never take account of the high costs and risks which attend entrepreneurship in this hazardous business, nor the simple fact that, unless he can find a patron, the composer must rely upon his publisher's business acumen to make a living for both of them. But there can be no denying the disorganization of composers in late nineteenth- and early twentieth-century Britain and the harshness of their working environment. In the lower reaches of the market they were as miserably placed as their fellow writers in Grub Street where 'the whole concept of authorship, implying intellectual property, copyright and contractual obligations, was irrelevant'.[8] Even respected musicians could get bad deals. A notorious example was Coleridge-Taylor, the black composer who sold the outstandingly successful and presumably remunerative *Hiawatha* outright, and later died in poverty. An appeal on behalf on his widow and children led to a long and acrimonious public correspondence, with the publisher refusing to 'disclose the secrets of our business' and leading musicians, including Stanford, voicing their distrust and antipathy to the prevailing type of contract. It was 'a mockery', claimed one of the trade's most persistent critics, 'to call such a document an agreement'. The artist was customarily 'in absolute ignorance of his rights and their potentialities, and he is dealing with a man whose business in life has been to study every detail of artistic property from the commercial viewpoint'.[9]

If it is true that British composers were weak and poorly organized, that they lacked the status and attendant self confidence of their French contemporaries, this still does not adequately explain the delay in establishing a performing right society. In the absence of initiatives from musicians, as in the case of SACEM, there was nothing to prevent publishers from taking the initiative, except the prevailing opinion among them that the balance of advantage lay

[7] Roth, op. cit. 60–4.

[8] Nigel Cross, *The Common Writer: Life in Nineteenth Century Grub Street* (1985), 126.

[9] G. Herbert Thring, in the *English Review*, repr. in the *Author*, June 1913, 270–3.

elsewhere: in sales of sheet music. More important than legislative enactments, public antipathy, contractual niceties, or even the bargaining power, social status, and disunity of musicians, were the peculiar requirements of the market place. More than in any other country, apart from the USA, where, significantly, performing right also had to wait until 1914, music publishing in England depended upon sales rather than performance.

'Autre pays, autre mœurs'

There was an enormous demand for sheet music in Britain. By the end of the nineteenth century annual sales were estimated to be some 20 million pieces[10] with 40,000 new titles, each printed in runs of at least 200.[11] Popular hits often sold 200,000 copies, even under normal conditions. Patriotic fervour in wartime could add enormous boosts to such titles as 'The Soldiers of the Queen'. Ballads and oratorios could sometimes command large sales for many years: 'The Lost Chord', 'The Holy City' (50,000 a year during the 1890s), and *The Crucifixion* are familiar examples. Even operas found many buyers, particularly in vocal score with piano accompaniment, or in two staves with words. One London printer, for example, opened his plant with a first order for 5,000 copies of Leoncavallo's *Pagliacci*, and sales of light operas and musical comedies were prodigious. If distribution of *The Merry Widow* was measured by 'trainloads',[12] there were native products, such as Sydney Jones's *The Geisha*, which were also immensely popular. Simple piano pieces and 'educational' music, mostly elementary piano tutors, scales, and exercises, were another large sector of the industry. Most purchases of sheet music were ultimately linked to ownership of pianos, which existed on a scale unmatched elsewhere in Europe. By 1910 there were, at the lowest estimate, two million pianos in Britain, far more than in France or Germany, and people were continuing to buy them, more eagerly than anywhere except in North America.[13] The piano was the centre of domestic entertainment, music shops were familiar in every high street, and sheet music was regularly purchased, by people of all ages and at every level of society. The French also bought pianos and music, of course, and sometimes a *café concert* song would sell 50,000 copies, but only in Britain and America were 'piano mania' and amateur performance the mainsprings of the music market.

[10] *Musical Opinion*, Mar. 1898.
[11] *Musical Opinion*, Aug. 1898.
[12] Roth, op. cit. 85.
[13] Ehrlich, op. cit. 91.

In these circumstances English publishers could be excused if they showed little enthusiasm for the bothersome, costly, unfamiliar, and unpopular business of collecting fees for performances. Some undertook the task: Oliver Hawkes, for example, had an agreement with Balfour Gardiner for his popular 'Shepherd Fennel's Dance'. The publisher collected performance fees, taking two-thirds.[14] If they wanted to exercise the right, publishers were required, by the Acts of 1882 and 1888, to say so explicitly on the title page of each piece. Far from doing this, most publishers of popular music would print a notice declaring that 'This song may be sung in public without fee or licence'. Particularly antagonistic to performing right were the firms whose mainstay was the 'royalty' or 'shop' ballad. Since they made a practice of *paying* leading entertainers to perform their songs, which carried on the title page the advertisement 'As sung by . . .', they were unlikely to exact payments for performance.

Prominent among these publishers was William Boosey, who had joined the family firm in 1880, and shifted to Chappell in 1894. Some of the ballads which he accepted and promoted became outstandingly successful, including 'Love's Old Sweet Song', 'The Holy City', and 'Roses of Picardy'. In those days his unequivocal opposition to performing right was frequently and forcibly expressed. He objected to 'foreign composers and publishers [who] insist upon vexatious rights of performance that never have been, and never will be, understood here'. He was convinced that such misguided people 'do not understand the strong prejudice in this country . . . which has necessitated, owing to notorious circumstances, recent legislation' (alluding to Wall's activities). He warned that persistence would lead inevitably to the rejection of their work.[15] Two years after that outburst William Boosey launched an attack on Alfred Moul, a French musician and business man living in London, director of the Alhambra theatre, and SACEM's first representative in Britain. Moul's tentative attempts to organize an English society were dismissed out of hand by Boosey. They were unnecessary, he argued, for several reasons: the 'trivial description' of most English concerts, many of them for charity; the 'extremely strong prejudice' of the British public following Wall's activities; and the great *sale* of small works under a royalty system which gave the composer an 'interest to have his music performed'. Therefore, Boosey concluded, *petits droits* were irrelevant in Britain: '*autres pays, autres mœurs*, they are impossible here', said the man who would eventually become first president of the PRS.[16]

---

[14] PRS Archives, Solicitors' file (Syrett), 20 May 1922.

[15] Letter to the *Era*, repr. in *Musical Opinion*, Dec. 1888.

[16] Letter to *Le Ménestrel*, repr. in *Music Trades' Review*, May 1890.

As SACEM pursued the interests of its members, controversy over performing right continued, with frequent appearances in court. There was, for example, successful litigation against the Comedy Theatre for unauthorized performance of a waltz song, 'Les Blondes', and against a Manchester concert agent who was responsible for the playing of a military march after refusing to pay SACEM's £5 fee for the 1890 season. His letter of complaint to the *Manchester Guardian* is a compendium of the arguments and rhetoric which, for at least another generation, would be employed against performing right. Claiming to be the only Manchester impresario to withstand SACEM's exactions, he warned against 'a new terror' which sought to protect foreign music but refused to publish a list, so that innocent offenders could be 'pounced upon for performing any one of these thousands of pieces', without being able to check beforehand. While no one would object to paying for a work of 'a high and important character', his recent infringement concerned 'an ordinary march—of no consequence'. Finally, in a burst of feigned altruism and aesthetic sensibility, he contended 'on broad and public grounds', that 'music is such a delightful thing that it should be free, and composers should be remunerated by the sale of copies, and not by vexatious restrictions'.[17] Reporting the case and ensuing debate, the *Music Trades' Review* advocated a boycott of all 'smaller French works' and ran a campaign against strange continental practices. The bureaucratic idiosyncrasies of cross-channel *droits d'auteur* were described:

On entering an opera or concert hall in Paris you come face to face with a long counter, presided over by three gentlemanly-looking individuals in evening dress, to whom your ticket is given, they replacing it with another, by which you are seated. These are the representatives of the 'Sociétés Roger' [responsible for *grand droits*], 'Souchon' [SACEM, who handled only *petits droits*], and the 'Assistance Publique', each to figure his receipts for the day.[18]

English practice was so different, and SACEM's difficulties there so acute, that M. Souchon was said to be preparing a complaint to the Berne Convention, against England's lack of co-operation [19]. The conflict was highlighted by court proceedings which also demonstrated how much harm Wall had done to the image of performing right. When, for example, William Boosey referred to the latter as 'a gentleman in Mr Moul's own line of business', this was sufficient for Moul to sue, successfully, for libel. He then announced that he would resign from SACEM and 'devote himself to the formation of a similar institution in this country'[20]. Meanwhile English music publishers

[17] Letter to the *Manchester Guardian*, repr. in *Music Trades' Review*, Sept. 1960.
[18] *New York Musical Courier*, repr. in *Music Trades' Review*, Oct. 1894.
[19] *L'Art Musical*, reported in *Music Trades' Review*, Sept. 1891.
[20] *Music Trades' Review*, Jan. and Feb. 1903.

were far more concerned about quite another matter; understandably, since it threatened to destroy their livelihood.

Pirates

Nowadays we associate 'piracy' with the illegal copying of records. At the beginning of this century it took the form of a trade in sheet music and, as at present, the law offered scant protection against unscrupulous use of new technology. Photo-zinc blocks, costing about ten shillings apiece, enabled printers to turn out thousands of sheets at a halfpenny each.[21] Since binding was unnecessary, pirated music was much more common than pirated literature, though very popular short items, such as Kipling's poems, suffered similar treatment. Processed in a few centres, mainly Liverpool and London, pirated copies of popular numbers were sold for a few pence: even the latest songs became available within days of their original publication. This material was openly hawked on the streets of London and provincial cities, in vast quantities and at a fraction of its legitimate price. Since there were no summary penalties for the offence, publishers could do nothing through the courts except seek an injunction and ultimate damages: useless remedies, in practice, for the street hawkers were 'men of straw'. Impotence begets violence. In the spring of 1902 one publisher employed a detective agency to seize 15,000 illicit copies from a van, 6,000 from a barrow, 8,000 from a hawker's lodgings, and a further 20,000 from 'some chambers near the Mansion House'.[22] There were a number of pitched battles, and frequent fines for assault. A group of publishers, including Boosey, Chappell, Hopwood and Crew, and Francis, Day and Hunter, formed a 'Copyright Association' to stop piracy and change the law. New legislation in 1902 attempted to improve matters by giving power to seize and destroy illegal stocks, but it still failed to create a criminal offence, and was therefore not really effective.

During the early years of the twentieth century estimates of the extent of piracy were so large as almost to defy belief, but they provide remarkable evidence of the market for 'dots' at a time when the general public still regarded music as something to be read, played and sung. Early in 1903, for example, it was reported that three quarters of a million copies of pirated music had been seized. Marches by Sousa and 'She was Only a Bird in a Gilded Cage', were available for twopence, 'The Lost Chord', 'Star of Bethlehem', and Leslie Stuart's popular duet 'Tell Me Pretty Maiden' for fourpence. Sousa,

[21] *Musical Opinion*, May 1904.
[22] *Musical Opinion*, Apr. 1902.

on a visit to London, complained to *The Times*, and Stephen Adams furiously reported that there were seven different pirated editions of his 'The Holy City' on the streets.[23] In June 1904 the Copyright Association seized over 109,000 titles, including the obligatory 'Holy City', selections from the opera *Cavalleria Rusticana*, the musical comedy *The Belle of New York*, and Edward German's *Merrie England*, and 1,250 copies of 'The Boers Have Got My Daddy'. John Abbott, who was Secretary of the Association, recalls the recruitment of 'an organised corps, consisting of ex-police officers and others with some knowledge of the pugilistic art' who raided street vendors and left visiting cards with the Association's address, inviting court action. 'Fights were a common occurrence' and magistrates would deliver 'trite remarks about taking the law into one's own hands', but it focused 'a spotlight on this extraordinary state of affairs' and the need for legislation to make piracy a criminal offence.[24]

In 1904 a Government report gave official recognition to these complaints. After examining publishers, composers, trade representatives, magistrates, police, and even Frederick Willetts, alias Fisher, self-styled 'King of the Pirates' and manager of 'The People's Music Publishing Company', the investigating Committee explained the extent and persistence of the trade. Between October 1902 and December 1903 there were 231 pirated editions of copyright music on the market; 460,000 copies had been seized in the Metropolitan Police District alone. Out of twelve civil actions successfully brought by William Boosey, at a cost of £500, only two had succeeded in recovering costs. Rights of seizure and destruction, available since 1902, were enfeebled: premises could not be entered by force and searched; nor could stocks be destroyed without serving the hawker with a summons—easily avoided by giving a false address. If it was argued that the public benefited from cheap music, said the Report, it had no right to do so by 'assisting to plunder a class on which the Legislature has conferred statutory rights of property, although the protection afforded by the statute has proved insufficient to deal with an evil which was not foreseen at a time when the Act was passed'.[25]

A sympathetic blue book was only one step towards victory over the pirates. There was considerable opposition from members of the public and some politicians. Many buyers were attracted by bargains

[23] *Musical Opinion*, Feb. and Mar. 1903. On piracy, see James Coover, *Music Publishing, Copyright and Piracy in Victorian England* (1985).

[24] John Abbott, *The Story of Francis, Day and Hunter* (1952), 31–2. The British Library has several volumes of pirated music, dating from this period, and collected by G. A. Preston, a leading pirate-hunter.

[25] Report of the Departmental Committee appointed . . . to inquire into the Piracy of Musical Publications (1904). *(Parliamentary Papers, vol. 79, pp. 227–381)*. See also the *Author*, Mar. 1904.

and few were deterred by allegations about 'filthy and unhealthy paper', or descriptions of the vulgar appearance of pirated music which, 'placed on a pianoforte in any respectable drawing room . . . would be shabbily out of place'.[26] Some were inclined to blame the publishers for self-inflicted wounds. Their business methods were criticized as old-fashioned, perhaps corrupt, certainly inefficient, including the quaint practice of 'double pricing', by which songs and piano pieces were regularly sold at half the marked price of four shillings. Discounts were thought to be arbitrary, profit margins excessive, and the risks of the trade, which publishers used as an excuse for high prices, were said to be greatly exaggerated. It was not unusual, therefore, for ordinary law-abiding people to regard piracy sympathetically, as a natural and not unwelcome response to exorbitant prices and easy profits, which had been enjoyed for too long by a monopoly, a 'ring whose sole purpose is to keep prices high'.[27]

As new legislation was debated in Parliament, these complaints, frequently voiced in the press, were reiterated and assembled into a general denunciation of music publishing. One MP declared 'the whole trade' to be 'rotten . . . in fact one of the most outrageous examples of a trust' [i.e. a monopoly]. Another expressed sympathy with composers, but refused to exonerate the publishers from blame. Leading the attack was James Caldwell, a Glasgow calico manufac-turer experienced in 'talking out' Parliamentary bills. He also compiled lists of grievances against the music publishers, included in an appendix to the Committee Report and a separate, widely distributed 'memorandum'. Undeterred by this opposition, and answering the now familiar accusations point by point, William Boosey continued to mobilize support for copyright reform by setting up a 'Musical Defence League' which called a 'Great Protest Meeting' at the Queen's Hall.[28] It was attended by Elgar, Parry, leading ballad composers, and several members of Parliament, with messages of support from Kipling, Conan Doyle, Stanford, and other prominent men. The assembly was informed that three million illegal copies had been seized in the past three years and, on behalf of composers, publishers, and music traders, insisted that the bill before Parliament should now be passed.[29]

With piracy and seizures continuing unabated, success was by no means certain. The President of the Board of Trade received a

[26] *Musical Opinion*, May 1903.
[27] *Musical Opinion*, Mar. 1903.
[28] *Music Trades' Review*, June 1904, and *Musical Opinion*, July 1904.
[29] *Musical Opinion*, Aug. 1904.

deputation from music traders, and promised his support for the bill.[30] The *Daily Telegraph*'s Parliamentary correspondent reported that 'opposition had been reduced to almost vanishing point'. But legislation was likely to be further delayed by an impending general election. In a dramatic attempt to force the issue, thirty-seven leading publishers announced that until the law gave them adequate protection they would cease all business; stopping new publications, advertisements, and artists' contracts.[31] It is sometimes assumed that this spectacular gesture was sufficient to ensure the passing of the new copyright act, but the argument is by no means self-evident.[32] Legislation often slips ' 'twixt cup and lip', and this was not to be the last occasion when the music industry would need infinite patience, guile, and a measure of luck, to see an act through Parliament. In any case, the publishers' proclamation was probably stronger in rhetoric than serious intent. As one commentator has pointed out, while declaring their innings closed, they were simultaneously paying high auction prices for copyrights of much-pirated songs, in evident expectation of a continuing game.[33] Meanwhile, an ingenious method of suppressing piracy was devised by making use of the conspiracy laws. After a trial which lasted nine days, spread over seven weeks at the Old Bailey, and which cost Boosey's firm, Chappell, 3,000 guineas, an enormous sum in those days, the 'pirate king' was sentenced to nine months, and his accomplices to fines and lesser terms of imprisonment.[34] The first major victory against the pirates, and a salutary warning to future offenders, it was followed by a similar prosecution in Leeds, costing another thousand guineas.

If the conspiracy laws were effective, they were also too cumbersome and expensive to provide a satisfactory alternative to new legislation. It was fortunate, therefore, that a capricious Parliamentary process suddenly produced a volte-face. The Musical Copyright Act of 1906 was passed, by means of adroit political legerdemain, largely thanks to the persistence and skill of T. P. O'Connor, who earned a reputation as the musicians' Member of Parliament. Contemporary appreciation of his achievement is attested to by the impressive list of musicians, playrights, actors, and political dignitaries who attended a celebratory dinner in his honour. Thus, it became, at last, a criminal offence to produce, sell, or possess pirated copies, or plates for making them; and the police were given rights of entry and

[30] *Musical Opinion*, Mar. 1905.

[31] *Musical Opinion*, May 1905.

[32] See McFarlane, op. cit. 93.

[33] Coover, op. cit. 119.

[34] There was extensive comment in the trade press. See *Musical Opinion*, Dec. 1905, *Musical News*, 6 and 27 Jan. 1906, *Music Trades' Review*, Nov. 1905, *Musical Times*, Feb. 1907.

search. Even this did not entirely eradicate the pirates—illegal sheet music continued to appear on the streets, and there were occasional seizures—but they were effectively contained. In 1911 the whole field of copyright was reviewed and tidied up in a new law which remained in force until 1957. It was, as we shall see, a necessary, but not sufficient, condition for the reassertion of performing right. For a quarter century piracy had been of supreme importance to the music industry; a threat to its existence which justified the publishers' obsessional determination to eradicate it. Unfortunately, as often happens after an arduous and successful campaign, ageing generals continued to fight old battles. Long after piracy had ceased to be more than an occasional irritant, some members of the Publishers' Association would devote their waning energies to mopping up its vestiges, while ignoring new problems and opportunities.

Starter's Orders

When Alfred Moul announced his intention of forming an English 'branch' of SACEM, in February 1903, he was presumably contemplating something different from the existing London office which merely represented French interests.[35] In the same month an apparently well-informed article expressed sympathy for the plight of English composers and claimed that their publishers had no interest in performing right, regarding it as an 'impediment to business'.[36] We know nothing about Moul's attempts to overcome these prejudices, except that he failed and was later said to have given up 'in despair'. His successor as SACEM's representative eventually completed the task, but he, too, is a shadowy figure, poorly documented and unfairly forgotten. C. F. James's piously detailed chronicle barely mentions Pierre Sarpy, despite his claim to be the Society's founding father. When a few English publishers began to give serious attention to the possibilities of performing right it was Sarpy who acted as their mentor. His experience was uniquely apposite, for he had pursued SACEM's interests in England with great energy, organizing a licensing system and appearing frequently in court, notably in the key case of *Sarpy* v. *Holland*.[37]

The time was ripe for reappraisal. In 1908 the Government began to prepare for a thorough revision of copyright legislation, and consulted interested parties, including the music industry. An international conference in Berlin had revised the Berne convention,

---

[35] *Musical Opinion*, Feb. 1903.
[36] The *Morning Advertiser*, quoted in *Musical Opinion*, Feb. 1903.
[37] See p. 30, fn. 13; the *Author*, Feb. 1908.

extending copyright protection to fifty years after the author's death, and modifying the rule on performing right: authors wishing to exercise it no longer had to print a notice to that effect. Therefore, if Britain was to meet international obligations it would be necessary to replace the Acts of 1882 and 1888 with an appropriate statute. Music publishers were asked if they would welcome such a change, and what sort of positive steps they might take to benefit from it. The publishers could reach no agreement, their Association reporting 'considerable divergence' to the Board of Trade. William Boosey was particularly critical of the proposed legislation, arguing that only confusion would result from any attempt to adopt the Berlin proposals. He was then appointed to a government committee for the revision of copyright law, whose report formed the basis of the 1911 Act.[38]

Twenty years later William Boosey devoted a chapter of his autobiography to these events, concentrating his account upon 'mechanical music' and its treatment in the 1911 Act. This, he argues, was 'the first blow' which altered the composer's position and his own attitude to performing right. Elsewhere, he alluded to his change of mind with an air of retrospective omniscience, suggesting that he already 'foresaw what was coming'. With a 'perfectly open mind as to the necessity of altering our methods of business according to changing conditions', he claims he was 'gradually becoming aware' that 'a composer's performing rights might even be more valuable than his publishing rights' and that foreign composers were already benefiting.[39] It is a muddled, self-justifying account of dimly recalled events, but, whatever the cause, the significance of this turn-round by one of the industry's leaders can scarcely be exaggerated. If acts of creative entrepreneurship largely consist of a correct perception, or better, anticipation, of market change, followed by decisive action, then Boosey's volte-face was an outstanding example. It was all the more remarkable for coming at a time when the music market was peculiarly unstable.

Publishers had suffered many vicissitudes since the 1890s, in addition to piracy. The demand for serious music appeared to be falling, as evidenced by attendance at Novello's Albert Hall and Chappell's 'Pop' concerts. Among several prophets of doom, the young Havergal Brian reported a 'crisis' in 1909, with insufficient opportunities for British composers, too many underemployed orchestras, and a multiplicity of poorly attended concerts without roots in

---

[38] *Report of the Committee on the Law of Copyright*, (Gorell Committee, Cmnd. 4976, 1909). *Minutes of Evidence Taken before the Law of Copyright Committee—Appendix*, (Cmnd. 5051, 1910). Sarpy's evidence is particularly illuminating: 210–13.
[39] William Boosey, *Fifty Years of Music*, (1931) 175.

the 'craving of the people'. It was a curious pre-echo of London concert life in the 1980s but, of course, without public subsidy.[40] The market for popular music was, as usual, far healthier; but, if the public's appetite was continuing to grow apace, its tastes were also slowly beginning to change towards a liking for American entertainment which soon became the prevailing mode. The old style English ballads, comic songs, and 'light music' were by no means dead, but new fashions were making themselves felt, and affecting the balance of power within the industry, at home and internationally. There were also the first faint rumblings of a technological revolution. Few music publishers were well prepared for future turbulence. Most of them were small family units, prone to the weaknesses which afflict such institutions: conservative management, usually recruited by family connection, with rare infusions of new talent; indifference to, or even distrust of, innovation; and insufficient financial resources to take a long view. It was a pattern familiar to later inquests on the 'British disease' in business. For an industry facing the twentieth-century upheaval in entertainment it could, indeed, have been fatal. Everything depended upon effective leadership and a reasonable semblance of unity. William Boosey was generally accepted as the industry's leader, but neither he nor most of his colleagues in the Music Publishers' Association were yet committed to performing right or the importance of the gramophone. In response to Government enquiries they aired views about the new trends, but continued to be more concerned with piracy and sheet music prices. When a leading French authority came to address them on the copyright implications of the gramophone, and to urge action, very few members bothered to attend the meeting.[41] They were demonstrating the innocent conservatism of small business men, but they had an excuse. The truly devastating impact of 'mechanical music' was not felt until twenty years later, with electric recording and radio. Meanwhile, for most of them, changes in risks and opportunities did not yet appear to be of sufficient magnitude, in those last years of peace, to necessitate drastic reappraisal of traditional ways of doing business.

Much legal ink has been expended upon the 1911 Act. For our purpose it is sufficient, putting aside mechanical rights, and complex questions of assignment, to say that it tidied up the law, establishing 'ground rules' for the next forty-five years. It recognized property in copyright beyond the mere right to print and publish, including the right to perform. Thus, it could be said to have facilitated the exploitation of performing right. But it did not in itself change the

---

[40] See Cyril Ehrlich, *The Music Profession in Britain since the Eighteenth Century* (1985).
[41] Music Publishers Association Archives, Committee Minutes, 1910–12.

balance of advantage for publishers between sales and performance. Nor did it guarantee that newly articulated rights, if desired, would be automatically secured. The former awaited a realignment of market demand which was only just beginning to make itself felt. The latter required organization and attack, for public acknowledgement of rights to intellectual property does not generally arise from instinctive human generosity; it has to be fought for.

The Start

In February 1912 H. S. J. Booth addressed some of his fellow publishers on the prospects of a performing right 'association' and the lessons to be learned from French experience. Director of Ascherberg, Hopwood and Crew, he was responsible for a substantial catalogue of predominantly light music, including the operetta *The Geisha*, which was a hit even in Germany; waltzes by Waldteufel and Ancliffe; and the British rights for *Cavalleria Rusticana* and *Pagliacci*. His opinions therefore carried weight, and he was confident that 'new profits' would be earned, without injury to existing business. SACEM, he observed, drew little of its income from theatres; most from concert halls and, notably, 'picture shows'. A rapid increase in the number of cinemas in London and the provinces, he argued, provided an unprecedented opportunity: 'the figures are dazzling'. There were, however, two necessary preconditions for success. Publishers must include all their works, not just a selection; and the implications of starting an organization through the publishers' initiative must be squarely faced. SACEM had been founded by authors and composers who had then 'admitted the publishers'. The reverse would be the case here, so 'if we are to be as influential as the French, we must *not* curtail the benefits of authors and composers'. If these conditions were met his firm would 'come in with the whole catalogue', but he was not prepared to waste time attending meetings 'unless we get to business'. More than a year later the industry was still vacillating. Some argued that the imposition of performing licences would be resented as a 'tax'. Others pointed out that it was already being paid to foreigners and that 'the French must laugh at us'. A few saintly and patriotic contributors to the debate pleaded that various categories of music user would have to be exempt, such as religious charities and organizers of military events.[42]

By November 1913 there had been sufficient progress for Sarpy to draw up a set of draft rules which were discussed by the committee of the Publishers' Association, initially without much enthusiasm. It was

[42] PRS Archives, Papers *re* formation, 15 Feb. 1912.

argued that the demand for a society came only from opera and theatre composers, song writers being 'very much against'; and that 'wholesale distribution of free copies' would be necessary. This was challenged by Oliver Hawkes, who cited French experience and warned that the burgeoning interest of English composers and authors in performing right was already being taken up by the Society of Authors which had established a 'collection bureau' to handle royalties for a fee of 15 per cent.[43] As Boosey pointed out, the most sensitive issue was the division of royalties between composer and publisher. In France the latter received no more than one third, in Germany one quarter. Booth and Hawkes suggested an equal split, but there was no general agreement, and, with barely concealed exasperation, Boosey announced his intention to 'get to work without further delay' ignoring those who were 'too nervous or not sufficiently interested'. It was a turning point.

On 23 December an agreement was drawn up to establish an association provisionally entitled 'The Authors', Composers', and Music Publishers' Society', to be organized 'upon lines similar to those governing the SACEM'. It was signed by the representatives of ten publishers: Ascherberg, Augener, Bosworth, Chappell, Feldman, Francis, Day and Hunter, Hawkes, Lafleur, Lengnick, and Schott.[44] The Performing Right Society Ltd. was formally registered on 6 March 1914 as a 'company limited by guarantee and not having a share capital'. A meeting at Chappell's, with William Boosey in the Chair, agreed that the Society's Committee should consist of eight composers or authors, and eight publishers, with one of the latter to act as Chairman. Each publisher contributed £50 towards preliminary expenses, at 4 per cent interest. A commemorative frieze celebrates the Society's founding committee (see pl. 2). Lionel Monckton (Vice-Chairman) was the celebrated composer of such musicals as *The Arcadians* and *The Quaker Girl*. Paul Rubens had written several successful shows, including *The Blue Moon*, and *Miss Hook of Holland*. Hermann Lohr was the composer of 'Little Grey Home in the West' and 'Where my Caravan has rested'. Herman Finck had already written the immensely successful light orchestral piece, 'In the Shadows', and was about to pen the music-hall recruiting song 'I'll Make a Man of You' ('On Sunday I Walk Out With a Soldier'). Henry Pether was the composer of 'Waiting at the Church' and other songs for such music hall stars as Vesta Victoria, Harry Lauder, and George Robey. Bennett Scott would eventually write more than a thousand songs, and was about to score with 'Take

---

[43] The *Author*, Feb. 1913.
[44] PRS Archives, Papers *re* formation, 23 Dec. 1913.

Me Back to Dear Old Blighty'. 'Adrian Ross' was the pen name of Arthur Ropes, a prolific lyricist. Harold Simpson was also a lyricist, and Worton David had written songs for Florrie Forde and Harry Champion.

The composers and authors were, thus, mostly representative of music-hall and a type of light music at which the English then excelled. A notable example was Charles Ancliffe, composer of 'Nights of Gladness', and the youngest military bandmaster ever to be appointed. The publishers were drawn from a wider constituency. In addition to William Boosey, (as Chairman), Booth, and David Day, there was, for example, Charles Volkert, a Director of Augener, Lengnick, and Schott. He had represented the latter firm in London since 1873 and was one of the most experienced and respected publishers of serious music in Europe. Another accomplished publisher was Arthur Edward Bosworth, who had started business in Leipzig, to protect Gilbert and Sullivan copyrights, before opening in London and then Vienna. His important catalogues included operettas by Zeller, light music by Moskowski and Ketèlbey, and the renowned Beringer piano tutor and Ševčik violin method. Pierre Sarpy was appointed General Manager and 'Secretary of the Company', his status attested by the adoption of 'Sarpierre' as the Society's telegraphic address, and by his salary of £1,000 a year, a high income at that time.[45] The Society's first general meeting took place at 32 Shaftesbury Avenue, where an office was set up in two small rooms, on 1 April 1914. The first name to be inscribed on the membership list was Liza Lehmann, composer of songs, piano pieces, a light opera which had been produced at the Prince of Wales Theatre, and the popular cycle 'In a Persian Garden'.

Reaction

The PRS was launched, but there was only a semblance of unity. The extent to which publishers and composers were still disunited soon became common knowledge, as the new Society made its first entry into the public arena. Opposition was at least as vociferous from within as from outside the industry, and much more damaging. Users of music might be expected to protest against paying for a service which they had been getting free. Such opposition could be countered by information and persuasion; but antagonism from publishers and composers, when it was not simply muddle-headed, was quite another matter. It suggested that there were fundamentally different conceptions of self-interest, and advertised the fact that a licence from the

[45] Ehrlich, *Music Profession*, 178 and 204–5.

Society was neither necessary nor sufficient to perform music belonging to non-members. These issues were openly discussed in the press, particularly in an extensive correspondence published by the *Daily Telegraph* throughout July 1914.

The opening article was largely based on an interview with William Boosey. Welcoming the Society, it explained that British composers would now be given opportunities which foreigners had long enjoyed, by enforcing the law and collecting 'nominal' fees from establishments which made use of their property.[46] Oliver Hawkes added support, claiming that the underlying demand for a performing right organization had come from composers, 'an irresistible wave . . . which no publisher can stop'. Englishmen, he explained, were writing 'charming light music' which was immensely popular but insufficiently rewarded. Finck's 'In the Shadows', for example, was popular throughout France, but Hawkes had repeatedly failed to secure fees for these performances.[47] There was even support from a prominent user of music. Daniel Mayer, a leading impresario, who was also mayor of Bexhill, donned both hats to welcome the Society. Like most holiday resorts his municipality already paid some fourteen guineas a year for foreign performing rights, and he thought that a few guineas extra would be well spent in supporting British musicians.

Equanimity was soon disturbed by J. H. Larway, one of Ketèlbey's publishers, who claimed that 'most of the houses in the trade' were opposed to an 'un-English' and 'inquisitorial' undertaking which would merely restrict sales in a country where they were the mainstay of the business, in contrast to continental publishers who depended on performance.[48] The composers' viewpoint was said to depend upon a distinction between writers of popular music, who would gain from the Society, and 'serious musicians', who already had such difficulty in getting their work performed that they feared new barriers. An 'eminent classical composer' who wished to remain anonymous, was quoted to this effect, and Joseph Holbrooke voiced the same sentiments 'from sad experience'.[49] John Francis Barnett, nearing the end of a long life of teaching and writing cantatas and simple piano pieces, was representative, in his ineffectual bewilderment and nervous indecisiveness, of several correspondents from the shabby genteel class who made up a large proportion of the 'respectable' Victorian music profession.[50] Songs, he thought, could not be protected, for every

[46] *Daily Telegraph*, 11 July 1914.
[47] Ibid., 13 July 1914.
[48] Ibid.
[49] Ibid., 14 and 15 July 1914.
[50] See Ehrlich, *Music Profession*.

means had always been sought to get them sung in public; free, of course. He would have greatly benefited from payments for perform-ances of such works as his cantata *The Ancient Mariner*, but the imposition of charges might have 'driven them from the concert room'. On the other hand 'very attractive' orchestral compositions would benefit. It was 'a very intricate question'.[51] There were no uncertainties in a forthright attack by Frank Allen, Managing Director of Moss Empires, the leading group of variety theatres. Shows like 'Hullo Ragtime' and 'Hullo Tango' at the London Hippodrome, said Mr Allen, *sold* songs, enriching publishers and composers, who should rest content with that state of affairs. He paid SACEM thirty guineas a year for a handful of inadequate rights, and he objected to paying another fee to an English society for even less, particularly since it did not represent the most popular compositions.[52] More surprising was a letter from the light music composer Montague Ewing, who would later become one of the Society's most fortunate and grateful beneficiaries. Claiming that composers were 'in a cleft stick'— refusing to join meant losing needed income, but joining would alienate some publishers—he concluded, lamely, that the only option was to stay out until publishers joined forces, which was 'a very remote possibility'.[53]

Several publishers were eager to advertise disunity. Boosey and Co., who published ballads and educational music, claimed that the Society represented less than half of the country's publishers and composers, and objected to its methods, particularly the failure to publish a list of protected works. Metzler (piano and vocal music, including Bizet and Sullivan) proclaimed their support for the *principle* of performing right, but refused to join because the initiative would fail without unanimity, and that was a 'hopeless' ambition.[54] J. B. Cramer and Co., with less tortuous logic, claimed to be 'neutral', and announced that they were not joining. Their 'song and dance music could be performed, as usual, without payment of any fee', but this did not apply to their operas.[55] Two directors of Novello were reported at considerable length. They had been sufficiently sympa-thetic to attend meetings and assist in drawing up rules. They were even willing to join, but only if fees were collected solely from those 'using music for the purpose of making money', such as cinemas, hotels, and restaurants. By contrast their own firm dealt with

[51] *Daily Telegraph*, 14 July 1914. Compare letters from Bonheur, Gilmer, Grover, and Parnum in *Daily Telegraph*, 17 July 1914.
[52] Ibid., 16 July 1914.
[53] Ibid., 15 July 1914.
[54] Ibid.
[55] Ibid., 14 July 1914.

hundreds of amateur choral societies, which were far more common in
Britain than abroad. Few of these worthy organizations could afford
fees, and they would be particularly inclined to avoid modern works if
required to pay. The Novello directors believed that similar reactions
could be expected from organizers of school concerts, and festivals like
the eisteddfods, all of which would suffer. As their final trump card
Novello announced that Elgar, whom they published, had recently
turned against performing right, renouncing the fee previously asked
for playing his violin concerto.[56] Many opponents of the Society
invoked the name of Harry Wall as a bogeyman. In an enormous
letter of several thousand words, the manager of the Drury Lane
Theatre gave dire warnings, claiming that Wall's activities had been
'a milder form' of what could be expected from the new institution.
The gloomy saga of past litigation would be dwarfed by future legal
difficulties.[57] Patriotism was also a popular theme: the Society was
described as 'an inquisitorial combine' and 'most un-English'.[58] The
conductor of a military band voiced more practical objections. He was
unwilling to list pieces played, and would rather boycott works than
fill in forms.[59]

There was some rallying to the flag. The case for the Society was
restated by Liza Lehmann, based 'not on cupidity, but on bare
justice', and by Volkert's colleague, W. Schecker. Lionel Monckton
made a detailed case, and refuted several objections. The new rage for
professionally performed background music in restaurants and hotels,
he explained, was replacing amateur domestic music-making. If
publishing value went down and performing value up composers
would suffer, unless they adjusted accordingly. Fears of exploitation
were misplaced since the Society merely sought to enforce existing
laws, and charge reasonable fees. It was impractical to issue a
catalogue.[60] A. E. Bosworth, writing with the authority of extensive
continental experience, pointed out that the German and Austrian
performing right societies had been opposed at their inception, by
owners of beer restaurants, of course, but certainly not by publishers.
Only 'the peculiarly English product, the royalty ballad', could
explain the strength of opposition from some London publishers. It
was idiosyncratic and fading, and must not be allowed to dominate
the whole of English musical life.[61] It fell to William Boosey to make a
final call to arms. After trading further blows with Novello, he

[56] Ibid., 16 July 1914.
[57] Ibid., 18 July 1914.
[58] Ibid. Letter from M. van Lennep.
[59] Ibid., 17 July 1914.
[60] Ibid., 15 July 1914.
[61] Ibid., 16 July 1914.

returned to the fray with typical pugnacity. Comparing the waverers to Canute, 'timid publishers and timid composers' content to wait and see, he dismissed objections from the firm of Boosey with its 'monotonous' ballads, and called upon the industry to display 'the courage of little brown mice'.[62]

And so it all began. An alliance of sorts had been formed, hardly glorious as yet, but convinced of the justice of its cause, and strong enough to claim some territory. It set to work.

[62] Ibid., 15 and 17 July 1914.

2

LOOSE ALIGNMENTS

Getting Organized

Sarpy's first tasks were to assemble a catalogue of music under the Society's control, to negotiate contracts of affiliation with foreign societies, and to issue licences to users in Britain. He was already at work in March 1914, in the hope that operations might start 'at any time within the next few weeks'. Member publishers were asked to submit lists of about one hundred of their principal works, preferably those 'in vogue' with reserved performing rights.[1] He visited Paris to arrange mutual representation with SACEM—the two societies agreeing to collect fees on behalf of each other's members—and made similar journeys to Berlin and Vienna. Home licensing was begun by offering the newly acquired British catalogues to existing SACEM licensees as an additional repertoire for an increased fee. Since most of the original contracts had been negotiated by Sarpy, he possessed unique knowledge of the market and of appropriate procedures, including the practical applications of the law, all of which were vital to the success of the new Society. The Committee gave him power to act quickly on their behalf, assigning rights personally to him, and allowing him to use 'his agents on the old lines he had been accustomed to'. Less costly and more effective than individual action by each publisher, this system was adopted from SACEM's mode of procedure at Sarpy's request, and was a remarkable demonstration of confidence by a group of highly individualistic business men, who were not accustomed to letting the reins out of their hands. Licences were taken up, apparently without much difficulty, by a number of important users of music: Moss Empires, despite its manager's complaints to the *Daily Telegraph*, the Alhambra and Stoll music-halls, the Lyons group of restaurants, the Savoy, Berkeley and Claridges hotels, and several seaside corporations were among the first holders of PRS licences. The London County Council also agreed to pay 100 guineas in future years for its band concerts.

The easiest way of extending the catchment area, beyond the preliminary take over of SACEM licences, was to deal with groups of potential clients through their trade associations, offering discounts

[1] PRS Archives, Volkert file, Sarpy to Volkert, 25 Mar. 1914.

for collective agreements. This was Sarpy's procedure, for example, in reaching agreement with the Incorporated Association of Hotels and Restaurants. Some groups of users were less accommodating. Early attempts to negotiate with the Cinematograph Exhibitors' Association, for example, were hampered by an unfortunate legacy. A few cinemas had been able to make unauthorized use of SACEM repertoire, and had so far resisted legal redress. Until that litigation could be settled, attempts to establish PRS contracts were bound to be difficult and inconclusive. Pantomimes were another potentially valuable source of income which remained elusive. The season was traditionally a peak of intensive musical activity, but the Theatrical Managers' Association refused to co-operate, bluntly observing that they did not need contracts with the Society since they could get their music free. It was their usual experience that publishers were 'prepared to pay for the privilege of having their songs introduced' into a pantomime. Discussions were delayed for another six months which, as Sarpy reported to his committee, was 'tantamount to shelving the matter'.[2] Even more embarrassing was the fact that the same theatres which were refusing to pay for the English repertoire were willing to renegotiate SACEM contracts, at increased fees, for French music which they mainly used for overtures and entr'actes. Feldman, a publisher whose line of business exposed him to conflicts of loyalty and self-interest, defended the theatre managers' right to resist high fees, but agreed that the proposed terms of ten, eight, and six guineas, respectively for first-, second-, and third-class theatres, were not unreasonable. He therefore promised to bargain with them and, if they remained adamant, 'throw in his lot with the Society': a notable, if temporary, declaration of allegiance by one of the leading publishers of popular music.

The loyalty of composers, many of whom felt vulnerable, was also put to the test. When Eric Coates joined the PRS, in August 1914, he was principal viola in Henry Wood's Queen's Hall Orchestra, and the youthful composer of some songs and a couple of orchestral suites. A few months later he resigned, after receiving warning letters from bandmasters, with the excuse that 'artists will not perform my works if a fee is demanded, and therefore it is detrimental to my interests to remain any longer a member'. Sarpy's tart response persuaded him to withdraw his resignation a month later, to begin a relationship with the Society, including membership of the Board, which was to prove of substantial mutual benefit.[3] Some composers took longer to commit

[2] PRS Archives, committee minutes, 20 Oct. 1914.
[3] PRS Archives, Coates file, 7 Aug. 1914; 20 Jan. 1915; 21 Jan. 1915; 4 Feb. 1915; *Performing Right Gazette*, Jan. 1928, 269–270.

themselves, John Ireland and Frank Bridge were both approached in
1918, but waited until 1924.[4] Bridge began to express interest in
1922—'He wants to join our Society at last. He is a front rank man'
wrote Volkert, his publisher, with justified enthusiasm—and soon
demonstrated a commitment which was quite extraordinary for an
active musician and teacher.[5] Replacing Monckton on the Committee
in 1925, he became the first serious composer of distinction to take an
active and sustained part in the Society's affairs.

Meanwhile the war had begun, bringing difficult problems for a
fledgling institution which was dependent upon close and frequent
international connections. An application for membership from the
distinguished publisher Breitkopf und Härtel had to be rejected as
'inopportune' with an invitation to re-apply 'at a more favourable
moment'. In similar mood, W. Schecker's resignation from the
Committee was reluctantly accepted, and his 'motives appreciated'.[6]
Even more serious was the fact that initiatives for co-operation with
performing right organizations in Austria and Germany had to be
abandoned immediately after they had been launched. Despite these
difficulties, however, the times were not wholly unpropitious for
launching the new Society. After a few months of uncertainty the
curiously distorted economics of war began to bring some benefits to
the music industry, and particularly to its indigenous practitioners
and products. Unprecedented conditions of full employment throughout the country, including plenty of jobs for women, greatly increased
the public's purchasing power. Shortages of goods in the shops left
more cash to be spent on entertainments, most of which entailed the
consumption of music. Servicemen on leave were spending freely and
taking music back to the trenches. The nation's musical expressions of
patriotism (chanting songs of recruitment and allegiance, boycotting
the enemy's tunes, or simply preferring its own) all tended to
concentrate demand on the Society's repertoire. Despite the exigen-
cies of war, therefore, it was possible for the Committee to achieve a
great deal in its first few months. Meeting on 5 February 1915 to
register new members and discuss, among other matters, how to
tackle the licensing of 'filmed songs' (the words of 'Little Grey Home
in the West' were being projected on a screen to the accompaniment
of a gramophone record) and the legal niceties of distinctions between
copyright ownership in Paris and London, the Committee's minutes
convey an air of satisfactory and continuing progress. Complacence

---

[4] PRS Archives, Schott file, 4 Dec. 1918.
[5] Ibid., 21 Mar. 1922.
[6] PRS Archives, Committee minutes, 20 Oct. 1914.

was short lived. At its next meeting, three weeks later, William Boosey reported his attendance at Pierre Sarpy's funeral.

An End to Diplomacy

The death of Sarpy was a calamity from which the Society did not fully recover for at least a decade. It was a grievous loss at the worst possible time, when policies and routines were only beginning to take shape, and alliances to be forged. A leader had died whose unique fund of experience, and ability to balance determination and tact, had been largely responsible for launching the enterprise, against all odds. His place was taken temporarily by H. S. J. Booth, who had some of the appropriate expertise but could not leave his publishing firm sufficiently to become a full-time administrator; and then, in March 1917, by John Woodhouse. A solicitor by training (he had witnessed the Memorandum of Association), office-tyrant by vocation, and litigant by temperament, Woodhouse was an accomplished maker of enemies. His post was reclassified as 'Controller', which had the right adamantine ring, with a touch of censoriousness (as the Oxford English Dictionary explains). If future progress in dealing with music producers and users would require an ability to shift between persuasion and insistence, there could be no doubting the Controller's preference. Tales of his tantrums became legends among the staff, but it has been argued in his defence that his notorious irascibility was induced by the rigours of his office, rather than exacerbating them. The present author sees little evidence for this belief. John Woodhouse was already in his late fifties when appointed; too late for acquiring unaccustomed tact. His contribution, apart from a measure of legal expertise, was to demonstrate that the PRS was not to be trifled with: doubtless a necessary image, but dangerous, if pursued too relentlessly. It can be argued that the Society was fortunate to survive his reign. His adventures in court were very costly, and not all of them were essential for the enforcement of performing right. He was unable to prevent a break up of membership which almost brought the organization to its knees. Above all, his universally acknowledged cantankerousness, which few other organizations would have tolerated for so long, influenced every relationship and damaged much that he sincerely attempted to achieve. Certainly it was an impediment to the building up of amiable public relations, without which it was difficult for an institution ultimately dependent upon goodwill to function. Fortunately, the damage was limited by the bluff good humour, and ultimate sanction, of William Boosey, and by the tact and common sense of C. F. James, who became Secretary in 1919. But this is to anticipate events which now require closer examination.

Throughout its early years the administration's primary task was to persuade users of music that it would be in their own interests to pay for something which they had previously expected to get free. This required persistently skilful advocacy, the establishment of a licensing system and, in the last resort, willingness to take legal action against defaulters *pour encourager les autres*. Litigation, rather than advocacy, was Woodhouse's strong suit, but he was aware that, in every case, success would depend upon accurate information about transgression. It was therefore essential to recruit a corps of 'agents', 'reporters', or 'inspectors'—nomenclature and function were not yet clearly defined. But suitable men were hard to find, train, and control, particularly for work in the provinces, where the evasion of licences was most common, and monitoring most difficult. 'I want to establish a more thorough visitation of unlicensed provincial establishments', he wrote in June 1917, 'but I am handicapped for want of musicians in provincial towns who would undertake the work of visiting these places and reporting on the music performed.' The cost of sending agents from London was 'almost prohibitive'. Since there were apparently no suitable men who could be taken on from 'provincial publishers of good standing', it was suggested that two 'well known music travellers' should divide the country, including Scotland and Ireland, between them, in addition to their normal duties as London publishers' representatives. Other possible recruits included an agent for a film company, described as 'a musician, very thorough and painstaking'; and the 'musical directors of touring musical comedies and revues who, though frequently duplicating towns, would by that very reason be in the position of being able to report repetitions of offences'. The handful of agents to be appointed were given lists of unlicensed establishments, and were paid admission costs, fares, and 7s. 6d. per visit, with a maximum of 15s. per day.[7]

A seemingly inexpensive and neat solution to many of these problems had been sought in the appointment of J. B. Williams in October 1915. For little more than £4 a month, plus a few shillings expenses, the Society expected to enjoy the inestimable benefit of advice and information from the Secretary of the Amalgamated Musicians Union. No one was better placed to get reliable facts and figures for grading music-halls and theatres—reporting the numbers of musicians employed and infringements of the Society's rights, even in the smallest and most remote provincial venues. It was a singularly

---

[7] PRS Archives, Francis, Day and Hunter file, June 1917.

unfortunate idea. In the first music-hall contracts, drawn up between 1915 and 1918, the cost of a licence was based on the number of instrumentalists in the orchestra, ranging from nine guineas for halls employing twelve or more, to four guineas for bands with less than eight players. This could be said to have faced Williams with a conflict of interest—a union leader was being required to provide information which might lead to some of his members losing their jobs. There was disagreement about these implications when the matter came to court; Williams dubbing the licence a 'poll tax', with the implication that heads would fall to avoid payment. More important than the intricacies of licensing and the precise terms of Williams's engagement, however, were the personalities of the protagonists. Two of the most litigious men in Britain were brought into conflict. The loquacious and abrasive union leader, whose career had been advanced by spectacular appearances in court, used to boast that he could 'paper his house with writs' and had been pointedly accused by some of his constituents of 'lining lawyers' gowns'.[8] The Controller was his natural opponent, pursuing a feud which eventually led to two separate but contemporary legal cases and a devastating boycott of the Society's repertoire by the Union. One of these lawsuits was simple, if costly: an absurdly gratuitous libel of Williams, tagged on by Woodhouse to a letter defending the Society's policies in the *Daily Telegraph*.[9] It was immediately challenged, of course, doggedly fought through the courts, and eventually adjudicated by the Lord Chief Justice, costing the Society over 500 guineas and generating much bitterness. The other court case arose from the boycott, to which we shall return. Nothing could slake the Controller's thirst for litigation. At the same PRS Committee meeting which heard of his libel costs a newspaper was reported to have described the Society's licence as 'a musical imposition'. The Society's solicitors were ordered to demand a retraction and apology for that 'libellous statement'.

Woodhouse's resort to the courts was sometimes more purposeful and relevant to the Society's immediate needs. His first action for infringement, in 1918, resulted in a notable judgement by Mr Justice (later Lord) Atkin, which provided invaluable authority and publicity. A cinema in Epsom was accused of performing 'Keep the Home Fires Burning' and 'If You Were the Only Girl in the World' without licence. The defendant claimed that his pianist had been told to extemporize and avoid copyright sheet music. He added the opinion that the PRS was merely 'engaged in the practice of fomenting and

[8] Cyril Ehrlich, *The Music Profession in Britain since the Eighteenth Century* (1985), 150–2, 180–5.
[9] *Daily Telegraph*, 10 Jan. 1919.

encouraging litigation in connection with Copyright'. Dismissing
these pleas and accusations, the judge explained that the Society
performed 'a very useful function', and proclaimed that its objects
were 'in every respect legitimate'. In a classic declaration of its right
to function he went on to say: 'One has very little sympathy when a
thief complains of the organization of the police force' but many
people otherwise 'honourable in every transaction of life . . . have very
loose notions as to the honesty of dealing with other persons' property
in such matters as copyright'.[10] This magisterial endorsement was a
valuable boost to the Society's morale, and gave users an incentive to
take up its licences—but only if they really needed its repertoire.
Unless the PRS could demonstrate its control over a substantial
proportion of music currently in demand, neither blandishment nor
legal insistence would guarantee custom. Unfortunately for the
Society, such control required more unity among publishers than was
yet forthcoming.

　　In the first few months of peace the Society rapidly lost its hold over
'popular' music. Feldman, Lawrence Wright, and the Star Music
Publishing Company resigned in January 1919, taking their composers and writers with them. By 1921 thirty-five firms belonged to the
Music Publishers' Association, of which only sixteen remained in the
PRS. Moreover, the apostates, the 'oustandings' as they were dubbed,
included every popular house except Chappell and Ascherberg. As in
1914, the industry brandished its disunity. 'We are not members of
the Performing Rights Society Ltd.' announced three leading rene-
gades in an advertisement prominently placed in the *Era*, the trade
paper, where it would be widely read and discussed. And they went
on to list twenty-three American publishers of popular music,
including that of Irving Berlin, for whom they were 'sole and exclusive
representatives' in Great Britain. Explicitly denying the Society any
right to demand fees for these works, they reiterated the challenge.
Their music could 'still be played without fee or licence. Any
interference with this liberty should be ignored, and the facts reported
to us.'[11]

　　The extent and seriousness of this disruption were profound, but its
causes are difficult to disentangle and assess, for there were clashes of
personality intermingled with cool, if ultimately wrong-headed,
assessments of self-interest. There can be no doubt, however, that
Williams did his considerable best to foment and accentuate ill-feeling
and disruption. At least one contemporary attributed the breakaway
directly to his activities, and Williams, who was nearing the end of a

[10] *PRS* v. *Thompson* (1918) 34 TLR 351.
[11] *Era*, 4 May 1921.

tumultuous career, certainly saw himself as a master strategist planning the Society's downfall. In a sustained campaign of provocation and abuse he ordered his members to boycott the Society's music and urged users to refuse its licences. The war, he told managers of theatres and cinemas, had reduced its catalogue to a nullity, with Austrian and German music removed as alien, nothing new from France, and the American 'Rag-Time catalogue of no use to anyone' because its publishers were 'quite willing that it should be used *free* by all and sundry'. Listing the publishers who had never joined the PRS, and gleefully announcing the latest departures, he deduced that some four-fifths of available music lay outside its control. His concluding call to arms was a skilful blend of fact, supposition, and wild conjecture. Managers should refuse to take up licences. The present level of fees was very low (an accurate and illuminating observation) and would soon be raised to the 10 per cent of receipts customary in France. Everyone should, therefore, join him in demanding a reform of copyright law, so that the purchase of a sheet of music would give one the right to perform it.

For members of his union, Williams's fraternal messages were simpler and peremptory. Musical directors should refuse to fill in the Society's forms, which required them to list every piece of music to be played. They had been engaged to conduct, not to act as mere clerks and 'common informers . . . supplying details to be used against musicians and employers elsewhere'. Such measures were 'a serious menace' particularly to 'the returning soldier musician'. Any manager considering the employment of a 'decent sized' orchestra would have to contemplate a 'fine of two guineas for every musician he employs over and above the number employed by his competitor'. Hinting darkly at the presence of 'pro-German influence' which might be responsible for unemployment among 'the dear boys who have done their bit', Williams then gave examples of allegedly extortionate increases: the fee for playing Debussy's String Quartet, should any Union members wish to do so, had been raised from five to forty-two shillings. Proceeding to organize the boycott, he dictated simple rules. Players, presumably having relinquished Debussy, were permitted to perform music published by Feldman, Star, Wright, and West, but should take care to avoid anything from Francis, Day and Hunter, the largest remaining popular publishers in the PRS. Their 'defeat' was to be the campaign's first objective, after which it would be necessary to 'tackle William Boosey', for Chappell would then be the only remaining enemy of any consequence. Music for forthcoming pantomimes should be carefully selected along these lines.

When the Society changed the basis of its theatre licences, obtained an injunction to prevent the boycott, and reached an 'amicable arrangement' with the Union, Williams changed tack with devious cunning. The 'poll tax' had merely been shifted from orchestral musicians to 'artistes', he alleged, and the new conditions were a 'patched up peace'. But he had to acknowledge defeat. The campaign had not met his expectations. 'We could have wiped the PRS out . . . we had them absolutely whacked', but the managers were not willing to refuse licences and 'risk proceedings'. He would 'let go' but was still determined to concentrate on copyright reform.[12] A few months later he was engaged, as James has recorded, 'to give the Society the benefit and advantage of his experience and services in a consultative capacity in connection with the Society's business.'[13] William Boosey, unsurprisingly, attempted to resign as chairman of the PRS, but was ultimately persuaded to stay.

This bewildering tangle of events was very damaging to the Society's image, structure, and morale, and therefore to its bargaining position. Francis, Day and Hunter left, or were driven out. They had been affected by the boycott, of course, but there was also fresh competition from new, post-war arrivals in Denmark Street, led by Herman Darewski. None of these firms showed any inclination to join the PRS. The Committee was in disarray, losing David Day, Worton David, Feldman, Pether, and Scott, who were replaced by a rather lack-lustre team. At the end of its first quinquennium the balance sheet looked bleak. Gross income had increased and was no longer dwarfed by expenses, but net income was barely £10,000 in 1919. Since the general level of prices had approximately doubled during the war, this sum was only equivalent, in pre-war pounds, to five times Sarpy's original salary: the founders had obviously expected much higher returns. After £1,800 had been remitted to SACEM, and £100 to the Italian Society, there was a paltry £8,000 left to distribute among 437 members, one-third apiece to composers, writers, and publishers. A slightly larger sum had been spent on administration and litigation. It was tempting to attribute these disappointing results to 'the greatest war in history', an impulse which no one resisted, but the excuse was unconvincing.[14] The music market had been buoyant, which should have been reflected in PRS receipts. Staff had been hard to get, but the amount of business never justified more extensive recruitment. In truth there was a growing sense of disenchantment and apprehension about the future. A year later William Boosey admitted as much in a letter to a colleague in SACEM. 'The Society

[12] PRS Archives, AMU file. See the *Performer*, 23 Jan. 1919.
[13] C. F. James, *The Story of the Performing Right Society* (1951), 30.
[14] PRS Committee's Report and Balance Sheet, May 1919.

has not made the progress that I anticipated' he confessed. Without 'the more important publishing houses' it lacked sufficient authority to impose its rules. Serious publishers, like Boosey and Enoch, might be persuaded to join in due course, but firms dealing with 'popular and ephemeral music' were staying out. It was, therefore, impossible to get users to obey the rules and submit programmes of works played. Until this was done the PRS would 'never be in a position to give real satisfaction either to our English members or to our Foreign associates'.[15]

One of the most remarkable facts in the history of the Society is that it did not merely survive these events, but recovered its nerve sufficiently to establish an effective unity and *esprit de corps* which it was never to lose again. Some credit for this must go to the man who, so far, has earned scant praise, for Woodhouse was a born fighter, and his sternest critics never accused him of giving up easily.

Survival

No sooner did the boycott finish than a new enemy appeared. The British Music Union Ltd. was an association of users, but, unlike the various trade organizations which represented their members in mutually helpful bargaining with the PRS, its sole purpose was to destroy the Society. Registered in November 1918 with a capital of £500, the BMU was essentially a group of dancing teachers, and did not attempt, initially, to represent a wider range of users. It invited subscribers to pay five shillings (later increased to one guinea) a year to receive catalogues of 'free music'. These would list material which could be performed without fee, for two quite distinct reasons: because copyright had expired, or because a publisher of current music waived claim to his performing rights. Dancers were primarily interested in the latter category, of course, which represented the real threat to the PRS. Ultimately, its best defence would be to regain the allegiance of the popular publishers, but for the moment it was given an opportunity to retaliate with Woodhouse's favourite weapon. The preface to the BMU's 1922 catalogue contained words which led directly to court. What proportion of the Society's fees, it asked, went to the salaries of administrative staff, rather than to 'the poor author and composer' who were 'solely meant to benefit' from 'the Act of Parliament under which the Society was enriching itself'?[16] For the ensuing libel case the litigants engaged the two most famous and expensive silks of the day, Patrick Hastings and Marshall Hall, with

[15] PRS Archives, William Boosey to M. Joubert, 4 Jan. 1921.
[16] *The Times*, 10 Feb. 1923.

supporting teams, to appear before the Lord Chief Justice and a special jury. After four days in court the defendants asked for a settlement, apologized for the libel, and agreed to withdraw the offending note, but not their catalogue. This technical defeat did not prevent their trade journal, the *Ballroom*, from hailing the proceedings as 'a great victory for uncontrolled music'.[17] Nor did it end the Society's troubles with the BMU, which changed its line of attack by promoting a private member's bill in Parliament. Seemingly innocuous, an impression which was sedulously cultivated by its backers, the 'Copyright (Musical Works) Bill' sought to 'restore the law' to its allegedly pristine condition before 1911. If enacted, it would again leave publishers unable to safeguard performing right except by printing a specific note of reservation on every copy of music.[18] This would have put the clock back, ignoring the exhaustive examination and explicit rejection of such printed notices which had preceded the 1911 reform. Numerous experts, including distinguished lawyers from Britain and France, Sarpy, Monckton, Sir Alexander Mackenzie, and William Wallace, who represented the Society of British Composers, had all spoken against the use of printed notices when giving evidence to the Gorell Committee in 1909.[19] The reinstatement of notices in 1924 would have offended against international practice, and wrought havoc among users, leaving them with a bewildering assortment of currently available music, to which were attached various legal requirements, according to its date and country of publication.

The BMU's bill was twice stillborn, in 1923 and 1924, but must be discussed because of its far-reaching consequences. Each occasion was fruitful of discord, giving the Society's enemies an opportunity to prepare for later warfare: assembling and developing their communications; testing and attempting to influence public opinion. The BMU lost no opportunity to extend its franchise, funds, and propaganda beyond the ballroom. Led by Cartwright Newsam, an unsuccessful music publisher, it found allies among a strange assembly of users, ranging from town clerks to restaurateurs and hoteliers, whose only common feature was a determination to continue using music without payment. Some Scottish Town Councils, for example, lobbied a Member of Parliament to advocate changes in the Copyright Act, a tactic which was rapidly adopted elsewhere.[20] The Parliamentary manœuvre also allowed journalists an opportunity to dig out old press

---

[17] *Performing Right Gazette*, Apr. 1923. *Ballroom*, Mar. 1923.

[18] 13 & 14 Geo. 5. Copyright (Musical Works). A Bill to Amend the Copyright Act, 1911. Bill 166, 18 June 1923.

[19] (Cd. 5051). See Ch. 1. n. 38, above.

[20] *Bioscope*, 24 May 1923. *Glasgow Herald*, 19 June 1923.

cuttings and refurbish ancient rhetoric. Thus, an article in the *Westminster Gazette* lamented that 'singing folk of a new generation are left uninstructed about the snare of copyright'. Its writer had discovered that 'decent publishers usually are quite nice about it', but some would 'exact ransom ruthlessly'. He supported the new measure, which would secure 'protection for the innocent' thanks to the good offices of some Members of Parliament whom he described as 'professional'.[21] It was a group of such men, led by the Members for Bootle and Oxford, who, professing their desire only to 'protect the innocent from the law', attempted to rush a 'very simple little Bill' through its second reading. The debate was conducted in an almost empty House, with fine oratory on behalf of 'innocent bandsmen in the North of England', amateur ladies singing 'Tit Willow', and similar victims of an organization which 'should not be allowed to act as they act and claim to be within legal rights'. Inevitably there were extended recollections of Wall; one Member of Parliament describing the PRS as 'much more violent and . . . discreditable' than the arch-villain had ever been. It was necessary, he proclaimed, to put an end to 'this existing scandal'.

Speakers in support of 'the great Society' claimed, with some exaggeration, that it represented 'the overwhelming majority of the largest publishers as well as the authors of musical compositions with the largest output'. But they were more scrupulous than their opponents in summarizing the complexities of copyright and its recent history. T. P. O'Connor, returning to a familiar battleground, adroitly outflanked the enemy by describing advocates of free music as 'a new race of pirates'. Music, he reminded them, 'is the product of a man's brain and . . . should be treated as the most sacred of all property'. Sidney Webb, who, as President of the Board of Trade, was the responsible minister, made a typically inconsequential speech, but was realistic about the international implications of performing right, and, as a socialist, appeared to be sufficiently concerned for the welfare of 'brainworkers' to lend them his support. The second reading was abandoned for six months, ending this second, and penultimate, attempt to demolish the PRS by Act of Parliament.[22]

One effect of these political skirmishes was to stimulate the Society's hitherto reluctant and desultory concern for public relations. Until 1922 communications with members and the outside world had been confined, apart from the odd pamphlet or writ, to the Committee's Report and Accounts, usually exiguous and uninformative, which was presented to a sparsely-attended and docile Annual

[21] *Westminster Gazette*, 9 June 1923.
[22] *Hansard*, 12 Feb. 1924, 813–30.

General Meeting. In July 1922 a quarterly *Performing Right Gazette* commenced publication, and there are other indications that the office was becoming slightly more conscious of the outside world. It began to collect press cuttings more carefully; partly, of course, in order to monitor the using of music, as hostile critics were quick to point out: a Member of Parliament accused it, ludicrously, of 'taking in every local paper, large and small'.[23] But the gathering of information and comment was a necessary part of a wider process of enlightenment. If users of music were to be encouraged towards a respect for intellectual property, PRS functionaries had continually to inform themselves about current behaviour, opinion, and response to the Society's initiatives. They also had to seek new channels of communication and influence. Thus, when Woodhouse learned that the BMU were organizing a lobby he sought advice about possible retaliatory moves, such as the engagement of 'a suitable Parliamentary Agent' to watch the Society's rights and interests. Having engaged one he was then counselled to write to the Prime Minister 'and other key figures', placing on record that the Bill, contrary to the soothing murmurs of its promoters, was highly contentious. The Controller's response to this advice was a document consisting of twenty-two pages of undigested gobbets from law textbooks, blue books, and court reports, which he sent to MPs in the hope of influencing their votes at the Bill's second reading. A brief covering letter made a few curt points about the Society's right to exist, but the significant information that it charged lower fees than other performing right organizations was relegated to page twenty, long past the point where most readers would have given up. But even this heavy-handed, unpersuasive advocacy was arguably an improvement on previous 'take it or leave it' attitudes. Henceforth, the office continued to receive reports of relevant Parliamentary activity from its agent, but made few attempts to communicate outside, apart from the limited readership of the *Gazette*.

Despite the continued disaffection of the 'outstandings', the Society's balance sheet had improved considerably by the end of its first decade. Gross income had nearly doubled, amounting to more than £42,000, of which some £28,000 was distributed among 557 members. Part of the gap between income and distributions was accounted for by legal costs. In 1923, for example, they exceeded £4,000, and were almost equivalent to the salaries of the entire administration, including the Controller. This was described by the Committee as 'inevitable in the pioneer work of establishing itself firmly and maintaining the rights of our members and repelling

---

[23] Ibid., 822.

attacks made from several quarters'. It then reported losing a case on 'a novel and highly technical point' of law which, 'after careful consideration', would be appealed to the House of Lords. In the following year it had to explain that losing the appeal had contributed to 'heavy legal costs which it is hoped will not recur'. It was difficult, of course, to draw the line between necessary and over-zealous litigation, but there is no evidence that members were sufficiently troubled by these costs to query them. If finances appeared to be neither princely nor always ideally apportioned, they were certainly more healthy than might have been expected after the collapse of unity, or than Boosey had anticipated in 1921. The proximate and apparently obvious reason for this improvement was the extension of licences. By 1924 there were nearly 5,500, an increase which could in turn be attributed to the administration, vigilance and litigation which accounted for high costs. That is how the situation was understood and interpreted by the Controller and his Committee. It was not a profound analysis. Improved yields were a result not so much of more intensive harvesting as of a fundamental change in the nature of the crop. The music industry, and with it the PRS, was enjoying huge benefits from a new source.

Plangent Cinemas

Cinemas provided an enormous stimulus to the music market during the 1920s. They were largely responsible for the fact that more live music was being performed by professional musicians than at any other time in the country's history. Films were silent, but they required a constant background of music which could not yet be provided by machines. The industry's economics, therefore, played into the hands of musicians, for a time. A branch of show business had at last caught up with modern industry in its ability to mass-produce a high-quality consumer good profitably at low cost—except in this one regard. Enormous quantities of music had to be supplied, separately from the main product, in the traditional, labour-intensive, 'handicraft' manner, to a thriving new industry which could afford to pay for a service which it regarded as essential. Until the autumn of 1929 suppliers of music, therefore, enjoyed a golden age. Every cinema, however small or remote, needed the services of at least a pianist for long hours throughout the week. Many of them employed groups of up to a dozen players, and 'super cinemas' in the larger towns and suburbs engaged proto-symphony orchestras. Everyone was playing simultaneously all over the country, in contrast to virtually every other kind of entertainment which, particularly outside

London, was highly seasonal and dependent upon intermittent tours. The cumulative effects upon the demand for music and musicians were, therefore, enormous. Instrumentalists enjoyed the benefits of an industry which provided some 80 per cent of their jobs, and publishers were similarly well placed. Most musicians, even performers of popular music, still played 'from the dots'. No doubt some impecunious bands got by occasionally with instrumental parts illegally pencilled from a piano score, and some cinema pianists played 'by ear', raising awkward questions of copyright. But pirated copies were no longer easily available and there was no cheap and practical means of photocopying. Sheet music had to be bought or hired in prodigious quantities.[24]

Some prescient members of the Society had always anticipated substantial returns from cinemas: it will be remembered that H. S. J. Booth had described their potential as 'dazzling'. But no one could have expected the boom to be so prodigious, and its timing so opportune. Proceeds from cinemas far exceeded music-hall payments—more than fivefold, by the mid–1920s. Members of the Cinematograph Exhibitors' Association, which covered most but not all cinemas, took out some 2,500 licences, approximately half of the total for every kind of user issued by the Society. Meanwhile, music-hall licences dropped from fifty-four in 1923 to thirty in 1925. Doubtless, this fall reflected antagonism to the Society and indifference to much of its current repertoire, for there were still several hundred music halls and theatres in existence, but it was also indicative of a steady and ultimately irrevocable change in public taste. In Victorian and Edwardian England music-hall was the fourth most popular pastime, after drinking, fornication, and sport. Now, in third or even second place, there was an entirely new form of entertainment which, ironically, and to the Society's immense good fortune, gave a new lease of life to music that was beginning to fade elsewhere.

The cinema's demand was heavily concentrated upon the 'light' music and popular classics still largely controlled by the PRS, as can be illustrated from advertisements in the *Gazette*. In January 1923 Metzler claimed to be 'the Pioneer Publishers of Cinema Music' with suites by Cowan, six books of pieces with various instrumentation 'for all and every type of picture' by Clutsam, and genteel 'popular songs' arranged by de Groot: 'A Lovely Little Dream'; 'I Love You, Ma Chérie'.[25] Ascherberg, Hopwood and Crew appealed to a wider

---

[24] Ehrlich, *Music Profession*, 194–204.
[25] *Performing Right Gazette*, Jan. 1923, 69.

market in October with 'dance and song successes which are eminently suitable for cinema, hotel and restaurant orchestras'. These comprised songs by Ivor Novello, and selections from musical comedies, waltzes, one-steps and fox-trots, including one by Tschaikowsky (*sic*): 'I Am but a Simple Country Maid'.[26] Later they announced 'The greatest HITS of the month' in the form of suites arranged by Roger Quilter from various sources, including Noel Coward's 'Poor Little Rich Girl', Cochran's review 'On with the Dance' and someone's 'The Rake' which promised to convey an 'impression of a Hogarthian orgy'.[27] For several years Ricordi offered the ubiquitous Tavan 'selections' which introduced thousands of people to opera and 'the classics'.[28] Then, there was a market, both lively and lugubrious, in background music classified by mood: 'Musical Directors of All Cinemas should not rest content' without

The Drama Collection: PATHETIC. Mourning in the home—the empty cradle; Funeral—the last journey—glooomy forebodings; Epilogue—peace after all trials; Affliction— anguish—cries of the tortured; Despair—unrequited love—cruel separation. DRAMATIC. Tumult—riots—confusion—panic; Extreme anxiety—horses stolen: Flight—in danger; Mystery—burglars in the house: SENTIMENTAL. Salvation—safety at last—unbounded joy—overwhelming relief.

Instrumentation and duration were matters of choice; and 'emotional intensity can be altered to the acting by exaggerating or softening the rendering of the expression marks'.[29] Livelier effects were available from Winthrop Rogers who offered 'Ditson's Music for the Photoplay' including 'agitatos, furiosos, mysteriosos, dramatic numbers etc.'[30]

Perhaps the most significant advertisements came from Bosworth, main publisher of Albert W. Ketèlbey, whose compositions included 'In a Monastery Garden', 'Sanctuary of the Heart', 'In a Chinese Temple Garden' and, above all, 'In a Persian Market'. The latter is an 'Intermezzo Scene' with explicit directions: 'the camel drivers gradually approach . . . the beggars in the market place . . . the beautiful Princess . . . the snake charmer' etc. The exemplar of exotic light music, this piece, or an extract from it, was probably more frequently played, at home and abroad, than any other work in the history of English music, with the possible exception of the national anthem. Not until outer space discovered Holst's *Planets* was there any rival in the quantitative stakes. Doubters should begin by estimating

---

[26] Ibid., Jan. 1924, 146.
[27] Ibid., Oct. 1925, 27.
[28] Ibid., Jan. 1925, 254.
[29] Ibid., July 1924, 206.
[30] Ibid., Apr. 1924, 186.

the number of film scenes requiring a melodic hint of the Orient, and multiply by the number of performances taking place. There were similar requirements for exotic background in other forms of entertainment, and some people simply wanted to listen to the music. In 1924 it was reported that one or other of Ketèlbey's compositions could be heard 'three or four times a day in most cinemas and restaurants'. The celebrated conductor Dan Godfrey noted that 'In a Persian Market' was the most frequently requested piece in his Bournemouth orchestra's large and eclectic repertoire. Ketèlbey, who had been elected to membership of the Society in November 1918, could therefore expect to be one of its main beneficiaries. This was indeed the case: by the late 1920s he was receiving more than £1,500 a year in performing fees. But this level of remuneration did not go unchallenged, and raised questions of general concern, both quantitative and qualitative, which were to trouble the PRS for many years to come.

Distributing the Fees

It soon became apparent that distribution of fees was a division of the Society's operations fraught with difficulty and requiring large numbers of staff. The controversy about payments to Kelèlbey and his publisher, Bosworth, is therefore, important because it raised, or exacerbated, many interrelated problems in this area. The Society's first exercises in distribution were based upon procedures which were too rudimentary to satisfy members and too ambitious to be practical. Attempts were made to collect records of actual performances from licensees, whose willingness to supply the information was made a condition of their licence. Woodhouse soon had to admit that this method was 'surrounded with great difficulty', and replaced it with a 'classification' system which was unacceptably clumsy and divisive. It is described by James as 'a classification of the members, based on their status and the character or type of their works, in conjunction with such data as were available regarding the extent of performance of their works', which begs more questions than it asks.[31] Reality is more interesting, and perhaps more instructive. Nothing connected with the process of distribution turned out to be simple. Complexities which might, at first glance, appear unnecessary, arose from rational attempts to appease conflicting interests and grapple with problems, as yet dimly perceived, which were intrinsic to the Society's functioning. The monitoring of performances and the appropriate

---

[31] James, op. cit., 25.

distribution of fees were, after all, the main purpose of the Society. These early experiments therefore deserve more than a euphemistic gloss, because the challenges to which they were a response would continue as long as the PRS itself, albeit with variations.

By the early 1920s authors, composers, and arrangers were being classified into no less than ten categories and, in addition, publishers were asked to grade them according to the 'popularity and sales' of their work.[32] Publishers were also graded, an exercise which inevitably caused dissension. In April 1923, for example, the loyal veteran Charles Volkert was moved to explain his absence from meetings where grades were discussed: 'I do not undervalue Cinemas, nor what Bosworth and Co. have built up for them . . . but I repeat that only Chappell, Hawkes, and Ascherberg are entitled to rank in first class, and I know our President shares my opinion.'[33] The persistence of such disagreements was an Achilles' heel, a potential threat to unity, and a constant reminder of the hazards attached to distribution. At their root was the immense difficulty of counting performances throughout the country, accurately, quickly, and economically. The forbidding scope of this exercise was only gradually perceived by those who had to undertake it; alternative statistical procedures and mechanization were not yet on the horizon. Were the fees paid out a reasonably fair reflection of performances which had actually taken place? Bosworth and Ketèlbey claimed that they were not. After organizing an independent check of performances in a number of cinemas, they submitted the results as evidence of underpayment, and demanded that such figures be used in calculating future distributions. Their colleagues were understandably opposed to this course of action, condemning it as divisive and likely to bid up costs by introducing competing monitors. Some feared that it would ruin Woodhouse's strenuous efforts to get 'complete' returns from licensees, as required by the terms of their licences. Anyone wanting to renege could take note that outsiders were now monitoring performances and he could gratefully relinquish any responsibility for the task. The Committee, therefore, refused to accept Bosworth's figures in allocating fees for 1924/5. Ketèlbey resigned, but was persuaded to return, and dissent was temporarily disarmed.

Even the staunchest defenders of the existing system were becoming increasingly aware of its inaccuracy, and there were many subsequent complaints. It functioned similarly to those ill-conceived computer operations which a later generation was to describe as 'GIGO' (Garbage-In-Garbage-Out), and for similar reasons. Returns of

[32] PRS Archives, Distribution Committee, letter to Sam Fox Publishing, 12 Mar. 1920.
[33] PRS Archives, Schott file, 5 Apr. 1923.

performances, the raw material for all subsequent calculations, were often grossly inadequate and unreliable. The Society could not yet expect to get anything like complete and accurate figures from the majority of users. There was, in the first place, a natural reluctance, on the part of band leaders and other designated reporters, to fill in forms conscientiously, after long, tiring sessions of playing, even if they were favourably disposed towards the PRS, and had not been encouraged by its opponents to resist the imposition of unwanted chores. It must also be remembered that Englishmen were not yet accustomed to the ways of bureaucracy, and tended to deride, or more often ignore, attempts to impose rules and demand information. Things were ordered differently in France where, despite Gallic strains of bloody-mindedness, the political, social, and commercial environment tended to be more congenial for SACEM's well-schooled procedures. In England the climate of opinion was not as antipathetic as in North America, but bureaucratic requirements had to be imposed against the grain. Not until the imposition of compulsory wireless licensing, with snooper vans to catch defaulters, did the British public begin to soften towards bureaucracy, a process which was, of course, vastly extended during the Second World War.

If it was impossible to get comprehensive and reliable basic statistics of performance, subsequent manipulation of such data as could be procured was very difficult, in the conditions of the time. The mere process of identifying which composition had been performed required access to information about an enormous and constantly growing repertoire, in diverse languages and sometimes exotic scripts, and a staff trained to process that information. Mistakes in the original returns had to be identified and corrected, a task which was frequently uncertain and always time-consuming. Many titles, particularly of popular songs and romantic ballads, were so alike as to be easily confused. 'Love', for example, was a fairly common initial word. The names of composers and writers (often pseudonyms, with several writers contributing to one composition) were commonly misspelled and misattributed. The next step was to identify and allocate precise rights to each work, often involving many interested parties in several countries, and a bewildering variety of fractional entitlements, which required exhaustive information and patient checking. Two examples must suffice, one elementary, another from a decade later, sufficiently complex to require expert attention, but by no means unique. 'Un peu d'amour' was composed by L. Silesu (foreign) and arranged by A. Wood (British); with words by C. H. Fisher (foreign) and 'A. Ross' (pseudonym, British). It was published by Digondé and Diodet (foreign) and Chappell (British). The *petits droits* in 'Waltzes from Vienna' were more complicated. Fees for compositions by Korngold and Bittner had to be allocated to four parties in the following proportions: one half and three equal sixths. Works by Clutsam paid equal quarters to four parties. Numbers by Hubert Griffiths also paid equal quarters. Earnings from the piano solo had to be allocated among six people in the proportions 20 per cent, 15 per cent, 2.5 per cent, 12.5 per cent, 25 per cent, and 25 per cent. Finally, the fees for brass- and military-band selections were divided among seven recipients in similar, but different, proportions.[34]

All of this work was extravagant in the use of labour, before the arrival of statistical sampling, cheap and simple calculating machines, and the computer. Administrative costs were therefore unavoidably high, despite the generally low level of clerical wages during the interwar years, and this in turn aroused criticism from the same members of the Society who were demanding constant improvements in the accuracy and speed of monitoring and distribution. It was a truly vicious circle of conflicting and unappeasable expectations. But these quantitative problems were simple in one respect. Given time and thought, which were admittedly not always in copious supply, they were susceptible to rational analysis and compromise. By contrast, a number of *qualitative* considerations, which also became inescapably attached to the distribution of fees, were of a wholly different order, requiring subjective assessments of individual pieces of music. Should performance of a popular song rank equally with performance of a symphony, and be equally rewarded? Should an elaborately scored orchestral composition earn the same as an equally long piano piece which had been written down more quickly and easily? If not, how were suitable 'weights' to be allocated? By duration perhaps; a forty-eight minute symphony earning sixteen times as much as a three-minute comic song? By some measure of labour input, or by aesthetic judgement about quality, prestige, seriousness of intention, and anticipated durability? Each of these suggestions was open to criticism, even disregarding motives of self-interest, and some, like proportionate simple rewards for effort, were too foolish to contemplate. Serious intentions were no guarantee of artistic achievement, as many Victorian composers had manifestly demonstrated; assessment by contemporaries rarely coincided with that of posterity; and aesthetic judgements were acknowledged to be subjective, even in an age more confident in such matters than our own. And what of durability? It was part of the conventional wisdom that popular music was ephemeral and the high earnings of a profitable number, therefore, momentary. A successful piece of 'serious' music, however,

[34] PRS Archives, Chappell file, 8 Dec. 1931.

was expected to bring in slower but more remunerative earnings. Thus, Fred Day, interviewed in the *Gazette*, sought to allay the 'alarm' of 'standard composers' by stating that 'the solid lasting thing always gets the best results of every kind in the long run'.[35]

Ketèlbey's earnings were again at the centre of such arguments. Disputing Day's contention, an anonymous writer in the *Musical Opinion* professed himself a supporter of the PRS, but 'upset' by 'the unfairness' of its distribution policies because their effect was to accentuate existing inequalities of income. Even a well-known 'serious' composition, such as John Ireland's song 'Sea Fever', he believed, could never earn as much in the long term as 'In a Monastery Garden'. Yet, Ireland was an unusually successful serious composer, while 'there are quite a few as fortunate as Mr Ketèlbey'. So a 'premium is placed upon the turning out of commercial music as compared with the composition of serious work'. An equitable and responsible policy, he suggested, would divide composers into two grades, popular and serious; and the latter should be 'allowed to divide the profits of their lucky and successful brothers by ten or some such figure'.[36] Self-righteous and simplistic, these views were probably representative of many 'serious' and academic musicians. If they seemed impracticable to the reduced and relatively homogeneous Society of the mid-twenties, they would certainly be unacceptable when the 'outstanding' publishers and composers returned. Yet, they articulated a real dilemma.

[35] *Performing Right Gazette*, July 1926, 101–3.
[36] *Musical Opinion*, Sept. 1926.

3

AN EFFECTIVE ALLIANCE

1926 was an *annus mirabilis* in the history of the Performing Right Society. Any year which registered Leslie Boosey, Vivian Ellis, and Gustav Holst as new members would be worthy of celebration, but in the year of the General Strike most of the musicians and publishers of Great Britain decided to bury their differences. The 'outstanding group' returned to the fold, bringing with them a number of firms new to the PRS. Twenty applied to join, or rejoin, at the beginning of March, including all of the leading 'popular houses' and such publishers as Boosey, Curwen, Elkin, Keith Prowse, Paxton, and Joseph Williams. Among the additional eleven applicants a fortnight later was J. H. Larway, who had been one of the Society's most unhelpful bystanders at its birth (see page 18). Unity brought an immediate increase and diversification of repertoire. In addition to a spectacular transformation in the range of dance and 'popular' music covered by a PRS licence, there were songs by Warlock and Vaughan Williams, and instrumental works by Rutland Boughton, Frederic Cowen, and Elgar. Even cinemas, already well served and still devouring live music, now had an even wider choice. Newcomers like Montague Ewing, and established favourites like Ketèlbey, whose 'In a Monastery Garden' was published by Larway, major accessions, which included the huge Sam Fox catalogue of American music for accompanying silent films, offered by Keith Prowse—all became available with a PRS licence.

The immediate reasons for this volte-face are less important than its effects; but they are, nevertheless, intriguing, because there is no simple explanation for these apparently last-minute conversions to performing right. James attributes them to falling sales of sheet music, but that decline, though already perceptible to those who wished to see, was not yet precipitous or universal.[1] Sales of drawing-room ballads were first in line for collapse, a fact of particular importance to the Boosey company. Many diverse kinds of music, having little in common except an ultimate dependence upon large-scale purchase by amateurs, would soon follow. But much else destined for oblivion was still being sustained by the silent movies—and by inertia, because

---

[1] C. F. James, *The Story of the Performing Right Society* (1951), 46–7.

fundamental changes in public taste take at least a generation to work their way through the market. Sales of 'educational' music, for example, actually enjoyed a minor boom at about this time, though the long-term trend would inexorably move downwards as the ownership of pianos declined. The ubiquitous 'piano in the parlour' was eventually driven out by alternative status symbols and forms of entertainment, a social revolution already perceptible immediately after the war, but taking about twenty years before it became everywhere apparent.[2] Meanwhile many publishers, including some who were highly alert to market trends, continued to regard sales of sheet music as central to their business, even when this conflicted directly with performing fees. Blackpool, an obvious focus of attention for show business, was a significant test case for their priorities. Its intensive season concentrated demand for music into a few hectic weeks, and there were later spin-off effects when people returned home wanting to rekindle holiday pleasures. In addition to shows, concerts, dances, a circus, hotels, and restaurants, there were innumerable music shops where the latest numbers were plugged by pianists and singers. When Woodhouse proposed to tighten up licensing in 1923 he was, therefore, immediately cautioned by an experienced publisher. There was no objection to insisting that Blackpool's places of entertainment take up PRS licences, he was told, but its shops should be left alone, because they were key points for advertising and selling sheet music.[3]

A house magazine published in August 1927 illustrates the continuity of this tradition. It alerts retailers to autumn business opportunities after the summer holidays. People will return from seaside resorts 'to office, mill and factory' with memories of such Feldman hits as 'We Must Have Another', the big 'social' number, presumably intended to be sung around the piano. There are advertisements for sixpenny editions of songs, a 'Communityland' collection and plenty of piano albums 'in various grades of difficulty'. Flourishing business in selections from *The Vagabond King* can be expected, proving that 'there is still a big public who prefer light classical music to jazz'; Florrie Forde is reported to have led an audience of 6,000 in singing 'When the Lovebird Leaves the Nest', and unprecedented numbers of trippers to Douglas will guarantee that Belfast dealers reap 'the benefit of the Feldman plug'. There is, to be sure, an advertisement for gramophone records, and a notice of newly acquired PRS membership, reminding 'bandsmen and artiste

---

[2] Cyril Ehrlich, *The Piano: A History* (1976), 184–7.
[3] PRS Archives, Chappell file, Goodman to Woodhouse, 22 Mar. 1923.

friends' that public performance requires a licence. But the general message of this lively publication is little different from pre-war days: sell sheet music to people who play and sing.[4]

If the Society's new allies were not simply running away from a dying traditional market, what had changed their minds? Ever since the breakup there had been repeated attempts to negotiate re-entry, by individuals on both sides of the divide. In February 1920 the Committee discussed an elaborate set of terms for readmission submitted by the 'Popular Houses', but failed to reach agreement. Representation, administrative procedures, and the allocation of fees were apparently the main points of difference.[5] The shift in public taste towards American popular music was a significant factor. The Secretary of the American Society of Composers, Authors and Publishers, the first American performing right society, which had also started in 1914, pointed out that most of its publisher members had contracts with English firms 'who are not allied with your Society'. He urged Woodhouse to strive for reconciliation and unity. Ironically, in the light of later American disunity, he added the boast that 'we accomplish it here . . . and are progressing very rapidly and successfully'.[6] A year later E. M. Goodman, a leading Chappell executive, who had been associated with that company since 1880 and a director since 1904, was tirelessly engaged in diplomatic overtures to the main dissidents, Feldman, Lawrence Wright, and Darewski. Such was his dedication to the task that he even braced himself to recommend a policy of 'patient and tactful persuasion' to the Controller. Yet nothing came of these discussions, which frequently broke up to an old refrain: should music-hall artistes pay or be paid for performing a song?[7] One publisher among the outsiders was notably less parochial: contemporaries used such words as 'professional' and 'modernization', then uncommon in the vocabulary or practice of English commerce, when applauding his business activities. A persistent champion of re-entry, Fred Day had sharpened his understanding of the music industry by experience at its main frontier of change. He had worked for Max Dreyfus, the emperor of American popular music who, with his brother Louis, had been associated with Gershwin, Kern, Porter, and Rogers and Hart. He had frequently revisited the United States, and was now leading a revitalized Francis, Day and Hunter, with a diverse and up-to-date catalogue handled by offices in New York, Paris, and (later) Berlin. Vivian Ellis

[4] *Feldmanism: The Magazine of the House of Feldman*, vol. 3 no. 9. Aug. 1927.
[5] PRS Archives, General Committee minutes, 4 Feb. 1920.
[6] PRS Archives, ASCAP to Woodhouse, 25 Apr. 1921.
[7] PRS Archives, Chappell file, Goodman to Woodhouse, 7 and 10 Jan. 1922.

began to learn his craft with the firm, working as a reader and song plugger, and in a delightful memoir confirms that Fred Day was the cynosure of Denmark Street.[8] Thanks largely to his influence, the Associated Publishers of Popular Music had been persuaded to debate performing right for several years, gradually educating opinion until an alliance, as Day later remarked, became 'practical politics'.[9]

A New Outlet

The case for unity received a powerful boost from a totally new source of revenue, potentially richer than anyone could yet recognize, easy to tap, but very difficult to organize for maximum benefit. It is a commonplace that established interests generally distrust innovation, even if its prospects are benign. A new technology, in particular, is almost always opposed and, if possible, kept out by guardians of the old. Radio, which would rapidly bring enormous benefits to many people in the music industry, was initially regarded by most of them as a usurper or, at least, a scapegoat for all kinds of difficulty. It must be admitted that many publishers were more adept than the rest of the musical establishment at assessing radio's potential. But even they were inclined to regard it as an experiment of limited extent and life expectancy.[10] The Society was quick off the mark, but Woodhouse proceeded slowly and cautiously, with typically legalistic circumspection. 'There is considerable agitation proceeding here on the subject of the broadcasting of music (music by wireless)', he wrote in July 1922, 'and it would appear to call for serious attention in regard to performing rights'. He was asking the Secretary of ASCAP for American reactions and proposals for dealing with the new medium. Concerned groups in England, he reported, were 'unanimous that performing right would be infringed where the performance is given and heard by the public, i.e. at the place of reception'.[11]

Caution continued to prevail for several years. Readers of the *Gazette* were assured that 'the recent developments in this country in regard to the dissemination of Copyright music by wireless are receiving the Society's attention'; and later that 'everything possible is being done to safeguard the interests of our members'.[12] At the next Annual General Meeting there was still no display of enthusiasm for the new medium. William Boosey announced that 'Acting in

---

[8] Vivian Ellis, *I'm on a Seesaw* (1974), 52–62.
[9] *Performing Right Gazette*, July 1926, 101–3.
[10] Cyril Ehrlich, *The Music Profession in Britain since the Eighteenth Century* (1985), 221–2.
[11] PRS Archives, Woodhouse to ASCAP, 26 July 1922.
[12] *Performing Right Gazette*, Oct. 1922, 28, and Jan. 1923, 51.

sympathy and co-operation with the joint committee of theatre and music hall and other entertainment managers', he had 'suspended negotiations with the British Broadcasting Company for the time being'. Broadcasts were being monitored and the matter would be pursued 'when the moment is opportune'.[13] One difficulty was that the Company refused to acknowledge that broadcasting was a public performance. It was willing to pay for the use of PRS repertoire, but would not admit formal legal responsibility. On the other hand the Society's choice of allies was ill-judged, for all had, or thought they had a vested interest in the past, regarding broadcasting with mingled condescension and fear, certain that it had no benefits to offer those whom they claimed to represent.[14] Perhaps, for some of them there was real self-interest and a grain of commonsense in this caution and apprehension, but composers and publishers required more foresight and a firmer commitment to the new medium. Moreover if the proclaimed aloofness of Boosey and Woodhouse was intended to imply that there had been hard bargaining with the BBC, subsequent events did not justify this boast.

The British Broadcasting Company began its regular service in November 1922, and the audience grew apace. There were more than half a million holders of radio licences in 1923, over one million in the following year, and two million by 1926. From the start, music occupied a considerable proportion of broadcasting time, even in Reith's austere schedules, so fees for performance were potentially valuable. But the Society was slow to reap this harvest. A PRS licence based on a fixed charge per station per year brought in about £1,000, and the yield barely doubled by 1925, equivalent to less than one-third of the fees from cinemas. Meanwhile, publishers outside the PRS made their own arrangements, beginning with a toughly negotiated fee of £1,000 for the first year's broadcasts of their repertoire, despite the fact that it was much smaller than the Society's. They then initiated a series of experiments with more complicated, but far more remunerative, procedures. Two shillings and sixpence was charged for each item per station, for the first 100,000 licences, increasing by sixpence for every extra 50,000, with a maximum of three shillings and sixpence per item. Then, in 1925 a new agreement levied differential charges. Dance tunes cost four shillings, and other music of less than seven minutes' duration five shillings, for each broadcast from a main station. 'Relay' station broadcasts were charged two shillings and threepence, and two shillings and sixpence, respectively.

[13] Ibid., July 1923, 104.
[14] Asa Briggs, *The History of Broadcasting in the United Kingdom*, vol.i. *The Birth of Broadcasting* (1951), 250–3.

In October 1925 the PRS Committee and non-member publishers agreed to seek 'uniformity' when negotiating broadcasting fees, and after further meetings, which doubtless encouraged hopes of wider co-operation, adopted a version of the latter's 'programme' system.[15] It resulted in payments, for the combined repertoire, of nearly £36,000 in 1926, approximately fifteen times the Society's previous revenue from broadcasting.

A True Alliance

The final step to unity was not taken without faltering, for there was a last-minute attempt in January 1926 to form a separate, breakaway society, which might have led to a disastrous long-term split between rival groups of publishers and composers.[16] It failed, and the conditions of reconciliation and unity were sorted out. High on the list was the establishment of a separate department to handle broadcasting fees, with an undertaking that they would be distributed 'as soon as practicable after collection'. C. J. Dixey, an accountant who had been handling broadcasting arrangements for non-member publishers, was brought in to run the new department. An increase in the scale and complexity of operations, all highly labour-intensive, required more space and staff. In 1921 the Society had moved its headquarters from Shaftesbury Avenue to better accommodation at a prestigious address: Chatham House, Hanover Square. Now, adjacent offices were acquired, the staff increased to eighty, and there was a considerable increase in the cost of salaries and wages, which approximately doubled between 1925 and 1929. The administrative structure was made more formal and elaborate, replacing the previous practice of leaving most decisions in the Controller's hands, with rare intervention by Goodman or William Boosey. Four specialist committees were set up: 'Broadcasting', 'Tariffs and Legal', 'Foreign and Colonial', and the quaintly named 'Gazette and Propaganda', all reporting to a newly-created Board of Directors, which replaced the former General Committee.[17] Not that its terms of reference became any narrower; a typical agenda would range from the Romanian Society's request for affiliation to the licensing of church halls in Bristol.[18] Instead of eighteen Directors there were now twenty-four, seven of whom were new members, but the old balance between composers, writers, and publishers remained unchanged, in a sense.

[15] PRS Archives, General Committee minutes, 22 Oct. 1925; 28 Jan. 1926; 19 Feb. 1926.
[16] Ibid., 7 Jan. 1926.
[17] Ibid., 13 Apr. 1926.
[18] PRS Archives, Board minutes, 9 Nov. 1926.

The new composer-directors were Harry Collman and two musicians of diverse background and accomplishment: W. H. Squire was a distinguished 'cellist who wrote light music; 'Horatio Nicholls' was using the *nom de plume* under which he wrote pseudo-American popular songs. Self-made to the point of caricature, this representative Tin-Pan-Alley figure had moved from a stall in Leicester market to a little shop in Denmark Street, writing most of the numbers he published, including the quintessential tear-jerker 'Don't Go Down the Mine Daddy'. He rapidly acquired half the street, was notorious for 'stunts', plugs, and showmanship, and was still capable of writing a genuine hit, such as the immensely successful 'Amongst My Souvenirs'.[19] In 1929 he shifted names and directorships to become Lawrence Wright, publisher-director.

At the Society's thirteenth Annual General Meeting, William Boosey claimed that composers and publishers were 'all represented and united' for the first time, and another dignitary greeted 'the year in which the Society became one hundred per cent strong'.[20] Since a few prominent firms and individuals still remained outside, neither statement was technically correct, but their essential truth could not be gainsaid. Total membership had increased from 564 to 855, and the PRS now controlled a very large proportion of currently performed music, amounting to about two million works. In addition to its domestic membership and repertory, the PRS also represented foreign societies through contracts of affiliation, which had been steadily extended since the war. An elaborate network of international co-operation was being steadily assembled, with constant communication between society officials, regular meetings, and conferences. By 1930 the holder of a PRS license was enabled in this way to use music from affiliated societies in Austria, Brazil, Czechoslovakia, Denmark, France, Germany, Hungary, Italy, Poland, Romania, Spain, Sweden, Switzerland, and the USA.[21] More countries were covered by mandates, as in the case of Norway and Finland, whose 'foreign relations' were handled by the Swedish society, and Portugal, represented by SACEM, until their own societies were set up.

The growth of membership and control brought two crucial problems. First, it was essential to increase revenue. In 1926 the influx of new members meant that the average level of payments per head— more slices from the same cake—inevitably fell, until the general level of fees could be raised.[22] The resulting upheaval caused upset within

---

[19] Ian Whitcomb, *After the Ball*, (1972) 162–3.
[20] *Performing Right Gazette*, July 1927, 216 and 213.
[21] *Special Report from the Select Committee on the Musical Copyright Bill* (1930), Q. 1428.
[22] *Performing Right Gazette*, Jan. 1926, 135.

the Society and, more acutely, among users. Moreover, control of an even larger proportion of copyright music smacked of monopoly, and this, too, would not long go unchallenged.

Prominent among the new members were two men of different background, but exceptional character and ability. Fred Day has appeared in earlier pages. Leslie Boosey will dominate later ones. He was William's cousin, and son of Arthur, the head of Boosey and Co. Born in 1887, Leslie was educated at Malvern and then offered the choice of 'varsity' or a job in Paris. Wisely choosing the latter, he worked at Durand et Fils, Debussy's publisher, where he acquired an excellent training: intimate knowledge of the French music industry, fluency in the language, and singing lessons in the eminent school of Jean de Reske, bringing him to a professional level of attainment which proved useful for his next task. Returning to the family firm he was told to organize its celebrated ballad concerts, a task which he performed with discrimination and fine discernment for a voice. He also joined the Territorial Army, and was commanding a company when war broke out. By some miracle he survived Loos, the Somme, and Ypres (two batmen were killed by his side, and a brother died in the same battalion). He was recommended for the DSO, but failed to get it because of a technicality. This experience of long service, survival, and scant recognition set a pattern for the rest of his life. Released from a prisoner-of-war camp, Leslie Boosey found his father dying and had to take over the firm after an absence of five years. Since ballads, still selling some 200,000 copies a year in 1919, were the mainstay of Boosey's business, Arthur had been a natural and energetic opponent of performing right. Leslie was more conscious of changes in the market place but, as he later recollected, could not bring himself to the point of reversing his father's policy for several years after taking over the firm. In 1926 the returning group of publishers begged him to join them and, after much soul searching, he finally agreed and was elected to the Board.

1926 was in every respect a watershed. A new alliance emerged, more complete than ever before and, as spectacular events were shortly to prove, far more resilient. A new era in policy and administrative style was also beginning to be shaped by new men. It was different in both content and demeanour: less abrasive, but with no diminution of authority or care for the interests of members. Although Woodhouse was due to retire, he was allowed to continue as Controller for a further two years, at his own request.[23] In April 1929 the job was given to C. F. James, who had been Secretary for ten

---

[23] PRS Archives, Board minutes, 13 Oct. 1926.

years; G. H. Hatchman, who had joined the staff in 1922, becoming Secretary. It was symbolic of the change that James took office under the more amiable title of General Manager.[24] Woodhouse became a 'Consulting Director', largely concerned with international matters, a position which he continued to occupy, with frequent attendance at Board meetings, until his death in 1948 at the age of eighty-six.[25] William Boosey took his own departure with greater despatch, retiring as Chairman through ill health in June 1929.[26] He died in April 1933 aged 69, and was justly mourned as a founding father. Without him, said T. P. O'Connor, there would have been no Copyright Act in 1911. Without his determined support, Pierre Sarpy might never have got the PRS started; and without the frequent exercise of his good judgement after the latter's death it might have foundered on the sands of litigation and rancour. But conditions were changing fast and his resignation was as well timed as had been his numerous interventions in the past.

An effective alliance had been forged by self-interest. It was now to be tempered by adversity. Between 1927 and 1931 the PRS faced and withstood three simultaneous onslaughts which tested its strength almost to destruction. The 'plugging controversy' was a conflict between some popular publishers and the BBC, seemingly trivial at first, which soon endangered sensitive negotiations with the Society's newest and potentially most important patron. Meanwhile, there was a reassertion of consumer resistance, again using Parliament as its agency but, significantly, excluding the BBC. Thirdly, and coincidentally, the silent movies suddenly collapsed, causing immediate and extensive unemployment among musicians and a precipitous fall in the demand for sheet music. Surviving all this required resourcefulness, determination to preserve hard-won unity at practically any cost, and a measure of good fortune.

Plugging Interlude

There was nothing new in plugging, even if the name was a recently imported Americanism. With luck and an ear for fashion, repetition of a song was known to be a familiar route to its popularity. Plugging pianists were advance troops in the scramble for cash, and it had long been common practice to pay prominent performers for bringing numbers before the public; so common that, as we have seen, adherence to the system had prevented some publishers from

[24] Ibid., 9 Nov. 1928.
[25] *PRS Bulletin*, Apr. 1948, 136.
[26] PRS Archives, Board minutes, 25 July 1929.

supporting the Society in its early days. But the size of the new radio audience was already giving new meaning to the conception of prominence, and the potential benefits of a plug. When the first reports of its exploitation reached the PRS Board late in 1926, disapproval was expressed and publishers were urged to stop paying dance bands to promote their numbers.[27] For the next two years the practice continued and was deplored by letter-writing members of the public, without attracting any general interest. The Association of Popular Publishers, responding to a remonstrance from the Corporation, appointed a 'vigilance committee' and passed a resolution, which welcomed co-operation from the BBC.[28] But the latter's concern was beginning to intensify, becoming an obsession as repeated attempts failed to eliminate plugging. According to a senior BBC official 'the evil' was rampant during outside broadcasts from fashionable hotels and night-clubs, an opinion which was confirmed by Harvey Grace, a leading church musician and editor of the *Musical Times*. It was 'common knowledge', he reported in the *New York Herald Tribune*, that favoured band leaders had been handsomely rewarded for announcing selected foxtrots, and it was 'some plug too'. Happily the BBC were now taking drastic action, in a manner which Dr Grace apparently believed would earn public approval. In future outside broadcasts only the place and name of the band would be announced, and the task would be performed by a BBC announcer. No dance tune titles would be given.[29] As an added precaution it had also been decided that if bands tried to shout titles they would be faded out between numbers.[30]

There was curiously little comment in the British press about this dramatic turn of events, though the *Daily Express*, allowing its patriotism to outweigh its antagonism to the BBC, applauded an end to the advancement of 'foreign' (meaning American) songs. The PRS, it advised, should collect more money for British composers rather than protest against 'drastic new orders'.[31] But the Society did protest to the BBC, claiming that it was an integral part of their agreement that music should be 'duly and adequately announced'. This was vigorously rejected by the Corporation, which refused to accept 'dictation from any outside body' about its presentation of programmes, and insisted that it had been driven to action because all other attempts to control plugging had failed.[32] Meanwhile, the

[27] Ibid., 9 Dec. 1926.
[28] Ibid., 15 Mar. 1928.
[29] *New York Herald Tribune*, 31 Mar. 1929.
[30] Asa Briggs, *History of Broadcasting*, vol. ii, *The Golden Age of Wireless* (1965), 86.
[31] *Daily Express*, 6 Mar. 1929.
[32] PRS Archives, Letters between PRS and BBC, 20 Feb., 4 and 6 Mar., 17 July, 1929.

diplomatic skills of Fred Day and Leslie Boosey were brought into play. In a series of visits to Savoy Hill, Day explained that popular publishers were bitterly resentful and warned that they would oppose renewal of the BBC's contract unless announcements were reinstated. Admitting their own inability to control plugging, they believed that only the BBC could do so by recruiting suitably knowledgeable staff to select dance music for broadcasting.[33] There were indications that the BBC was beginning to move in this direction, such as the appointment and promotion of Jack Payne. It welcomed Day's 'sincere efforts', but was not prepared to extend confidence in his goodwill more generally to Denmark Street.

Throughout months of intense argument, preoccupation with plugging appeared to be threatening the entire structure of broadcasting fees. In the words of a BBC official there was an 'impasse . . . our amicable though protracted negotiations appear to be doomed to failure' because 'the public interest is heavily engaged in the prompt and effective suppression of . . . a growing menace'.[34] Woodhouse, who was still conducting the correspondence, expressed concern without giving way. Anxious to co-operate in the elimination of 'a very pernicious system', the Society, nevertheless, insisted upon its 'absolute right to state the terms upon which we will allow our repertoire to be used by your Corporation in all its aspects'. He urged the BBC to sign its contract.[35] This show of strength concealed dissensions which were articulated at a meeting of Society officials and the Associated Publishers of Popular Music. Some abrasive publishers were eager to fight by refusing permission to broadcast their material. Others argued, correctly as things turned out, and with a better understanding of popular taste than Dr Grace, that 'public agitation' would force the BBC to climb down. Woodhouse suggested a renewal of the licence for an interim year without insisting upon announcements, and was supported by Leslie Boosey, who expressed concern that the BBC, if pushed too hard, might seek intervention from the Government. It was decided, with some dissent, to buy time by adopting the Controller's proposal.[36]

During the summer it became evident that the BBC was losing its battle. In the outcome plugging was never completely eliminated, despite innumerable meetings, resolutions, and suggested procedures.[37] But on the immediate question of announcements the BBC was forced

[33] PRS Archives, F. Day report, 16 May 1929; letter to C. F. James, 18 July 1929.
[34] PRS Archives, BBC to PRS, 6 Mar. 1929.
[35] PRS Archives, Controller to BBC, 6 Mar. 1929.
[36] PRS Archives, Meeting of Associated Publishers of Popular Music at PRS, 14 Mar. 1929.
[37] Briggs, *Golden Age*, 85–6.

to retreat, reintroducing them in October 1929. The *Melody Maker* proclaimed 'unconditional surrender', welcomed 'restored sanity', and dismissed a euphemistic gloss of the episode in the *Radio Times*. Dance music, it concluded, required a 'judicious expenditure of cash and gumption'.[38] In these changed circumstances Boosey was able to prepare the ground for better understanding between the two institutions. Most important was a series of letters to, and meetings with, the Director-General of the BBC. The PRS, Boosey explained, had no regard for plugging, though to call it 'abominable' was 'losing your sense of proportion a bit'; but it could not allow 'the precedent of using a man's music without making acknowledgement'. Although any suggestion of a separate agreement for dance music would be 'entirely contrary to the spirit of unity we have endeavoured to create in the Society', there would be no question of refusing a licence.[39] It was the beginning of a working relationship between the two men which was to prove invaluable in future negotiations. A contract was signed which would at least 'bind the parties of goodwill'.[40] A patched-up arrangement, with crippling financial limitations, it was completed not a moment too soon, for enemies were at the gates.

'An insult to the craft of music'

The rise and fall of the 'Tuppenny Bill' is one of the most celebrated incidents in the history of the PRS. Documented by a massive Parliamentary Report, replete with evidence and opinion, it attracted widespread interest and comment, in newspapers and among a public hitherto not much concerned with the Society's activities.[41] The debate was more animated and, at least outside Parliament, generally better informed than during the comparatively minor skirmishes of 1923 and 1924. Its effects upon the PRS were profound and long-lasting. New leadership and the foolishness of its enemies gave the Society an opportunity to close ranks, mobilize support, and attempt to educate public opinion, arguing its case with confidence and aplomb. The campaign ended in a resounding victory which made the defeated look mean and foolish, and was sufficiently decisive to dissuade further outbreaks of destructive opposition for another generation. But all this took three years to achieve, and the fact of success does not mean that it was never in doubt. History should not

---

[38] *Melody Maker*, Nov. and Dec. 1929; *Radio Times*, 1 Nov. 1929.
[39] PRS Archives, Leslie Boosey to Sir John Reith, 6 and 24 Dec. 1929; Reith to Montgomery, 30 Nov. 1929.
[40] PRS Archives, BBC to Leslie Boosey, 10 Oct. 1929.
[41] *Special Report . . . Copyright Bill*, (see n. 21).

be read backwards, with Panglossian hindsight. The Tuppenny Bill, for all its ineptitude and foolish malevolence, represented a significant threat by determined and resourceful adversaries. Its demolition was a triumph for justice and common sense, assisted by intelligent leadership. Complex information was lucidly presented with, for once, a minimum of legalistic obfuscation. Tortuous arguments of attack and defence were unravelled patiently and without undisciplined rancour. Most effective of all, perhaps, was the exercise of public ridicule in the Society's defence, by two great masters of that martial art.

The initial attack came from a familiar quarter. Despite its pretentious title and demeanour, 'The International Council of Music Users Ltd.', registered as a company in October 1927, began life in much the same form as its defunct predecessor, the British Music Union Ltd. Its governing body originally consisted of a dancing teacher, the secretaries of three catering associations, two prominent hotel managers, and a Musicians' Union official. Later, they were joined by more dancing teachers, hoteliers, and restaurateurs, and J. M. Glover who, after presiding over the early numbers of the *Performing Right Gazette*, had changed sides to edit the *Theatrical Managers' Journal*. It was a simple matter, then as now, to marshal a lobby, though slower perhaps. For the next two years the ICMU steadily tried to influence opinion in Parliament and among the public. Anecdotes and odd snippets of misinformation were fed to the press by Captain (or Major: the rank varied) J. Russell Pickering, the Council's secretary, an accountant who had managed Bertram Mills Circus, and was later to move on to holiday camps and the Royal Opera House, Covent Garden.[42] His new organization, he informed the *Era*, was 'purely defensive and in no way aggressive', aiming to 'protect the interests of those performing music in public'. It would even benefit publishers (there was no mention of composers) 'as it is by performing music that it becomes popular'. The *Daily Sketch* forecast 'a big fight' because performing fees for 'modern popular music' were 'much too high'. The public, the *Sketch* reassured its readers, was about to rebel throughout Europe by 'dancing the barndance and polka'. The absurdity of such reports is partly explained by the existence of widespread distaste for and antagonism towards the growing influence of American popular culture, in films and music. It was particularly strong among the articulate middle class and middle aged. The BBC was no stranger to such prejudice, and its austere journal, the *Listener*, which commenced publication in

[42] *Daily Sketch*, 4 and 7 Nov. 1927.

1929, was even capable of sharing gossip with Fleet Street for the good of the cause. Thus a music critic welcomed 'a thoroughly English dance in 6/8 time, somewhat related to Sir Roger de Coverley, that shall supplant the hated thing' (meaning American popular music) and added the premature epitaph, 'Who hears "Alexander's Ragtime Band" now?'[43]

Subscribers to the ICMU were asked to contribute fees equivalent to 10 per cent of their PRS licences, up to a maximum of twenty-five guineas.[44] None of them appeared to be quite sure what was being offered in return, though a 'library' was mentioned.[45] Did this imply provision of alternative 'free' music—barn dances, polkas, and the Sir Roger de Coverley, perhaps—or was the Council offering to act as an intermediary, pledged to reducing the cost of PRS licences? Or were its ambitions more simply destructive? Exasperated, reasonably for once, by the enthusiasm of Bournemouth's municipal authorities for these nebulous enticements, Woodhouse demanded of its leading musician 'what do they suppose this Council of Music Users can do for them (in return for) ten per cent of the fee they pay to us for a very solid and valuable privilege?' Sir Dan Godfrey could only reply that he had not been consulted by his employers, but that the Town Clerk supported the venture and it was backed by 'prominent names'.[46] Support for the ICMU was similarly enthusiastic but ill-defined in Scotland where, as in 1923, some town councils proclaimed eager, incoherent, and diverse support for the Society's enemies. Dundee councillors, for example, appeared to expect a supply of 'free music', a PRS licence reduction from sixty to five pounds, *and* 'a national , opposition strong enough to bring the issue into Parliament'.[47]

When communicating privately with the PRS, as distinct from the rhetoric of its public utterances, the ICMU was conciliatory in tone and ostensible purpose. It purported to act as an association of associations, in quest of uniform licensing and 'reasonable fees'; and spoke soothingly of 'harmonious relationship and co-operation'.[48] The Controller's response was characteristically robust. Letters to important and self-important dignitaries were phrased, indiscriminately, *de haut en bas*, usually beginning with a remonstrance or reprimand even when they ended with invitations to further discussion, and not hesitating to dismiss serious arguments as 'child-

---

[43] *Listener*, 31 July 1929.
[44] *Era*, 30 Nov. 1927.
[45] *Dundee Courier and Advertiser*, 17 Apr. 1928.
[46] PRS Archives, Correspondence between Woodhouse and Godfrey, 6 and 7 Feb. 1928.
[47] *Dundee Courier and Advertiser*, 17 Apr. 1928.
[48] PRS Archives, Pickering to Woodhouse, 6 July 1928.

ish'.[49] Although this was his customary demeanour, he now showed signs of being taxed beyond endurance. Fired by rightful indignation and customary spleen, he was also encouraged by recent success in court against the *Hotel Review*; an action which had elicited costs, an apology, and an admission, particularly important in the light of subsequent events, that PRS tariffs were 'no more than a fair charge'.[50] Nor was there much tact or diplomacy from William Boosey, who engaged in a vigorous correspondence about 'The Music Users' Revolt'. He drew attention to the fact that a luxury hotel was paying its band £1,000 a week while complaining about performance fees of less than £200 a year. He took a side swipe at the Musicians' Union, then at a high peak of success, power, and complacency; for silent cinemas were still alive with the sound of live music. Its current leaders, said Boosey, were 'the spoilt darlings of the profession . . . without the excuse that restaurant keepers have of not understanding anything about the subject in dispute'.[51] These early reactions to the ICMU were sufficient evidence that, despite Pickering's honeyed tones and the slow run-up to open conflict, feelings ran high and much was genuinely at stake.

The masquerade of negotiation continued for a time, but disparities were too acute for compromise. A prime example of irreconcilable difference, which was later subjected to scrutiny by the Parliamentary Select Committee, was the reiteration of old complaints about programme returns. Faced with the demand that its licensees should no longer be required to list works performed, the Society explained that the whole system of distributing fees depended upon this information. Refusal to supply it would be sufficient reason, in itself, for abandoning further discussions. This, as Leslie Boosey pointed out to the Committee, had probably been the ICMU's intention, but its other demands were similarly unacceptable. It was presumptuously setting itself up as an agent for the renegotiation of long-term contracts which had already been settled. Above all, it was demanding absurd reductions in fees, down to a minimum of two guineas, in place of the existing five guineas.[52] There was little doubt that such demands were deliberately provocative and pitched at levels which invited rejection. The next step for the ICMU was to 'introduce a Bill into Parliament with the avowed object of removing the necessity for the existence of the PRS'.[53] It came to the House on 22

---

[49] PRS Archives, Woodhouse to various correspondents, 6 and 9 Feb. 1928; notes of meeting with ICMU deputation, 3 Apr. 1928.

[50] *Performing Right Gazette*, Oct. 1928, 362.

[51] *Evening Standard*, 1 July 1927, repr. in *Performing Right Gazette Supplement*, July 1927.

[52] *Special Report . . . Copyright Bill*, Q. 2996–3000.

[53] Ibid., Q. 3000.

November 1929 and soon received a second reading without a division. At that moment the PRS faced the worst crisis in its history.

The Musical Copyright Bill proposed two amendments to the 1911 Copyright Act:

(1) to make it compulsory that a printed notice of reservation of those rights should be printed on every copy of the work as a condition of the retention of the performing rights in musical works, and
(2) to provide a compulsory licence in respect of performing rights, in so far as they have been retained by printing the required notice, with a fixed maximum applicable to the fee which the owner of performing rights may demand from the music user.[54]

The first amendment merely repeated the British Music Union's gambit of 1923, and was open to the same objections. It was attempting to ignore the mass of evidence which had preceded the 1911 Act, the existence of international agreements, and the widely acknowledged belief that chaos would result from insistence on printed notices. The second amendment was new, deceptively simple, and malevolent. This was the clause which gave the bill its nickname, for that derisory sum was intended to cover the performance right of a work in perpetuity. It proposed that any composition, regardless of its size, type, or quality, could be performed by anybody anywhere, for the single payment, regardless of the cost, remuneration, or character of the event. Thus, the BBC would have been able to broadcast a piece of music whenever it pleased, for the price of a copy plus twopence. It is remarkable, therefore, that they gave no support to the tuppenny men, despite current arguments about plugging. In December 1929 the PRS Board 'noted with satisfaction' that the BBC were 'not concerned with the promotion of the Musical Copyright Bill of which they did not approve'.[55] At the same meeting it discussed tactics for dealing with the Bill, in ways which indicate a new maturity, and sensitivity to public relations. Note was taken of an article in a Birmingham newspaper which, it was agreed, could well be libellous but, on this occasion, the matter was put aside; litigation would *not* be undertaken. Energies would be better concentrated upon assisting the meetings of various friendly groups and associations, in what amounted to the Society's first extended exercise in systematic briefing. Most auspiciously it was decided to reprint and circulate a recent article in *Punch*.[56]

The article, 'Why Twopence?' was by A. P. Herbert, a man whose

[54] Ibid., p. iii.
[55] PRS Archives, Board minutes, 12 Dec. 1929.
[56] *Punch*, 4 Dec. 1929, repr. in *Performing Right Gazette*, Jan. 1930, 494–5.

diverse talents had already brought him to prominence. Barrister, author, librettist, and, later, Member of Parliament, he would subsequently espouse many a worthy cause, from the reform of divorce and obscenity laws to the author's public-lending right, but never was his mordant pen employed to such devastating effect as in December 1929. In a superb polemic he tore the hapless Bill apart with logic and ridicule. This 'fantastic measure' which set out to destroy the livelihood of composers was being promoted by self-styled socialists who preened themselves as 'champions of the producer'. Were their two pennies intended to be shared by composer, publisher, and writer? Was tuppence intended to purchase the right to perform foreign, as well as British works, or to sanction the manufacture of 100,000 gramophone records? Why, then, restrict this new system of statutory flat rates to *musical* works? Why not a tuppenny *Saint Joan* or *Forsyte Saga* or Chaplin film? If tomorrow's *Mikado* and *Meistersinger* could be performed for tuppence then 'for a bob you could run a repertory season'. The Bill's promoters accused the PRS of 'iniquities', such as 'collecting money due to the creator and handing it over to him', or sending inspectors 'to detect widespread stealing'. The Society's allegedly 'harsh terms' amounted to 0.5 per cent of a rich hotel's music bill; the remaining 99.5 per cent going to executants who were apparently exempt from denigration as 'warts' or 'vampires'— scholarly terms which had been applied to the PRS by a University MP. Despite its stately progress so far—a successful second reading and referral to a Committee merely for amendment—the Bill was rotten at its heart, embracing a 'stinking' *principle*: that 'composers alone of the world's workers shall have their earnings limited by law, shall be forbidden to organize themselves and to sell their work to whom they please for what it is worth'. Members of Parliament had disgraced themselves by allowing this ridiculous measure to slip through; most speakers displaying 'an ignorance of the subject so profound as to make it impertinent of them to speak at all'. One had betrayed the prevailing philistinism and contempt by speaking of 'the long-haired fraternity which composes music'. The bill, concluded APH, was 'the most unjust, unprincipled, muddle-headed, ill-drafted, unworkable measure that was ever printed by His Majesty's Printers. No man should waste a minute in attempting to amend it; it must be killed dead, as an insult to the craft of music'.[57]

More succinct and equally damaging was a cartoon, 'Tuppence', by David Low, which appeared in the *Evening Standard*. Overlooked by the shades of Wagner, Sullivan, and Chopin, a mendicant Elgar, with

[57] Ibid.

dog, upturned hat, and begging bowl, sits at a street harmonium to accompany George Bernard Shaw in selections from *Gerontius* ('All my own composition'). Two comfortable citizens stroll past, arm in arm: a Scotsman with music case holding 'cheap music for the Caledonian Choral Society' and a bowler-hatted English Labour politician, who tosses tuppence into the hat. The Scotsman remonstrates: 'For why did ye no mak' it a penny?' It was an appropriate rebuke in more than one sense, for the Bill's promoters had given hostage to fortune by choosing so derisory a sum. Threepence or even one penny might have sounded more innocent. It was singular folly to choose tuppence, and singular cunning for the Society's friends to turn the paltry sum to such devastating effect. By trifles like this are political campaigns won and lost. No one could match APH's eloquence, or Low's pungent derision, but there was no lack of articulate support. Outrage was forcibly expressed by practically everyone concerned with music and the arts in England. A protest by the 'Confederation of Arts' announced its 'determined opposition' to legislation which would be 'disastrous to the native composer and the art of music'. Its signatories included many composers, of course, but also Arnold Bennett, Roger Fry, Pinero, Rothenstein, Gilbert Scott, George Bernard Shaw, Sybil Thorndike, Virginia Woolf, and the heads of RADA, the National Gallery, and the Wallace Collection.[58] There was one apostate voice. Ralph Vaughan Williams had become a reluctant member of the PRS when his publisher, Curwen, joined in 1926. Indifferent to the collection of performing fees, he had often expressed concern about the licensing of 'small musical entertainments in country villages', and was regarded as 'more inclined to criticize than to assist the Society'. It was therefore not unprepared when he wrote to *The Times*, arguing that the Bill's promoters were 'voicing a very real grievance', and warning against 'tyranny and intimidation'. Nor could he have been much surprised to be admonished by the Board, for private criticism was very different from public disloyalty at a time of crisis. The incident closed with his proffered resignation, which could not be accepted for four years, under the Articles of Association.[59] In later years RVW and the Society were to enjoy an amiable and mutually beneficial relationship, but at this time their views were poles apart, and the composer was odd man out. There were deputations to the House of Commons representing the Incorporated Society of Musicians and the Union of

[58] *The Times*, 25 Jan. 1930.
[59] PRS Archives, R. Vaughan Williams file, Memorandum, 31 May 1927; Leslie Boosey to R. V. W., 13 Dec. 1929. Letter to *The Times*, 10 Dec. 1929.

Graduates in Music.[60] If some of this furore was orchestrated from Hanover Square, where Leslie Boosey was preparing an elaborately documented case for the Select Committee, the diversity and distinction of the protesters, many of whom were not easily lobbied, suggests a spontaneous outburst of anger, apprehension, and contempt.

Press comment was equally condemnatory. *The Times* observed that broadcasting had enormously increased the audience 'which consumes and ought therefore to pay for music' yet the idea of 'music for nothing' had become all too common, and musicians were expected to live on little else but publicity. The twopenny proposal was 'preposterous'.[61] The *Daily Telegraph* was scathing at greater length. The proposed reform was 'simply a law to enact that music can be stolen'. The 'grievance' of which its supporters complained was merely that they were expected 'to pay for using other people's property'.[62] Returning to the fray a month after the second reading, which it described as taking place 'amid outpourings of ignorance and sentimentality on both sides of the House', the *Telegraph* advanced a simple explanation for the extraordinary lack of reasoned criticism: 'the Bill is so blatantly iniquitous that there is no matter for argument'. Long discussion had demonstrated that 'no person of authority or public credit will now attempt justification of its provisions'.[63] The *Morning Post* rehearsed arguments which were now becoming familiar about the Bill's absurdities and the composers' needs. It also explicitly defended the PRS. Far from being 'a tyrannous body, which sat like a vampire on composers', the Society's whole purpose was 'to protect them'.[64] The *Observer* expressed its outrage at the Bill's ignorance and indifference to English music and to international commitments.[65] The *Daily Mail* attacked the 'fantastic injustice' of a 'preposterous Bill' and denied that PRS fees were arbitrary, excessive, or ill-defined. On the contrary, 'The Society has a fixed scale of charges, easily obtainable by any enquirer'.[66] The *Evening Standard* described the Bill as 'outside the bounds of sanity', and repeated criticisms which must have become familiar even to casual readers.[67] And that is surely the significant point. In a few weeks of intensive, reiterated argument, of which only a sample has

[60] *The Times*, 6 and 15 Feb. 1930.
[61] Ibid., 7 Dec. 1929.
[62] *Daily Telegraph*, 23 Nov. and 3 Dec. 1929.
[63] Ibid., 21 Dec. 1929.
[64] *Morning Post*, 25 Nov. 1929.
[65] *Observer*, 1 Dec. 1929.
[66] *Daily Mail*, 18 Dec. 1929.
[67] *Evening Standard*, 2 Dec. 1929.

been cited, the Society had received sufficient publicity to make its case, for the first time, justifying its existence to reasonable men.

'A convenience and almost a necessity'

Such was the general conclusion of the Select Committee, after fourteen days of proceedings, spread over twenty-three weeks, and a Report which mustered 270 double-column pages of evidence and eleven appendices. Every conceivable form of attack had been mounted against the PRS. Harry Wall was given yet another innings: 'the methods of the Performing Right Society resemble those of Mr Wall, but their powers are enormously intensified'.[68] The Society had been accused of misdemeanours large and small, plausible and inconceivable. Its fees were said to be 'arbitrary'[69] and extortionate.[70] It was accused of 'intimidating' those who refused to take out its licences,[71] and 'campaigning' against Sunday Schools and Churches.[72] Its activities were alleged to be responsible for every misfortune which had befallen every disgruntled music trader, leading to 'reduced sales of pianos, sheet music, gramophones and records'.[73] In reply to this flood of special pleading and abuse, Leslie Boosey had patiently assembled a watertight case. Every inaccurate fact, wild accusation, and irresponsible smear was quietly refuted. Even Harry Wall was gently laid to rest.[74] This exercise of unruffled authority entailed keeping a firm check on Woodhouse, who never appeared before the Committee unaccompanied by Boosey and James. Despite frequent provocation there were no outbursts of spleen from the PRS side. It was a sensible precaution, for sweetness and light was both necessary for immediate goodwill, and sufficient of a novelty to require confirmation that the new attitudes had come to stay. That they were new, and welcome, was made quite explicit by the BBC. Refusing again to join the attack, the BBC, nevertheless, insisted that its harmonious dealings with the Society were of recent vintage. 'During the time that Mr Woodhouse was Controller of the Society our relations were anything but amicable, and frequently at a point of considerable strain': there had been 'peremptory demands, often based upon incorrect facts or untenable assumptions'. But now all

---

[68] *Special Report . . . Copyright Bill*, Q. 927.
[69] Ibid., Q. 495, and p. 279 para. 8.
[70] Ibid., Q. 945 *passim*.
[71] Ibid., Q. 505.
[72] Ibid., Q. 1665.
[73] Ibid., Q. 1234.
[74] Ibid. 305.

was changed and the BBC reiterated its opposition to the Bill, though it continued to grumble about plugging.[75]

Did the users have any genuine cause for complaint? Shorn of its unreasonable and unreasoning antagonism, their protest to the Committee contained two arguments which required an answer. First, by refusing to issue a catalogue, the PRS was concealing information about what music was covered by its licence, and charging for unrequired products: 'the intrinsic value of the music contracted for was and is unknown'.[76] Secondly the Society was a monopoly, capable of arbitrarily increasing the cost of its licences, and leaving users uncertain about, and unable to protect themselves from, further increases. In so far as the first of these complaints was an innocent request for information it could be met by goodwill and improved circumstances. The Society's avoidance of catalogues had originally been due to economics and apprehension. The provision of such a service would have been prohibitively time-consuming and costly; it would also have given damaging information to the consumer groups who were trying to organize supplies of 'free music', particularly during the Society's period of disunity. Now, with greater unity, higher gross income, wider control of repertoire, and a larger, more amiable, administration, the Society could begin to respond to the request. Extensive lists of publisher members began to appear in the *Gazette* in April 1930. But this did not allay doubts about paying for unwanted music; nor could such complaints possibly be appeased. Like all performing right societies the PRS operated a system of blanket licences which entitled the holder to perform any and every work in its repertoire, but could not possibly be custom-tailored for individual licencees. To composers and publishers it seemed self-evident that this was a tremendous bargain. To those users who wanted only a small part of the Society's repertoire, its offered product might appear to be undifferentiated and expensive. How were bargains to be struck which might satisfy both parties? Talk of 'intrinsic value' merely begged the question, but any attempts to determine licence fees by market bargaining raised a second, even more intractable, question of monopoly power. The Committee pronounced on these difficulties, to curious and unhelpful effect.

The obvious and immediate outcome of the Committee's deliberations was a report of the Bill 'without amendment'. It was the parliamentary equivalent of sudden death, and with this 'contemptuous epitaph'[77] no

---

[75] Ibid. 326.
[76] Ibid., Q. 768.

more was heard in Parliament of the Musical Copyright Bill. But there was a sting in the tail of the Committee's conclusions. It supported the PRS by refusing to 'place any obstacles in the way of composers forming an Association for the purposes of protecting their performing rights'. It even claimed a position in society for such an association as

undoubtedly a convenience and almost a necessity, both to the composer, music publisher and the user of music who would be considerably embarrassed if he had to deal separately with each piece of music performed. In fact it may be said to be the only practicable way in which the composer can collect his fees for performing rights in any adequate manner.

The Committee argued, however, that in order to function effectively, the PRS had been forced to become, in effect, 'a super-monopoly of the monopolies conferred upon composers by the Copyright Acts'. It could conceivably 'abuse its powers by refusing to grant licences upon reasonable terms . . . contrary to the public interest'. In those circumstances, the Committee concluded, it should be possible to 'appeal to arbitration or to some other tribunal'. Since any legislation to this effect would conflict with international copyright obligations, 'the Board of Trade should keep in touch with the position' in preparation for the 1935 International Copyright Union meeting, in case there should be any need to deal with abuse of monopoly privilege.[78]

It should be emphasized that these rumblings about *possible* abuse of monopoly power were never intended to criticize the Society's actions up to that date. Indeed the senior official at the Board of Trade who was most qualified to pronounce on these matters had explicitly absolved the PRS from any such imputation. He 'had gone thoroughly into the situation and had satisfied himself that there was no abuse whatever by the Society'. On the contrary, it was his view that the existing level of fees was 'futilely small'.[79] Nevertheless, in its hour of triumph the Society was branded as a 'super-monopoly of monopolies', and given a sword of Damocles—the threat of some future tribunal. In practice, the latter was probably more damaging. In those days 'monopoly' was not an instinctive word of derogation in Britain. Monopolies and restrictive practices were commonly accepted with equanimity. Most goods entering retail trade were subject to resale price maintenance; competitive pricing and independent and

[77] *Daily Telegraph*, 12 July 1930.
[78] *Special Report . . . Copyright Bill*, p. vi.
[79] PRS Archives, Notes of interview with Sir William Jarratt and Mr. B. G. Crewe at Board of Trade, 24 Apr. 1930.

outspoken consumer reports were unknown. The public's recent acceptance of a broadcasting system which established the BBC as sole broadcaster, and imposed compulsory licences was, of course, peculiarly relevant to the Society's position. In his history of the BBC Lord Briggs has explained how the concept of monopoly was contentious in 1923 but 'almost universally accepted' by 1925.[80] In any case the PRS could always deny that it possessed absolute monopoly powers, because some publishers were still not members, and there was a vast public domain of music which had fallen outside copyright, including the greater part of the 'classical' concert repertoire. The brand of 'monopoly' was therefore no great burden for some time. It was ironic that the sword should cause more hurt since, as events turned out, its threat remained chimerical for a quarter of a century. The meeting of the International Copyright Union, for which the Board of Trade was supposed to prepare, was delayed until 1948 by the politicial upsets of the 1930s and by the Second World War. A performing right tribunal did not become a reality until 1957; but throughout the intervening period it was reasonable to assume that some such court of appeal would soon be set up. Undoubtedly this expectation influenced the Society's tariffs. Its negotiations generally tended to be cautious and 'responsible'; and there was continued acquiescence in 'futilely small' fees, far below those charged in many countries, particularly France, despite frequent criticism from members and occasional misunderstandings with affiliated foreign societies. Ernest Ford, for example, who was head of licensing for many years, recalls a long discussion at cross purposes with a SACEM official who had been assuming that the Society's annual cinema tariff of three guineas was a weekly or, at least, a monthly, charge!

It could be argued, therefore, that the defeat of the Tuppenny Bill was in some respects a Pyrrhic victory. But it was none the less a victory, for good sense, for music, and for the Society's first comprehensive articulation of policy. As the *Musical Opinion* exclaimed, 'If the composers of this country have not sent a vote of thanks to Mr. Leslie Boosey for all the time and energy he gave to the preparation and strengthening of the case against the Bill they ought to be ashamed of themselves'.[81] They did not, and presumably were not, but Boosey faced too many new challenges to spare much time for pondering ingratitude. The silent cinema had collapsed, the depression begun, and his super-monopoly of monopolies had to be led in negotiations with a super 'monopsony' (in the economists' jargon), the largest user of music the country had ever known.

[80] Asa Briggs, *The BBC: The First Fifty Years* (1985), 86.
[81] *Musical Opinion*, Sept. 1930.

4

NEW HORIZONS

By 1930 the market for printed music had lurched into a steep decline which continued throughout the decade. The experience of six leading English publishers is representative of a general malaise. Their world sales of sheet music fell from £537,000 in 1921, to £318,000 in 1929, and £185,000 in 1935. Within this group of firms, as elsewhere in the industry, the 'popular' publishers did particularly badly, one falling from £71,000 to £14,000 over the same period, another from £55,000 to £9,000. A leading London retailer reported that its sales of sheet music from all publishers had fallen by half between 1926 and 1935, despite the fact that the music industry was far more concentrated in the metropolis than it had ever been in the past.[1] Cinemas left the market completely and for ever. Live musicians had been replaced by sound tracks within a few months of *The Jazz Singer* coming to town in 1929, repeating the American experience of 1927. Almost overnight there was no longer any need for a large and steady supply of 'photoplay' or 'background' scores and instrumental parts, to thousands of British cinemas, as distinct from a handful of sound recording studios. Huge stocks of such paper were therefore accumulated in warehouses, never to be used again, and were eventually destroyed. Although notes which were not specifically intended to accompany silent movies continued to be bought and hired for another generation, the market for most forms of printed music, particularly of the lighter category, was stunned by the coming of talkies. A massive haemorrhage should not, however, be confused with terminal decline. 'Light' and 'tea shop' music, continued to be sought, as background to eating and drinking, though not yet to working or shopping; and sometimes for direct listening, rather than overhearing. All of it was played from the printed page; and players, even in dance bands, were still expected to read. Instrumentation ranged from café or 'syncopated' piano, and the ubiquitous piano trio, to inflations and concoctions for symphony orchestra. On one occasion Ketèlbey conducted the Concertgebouw Orchestra in his own compositions.

[1] PRS Archives, BBC arbitration 1937. 'Comparative statement relating to sales of sheet music, mechanical royalties, performance and broadcasting fees of publishers and composers: 'Prove' of Keith Prowse and Co. Ltd.' See also Cyril Ehrlich, *The Music Profession in Britain since the Eighteenth Century* (1985), 210–11.

If technology had taken complete control of music in the cinema, its seizure of music in the home was scarcely less rapid and complete. Radios were transmogrified in a few years. The 1920s contraption of cat's whisker and earphones, listened to and often assembled by individual enthusiasts, was replaced by the 1930s family wireless set. Fixed to its plug in the living room, it soon became the acknowledged centre of home entertainment. The advance of broadcasting was undeterred even by the economic depression. There were five million holders of wireless licences by November 1932. Three years later 98 per cent of the population were equipped to listen to one BBC programme and 85 per cent had a choice between two.[2] The gramophone also took a great leap forward with electrical recording and playback. Acoustic horns, wind-up motors, and soundboxes were replaced by microphones, electric motors, pick-ups and loudspeakers. Record players could be connected to the radio for a few pounds. Similar in performance, but not in appearance and cost, were the radiograms, their massive cabinets a new symbol of status and participation in the splendours of modern technology. One model already claimed to reproduce 'the complete range of audible sound', and another, whose 'faithfulness of reproduction' was merely 'remark-able' was allowed to enter the king's apartments.[3] Displacing the piano as centre of home entertainment and 'household orchestra', these new consumer durables required no sheet music; and so another slice of the publisher's market was lost. Of great importance to the Society was the fact that radios and electric gramophones began to roam away from home and nudge their way into public life, as hotels, restaurants, and dance halls experimented with canned and broadcast music. The equipment was clumsy, and the sound was not good, despite claims made for its fidelity, but it could be amplified and relayed to subsidiary loudspeakers. Above all it was cheap. Record players displaced musicians at little cost, and broadcast music was a free good: performances, unlike equipment and wireless licences, were grabbed for nothing, literally from the air.

Despite these manifest disadvantages to the producers of music, not everything was negative in the new developments, for the same forces which were destroying the market for printed music were also responsible for a huge increase in its performance. Nor was it simply a matter of technology, for innovation was merely the latest and most spectacular aspect of a fundamental revolution in the extent and use of spare time. Despite the depression, increasing purchasing power was being concentrated upon the new leisure goods and services by

[2] Asa Briggs, *The BBC: The First Fifty Years* (1985), 110.
[3] *Music Trades Review*, Dec. 1927. *Musical Opinion*, May 1929.

shorter working hours and improved transport (cars, buses, tube
extensions) which brought people to town, to shop, and be entertained. At every social level, from the working to the idling classes,
there was profit to be made from leisure: night-clubs, road-houses,
dance-halls, skating-rinks, restaurants, Lyons tea-shops and 'corner
houses' which capped the enjoyment of a night out, all flourished
during the 1930s. Even the public house, once the main, exclusively
masculine, drain for spare cash, was beginning to woo modernity,
catering for women, selling less beer, and offering a little more comfort
and amenity, including music. 'Going to the pictures' became, in A. J.
P. Taylor's phrase, the essential social habit of the age, a 'best buy' in
a decade of bargains. The new luxury cinemas offered continuous
entertainment for the whole family. They were classless, delightfully
time-consuming, very cheap, warm in a cold decade, and far more
comfortable than the old theatres and music-halls. By the late thirties
some twenty million cinema tickets were being sold each week, at a
typical price of ninepence. It was, in the language of the times, a super
colossal market, but it was dwarfed by radio. In terms of potential
audience and hours of entertainment, the BBC suddenly emerged as
the monopolizing impresario for the biggest show the country had
ever experienced. By the late thirties it was broadcasting fifty hours a
day; and nine million people were paying ten shillings a year for its
compulsory licences.

Adjusting to the New Environment

The common factor in this maelstrom of profitable activity, which
attracted so large and growing a proportion of the nation's expenditure, was that it required copious and frequent infusions of music.
Unfortunately, there were few guarantees that suppliers of this
essential service would be paid, and none that they would be
adequately reimbursed for their work, without determined bargaining. It was the Society's duty, of course, to see that this was done, but
there were new difficulties and constraints. A prime task was the
effective licensing of new users. Mere identification became a far more
burdensome task when repertoire belonging to the PRS could be
tapped simply by installing a loudspeaker. Without a large corps of
inspectors, comprehensive monitoring was impossible. Even a modi-
cum of surveillance was costly in times of rapid technological and
social change, when markets were being realigned and expansion or
contraction could be perceived only slowly, and hardly ever anticipated. Patterns which are clear in hindsight—the changing geographical location of many centres of entertainment, for example,

with a pronounced drift to the South—were slow to come into focus. In 1937 C. F. James explained the procedure by which half a dozen inspectors 'move round the country . . . but it is a very slow business'.[4] In the case of existing licence holders the essential problem was one of adjusting fees sufficiently to take account of the increased scale of operations and profitability. Cinemas were an obvious example. In 1930 they were still being licensed under terms which had been worked out in the 'silent' and 'fleapit' days of 1924, with the ludicrous result that luxurious 'super' cinemas were paying annual fees as low as £14, and small houses 28s. After long negotiations with the Cinematograph Exhibitors' Association, representing over 4,000 cinemas, a new four-year agreement reassessed licences on a graduated scale according to the cash value of each theatre's seating capacity.[5] The terms were not onerous, yielding about one-tenth of a penny for a performance of a short piece, to be shared between composer, author, and publisher. In 1934 this agreement was renewed for another five years, at similar rates and even with reductions for the smallest cinemas. The negotiations were reported, without irony, to have been 'friendly and amicable'.[6]

A more positive stance was required to deal with the public 'rediffusion' of broadcast music. First it was necessary to establish that the use of a radio to entertain one's customers was a 'performance', and therefore liable to infringe PRS rights. The key case, *PRS* v. *Hammonds Bradford Brewery Ltd.*, raised complex points of law and was taken to the Court of Appeal by Hammonds, but its outcome gave unequivocal support to the Society. Its clearest articulation, by the Master of the Rolls, took the form of a citation from a similar ruling in the United States:

There is no difference in substance between the case where a hotel engages an orchestra to furnish the music and that where, by means of the radio set and loud speakers here employed, it furnishes the same music for the same purpose. In each case the music is produced by the instrumentalities under its control.[7]

Immediately after this decision there was a flurry of excitement in the trade press. Rumours were spread about an imminent campaign of 'extortion' by 'tyrannous laws'. The Englishman's castle would be invaded in a drive to impose PRS licences upon every kind of business

---

[4] PRS Archives, BBC arbitration 1937, vol. iv, 6–7.

[5] *Performing Right Gazette*, Apr. 1930, 526.

[6] Ibid., Apr. 1934, 249.

[7] *PRS* v. *Hammonds Bradford Brewery Ltd.* (1933) 1 ch. 855. *Performing Right Gazette*, Apr. 1933, 154, and Oct. 1933, 192–6. For legal interpretation see Gavin McFarlane, *Copyright: The Development and Exercise of the Performing Right* (1980), 123–5.

using, or even selling, radios. It was alleged that the use of
loudspeakers in hotels and public houses would cost between £5 and
£30 a year, that the PRS would derive up to £100,000 from this source,
and that, therefore, 'thousands of hotel keepers have got rid of
gramophones and radios'.[8] Nothing could have been further from the
truth. Having established its right to be paid for the commercial use of
broadcast music, the PRS was anxious to proclaim the modesty of its
expectations. 'We want to collect from the air what we have lost on
paper' said Boosey in a press announcement following the court
decision, but 'we are not out to make the owners of public houses . . .
pay a large sum'.[9] It was later announced that licences for public
houses would range from one to three guineas, and that there was no
question of licensing shops demonstrating radios for sale, despite the
fact that such demonstrations were 'performances' in the eyes of the
law.[10]

Why was the PRS so reluctant to adjust its sights, so very cautious
in adjusting old licences and imposing new ones? It was an attitude
which became most apparent in the Society's dealings with the BBC,
and was to accumulate difficulties for the next generation of
negotiators. Several explanations are possible. There was the influence of the prevailing economic climate. At a time when many
business men considered themselves fortunate to have survived the
1929 crash, unemployment was at unprecedented levels, and the
general public was becoming inured to the economics of depression, it
was difficult to insist upon the fact that many of the Society's patrons
were engaged in a prosperous and expanding sector of the economy.
Among its members, in contrast, there were many who had recently
been grievously hurt, by the depression in general and by the collapse
of the silent cinema. There was now a chronic over-supply of
musicians in relation to the demand for their services, even more
acute than in the past. Docility, modest expectations, unwillingness to
drive hard bargains, all characteristic traits in the 'respectable'
branches of the music profession, were reinforced by recent experience. Finally, among some Board members and functionaries a desire
to consolidate goodwill after the Tuppenny victory was, perhaps,
backed by apprehensions about arbitration.

To counterbalance these inducements to caution there were
murmurs of discontent, and even occasionally raised voices, from
some members. The collapse of sheet-music sales, and a slump in the

---

[8] *Hotel and Boarding House*, Dec. 1933.

[9] *Evening Standard*, 13 Oct. 1933.

[10] *PRS* v. *Hammonds Bradford Brewery Ltd.*, *Performing Right Gazette*, Apr. 1933, 148, 154, and
Jan. 1934, 214–6.

market for gramophone records after 1930, greatly concentrated the minds of the more active composers and publishers upon alternative sources of income. Performing fees were therefore scrutinized and challenged with impatience; their level, accuracy, and speed of payment subjected to mounting criticism. Some of the 'popular' publishers were particularly vociferous, for a variety of reasons. Their style of business tended to be aggressive and mindful of margins and turnover, requiring speedy settlement of accounts: no shabby-gentility for them. Their peculiar vulnerability to volatile tastes had been responsible for many casualties in the immediate aftermath of the 1929 crash; and survivors were likely to fight desperately for continued survival. Finally, there was a tendency, as so often happens, for recent converts, in this case to performing right, to be most zealous in pursuit of their new-found faith. 'We are naturally looking to the performing right fees to make up to us for what we are losing in other directions', wrote one of the 1926 recruits in 1930, as he mounted an assault upon the administration which included angry letters, accusations of 'diddling' and delay, and visits from his accountant, a lady assistant (surely rare in those days) who, as one battle-scarred official complained, 'was prepared to become unpleasant'.[11]

This dispute was merely the latest and angriest expression of a more general discontent. Feeling was widespread that the general level of fees was unacceptably low, and their distribution slow and unreliable. The former complaint had little immediate effect, for reasons already suggested; the latter problem continued to be intractable, despite considerable effort and expenditure. In March 1927 the Distribution Committee noted that 30,000 programmes remained to be analysed for the nine months ending in the previous January, and that it would be impossible to complete the task in time for the annual distribution next June.[12] By November it was estimated that current rates of progress would lead to a backlog of more than 25 per cent: approximately 33,000 programmes out of 142,000 would remain unexamined. It was therefore proposed to deal with only 'a proportion', casually touching upon the relevant, but difficult, concept of statistical sampling, with its attendant hazards.[13] The next few years brought little improvement, as members continued to enquire and complain about their fees. Complaints from popular publishers were usually simple allegations that the sums of money they were receiving were not commensurate with their

[11] PRS Archives, Campbell Connelly file, 17 July 1930; 23 Jan. 1931; 29 Jan. 1931; 16 Feb. 1931; 22 May 1931.
[12] PRS Archives, Distribution Committee minutes, 8 Mar. 1927.
[13] Ibid., 29 Nov. 1927.

perception of the public's demand for their music. 'Serious' musicians were sometimes more difficult to handle because their grievances often implied, if they did not state, the assumption that they deserved to be paid more for *better* music. Increasing sensitivity about these matters was probably inevitable after 1926; a necessary price for unity. Dealing with it required tact, and sympathetic knowledge of a wide and eclectic repertoire, if complainants were to be appeased and that unity preserved.

Frank Bridge was their most persistent and vigorous champion among the Society notables, but they also found other sound-boards. In 1929 a 'Memorial' from the Incorporated Society of Playwrights, Authors and Composers, on behalf of forty-three composers of 'serious' music, was referred to the Distribution Committee. The essential burden of complaint was that the existing 'weighting' of performances for allocation of fees failed to do justice to the *quality* of their music.[14] Classification procedures were re-examined and an elaborate 'points' system worked out, ranging from 1 point for a dance tune, via 20 for a symphonic poem of twelve minutes, to 240 for an hour's work.[15] The Committee devising this arcane system, which included Frank Bridge and Fred Day, was chaired by one of the Society's most exotic characters, who had joined in 1917, and was appointed to the Board in 1924. George H. Clutsam was born in Sydney in 1866, toured as a young pianist in India, China, and Japan, settled in London in 1889, played as Melba's accompanist, and was a critic for the *Observer*. As a composer he began seriously with two operas, one of which was conducted by Beecham, but achieved commercial success with lighter things. There were songs, notably 'I Know of Two Bright Eyes', and 'Ma Curly Headed Baby', memorably recorded by Paul Robeson, and several musical comedies. Far the most successful was *Lilac Time* and its film version, with Richard Tauber, *Blossom Time*. Known to Schubertians for turning the first song of the *Winterreise* into a waltz, and a section of the G major 'Fantasy' Sonata into a drinking song, this highly remunerative concoction was similar to a German piece entitled *Das Dreimäderlhaus* and, therefore, subject to copyright disputes. The Clutsam version, which was first staged in London in 1922, had a libretto by Arthur Ropes, one of the Society's founding fathers, who became its Vice-Chairman in 1924. When Ropes died in 1933 his place was taken by Clutsam, who continued in that office until 1949.[16] A key figure in the

[14] PRS Archives, Frank Bridge to Woodhouse, 19 Nov. 1928; Woodhouse to William Boosey, 21 Nov. 1928.

[15] PRS Archives. Distribution Committee minutes, 17 and 26 Apr. 1929.

[16] Ropes's obituary is in *Performing Right Gazette*, Oct. 1933, 202.

Society for several decades, Clutsam was not among its distinguished composers, but he was willing to devote endless time to its affairs, and was familiar with a large repertoire. 'There was little you could teach him about any branch of music', said Eric Coates, his friend and admirer.[17]

If the Society could claim to be making serious attempts to improve the distribution of fees, it was unable to provide much tangible benefit without a substantial increase in income. Hopes centred upon broadcasting.

Looking for a Yardstick

The 1929 BBC agreement marked a complete break with the past, not because the payment of £45,000 was £6,000 more than in the previous year, but because it was based upon a significantly new concept. Previous levies had been worked out, with great effort and delay, from a complex scale of fees linked to the duration of each work broadcast. The 1929 agreement abandoned these labyrinthine exercises and was based instead upon the current number of wireless licences. It was simpler, more expeditious, and gave the Society a stake in the growth of the radio audience. Subsequent contracts used the same formula, but with two severe constraints. Total payments to the PRS were limited to a fee equivalent to 5 per cent of the BBC's receipts from wireless licences; a sum which was itself barely half of what the public paid, the rest going to the Post Office and Treasury. Additionally in 1932 the PRS was made to bear a share of the BBC's 'voluntary contribution' to the Government, which had been exacted as a result of unexpected and highly resented interference by the notorious 'May Committee' on public finance.[18]

These circumstances exacerbated the tensions of a bargaining process which was already laborious and intractable. In contrast to the Society's dealings with other users of music, its relationship to the BBC was in every sense unique, and without useful precedents. Because radio was already the largest user of music, and still growing apace, it had to be made to pay adequately. But how was adequacy to be measured? Since anyone seeking access to Britain's radio audience was effectively limited to the BBC's programmes, the PRS, exercising its near monopoly of supply, was set to bargain with a powerful single buyer. The Corporation's bargaining power was, of course, far greater than that of any other group of PRS licensees, limited, in the last

---

[17] Eric Coates, *Suite in Four Movements: An Autobiography* (1953), 196.
[18] Asa Briggs, *History of Broadcasting, vol. ii, The Golden Age of Wireless* (1965), 378–80.

resort, only by an inability to function for long without using the Society's repertoire. Hard bargaining could be expected from both sides, not because of the bargainers' innate obstinacy, but because they were ultimately responsible to importunate clients, for whom the stakes were high. The natural inclination of any monopsony to hold down its level of payments, because there is no competitor to bid them up, was reinforced, in the BBC's case, by Government parsimony. This still left the Corporation with a substantial income which increased threefold between 1927 and 1936, but its officials worked in an atmosphere of caution and thrift, despite frequent accusations of profligacy by their enemies.[19]

Not that bargaining was influenced solely by financial considerations. There was a political dimension, a tendency for the BBC to play the patriotic card, when fixing low rates for Empire broadcasts, for example, or assuming that 'the nation's burdens' must be shared; arguments which would not, in peacetime, have been considered relevant to normal commercial transactions. Nor were BBC officials, seemingly forgetful of their own privileged position, slow to accuse the Society of abusing its monopoly power.[20] The Reithian ethos also had its influence: a paternalistic sense of responsibility for providing a public service, which took little account of popular taste and was disdainful of commerce in general, and show business in particular. Last, but not least, there were differences in ways of conducting business. BBC functionaries were high priests of the written word, always preferring paper to talk, masters of the lengthy memorandum, for whom bargaining was a slow, formal, fully documented process, with no short cuts: in the Society's archives BBC correspondence rapidly exceeded that from any other source. While Leslie Boosey and the PRS staff were usually capable of handling all this with equanimity and the required decorum, they also had to represent constituents who were accustomed to more boisterous and informal business procedures, and who expected quick results.

A gulf separated Savoy Hill (and, after 1932, Broadcasting House) from Denmark Street. In some respects it had been deepened by the plugging crisis. But that absurd episode had strengthened the Society's hand in at least two ways. It taught the BBC's mandarins, perhaps for the first time, that they must take some account of the public's desire to be entertained, and make occasional gestures towards popular taste. When dance music was allowed a little more prominence, under Jack Payne, and later Henry Hall, it represented

19   Ibid., 379–80 and 483–4.
20   BBC Archives, BBC to James, 12 Aug. 1931.

only a slight lightening of austere schedules, but it also served as a reminder that this repertoire was indispensable to the BBC.[21] Secondly the plugging crisis had again demonstrated the Society's unity, for the BBC had failed in its attempt to separate dance music fees from the rest. Equally significant for future bargaining had been Boosey's ability to maintain a united front when Reith attempted to separate performance fees for dance music from the rest. The alliance was still holding together, but its young Turks were spoiling for action.

These crucial negotiations were being conducted in an economic climate of unprecedented severity. In 1932 the economy was approaching the bottom of the worst slump in its history. It was a gloomy year for almost everybody, but there then began a slow recovery which was practically continuous until 1937. The BBC's crumbling defence of the 5 per cent ceiling reflected these improving conditions, both in the general economic climate, and in the Corporation's financial confidence. At first it argued that the ceiling was necessary protection against having to pay out fees which would lead it into 'bankruptcy'. But the 'oppressive and inequitable' curb was losing the PRS at least £5,000 a year by 1933. The Society was so determined to get rid of this constraint that it was even prepared to go to arbitration, if all else failed, despite the familiar hazards, of which Boosey was reminded by nervous members.[22] After further tortuous negotiations the BBC agreed to abandon the ceiling, but continued to impose constraints upon the Society's stake in the growth of the radio audience. The four-year agreement of 1933 embodied a sliding scale of payments which *fell* as the number of wireless licences increased: $5\frac{1}{2}d.$ per licence for the first million. $4\frac{1}{2}d.$ for the second, and so on. The excuse was that similar limitations were being imposed by the Government upon the BBC.

Hobbled in these devious ways by official cheese-paring, the Society's income from broadcasting lagged behind the growth of its radio audience until 1933, and then began to catch up. Between 1929 and 1936 the number of wireless licences increased from 2.6 to 7.3 million, and payments to the Society rose from £45,000 to £115,000. There were additional small disbursements for broadcasts to the Empire. This was a substantial increase in aggregate income from the

---

[21] Briggs, *Golden Age*, 86–9. Jack Payne, *Signature Tune* (1947). On austerity and popularizing, see Briggs, *First Fifty*, 129–31. On mandarins and music policy, see Paddy Scannell, 'Music for the Multitude? The Dilemmas of the BBC's Music Policy, 1923–1946', *Media, Culture and Society* (1981) 3, 243–60.

[22] PRS Archives, Draft letter to Goldsmith, BBC, 5 Jan. 1933. A. W. Ganz to PRS, 16 Jan. 1932.

BBC but, since it took no account of the *quantity* of music being broadcast, it was insufficient to provide an equivalent improvement in the fees paid to individual composers and publishers. The Corporation made lavish use of their property. By the mid-thirties figures collected by the Union Internationale de Radiodiffusion showed that over 70 per cent of British broadcasting time was taken up by music, far more, incidentally, than in most other European countries.[23] After allowing for a proportion of non-copyright music, and dramatic works, such as operas, which were not under PRS control, it was estimated that 65 per cent of the BBC's schedules was being filled by the Society's repertoire. The number of performances being broadcast had increased almost fourfold since 1929, while the BBC's payments had increased less than threefold. The amount available for distribution *per work* had actually fallen.

An opportunity to challenge these financial constraints came in 1935 with the Government's appointment of the Ullswater Committee to report on the condition and future of the BBC. A meeting and a brief, but warmly amiable, correspondence between Reith and Boosey clarified their positions. The latter reported that he had asked to give evidence, and that there was among PRS members 'a very strong feeling that even twice as much as we are getting would not compensate the members of our Society for the disastrous effects of broadcasting'. Assuring Reith that there was not 'the remotest idea of holding the BBC up to ransom', he added 'as you rightly say the great difficulty is to find a "yard stick" '. The great man responded cautiously, but not unhelpfully. 'You know that we shall be asking for a higher percentage of the licence fee', but any PRS appeal should be made 'quite independently of us', in order to guard against suppositions that, in the event of the BBC's getting more cash, it would be 'morally committed' to pay more for its music. In addition Reith thought it 'a very good plan if you were to recommend the establishment of statutory arbitration machinery'.[24]

While the Ullswater Committee deliberated, its relevance to the Society was noted by a few commentators. The *Stage*, for example, reminded its readers that

a stall-holder in a West End theatre has to pay more than 10s. for two or three hours of entertainment; a film-goer as much for a few visits to a kinema. The BBC can give 4,000 or 5,000 hours of entertainment for 10s. simply because its terms to composers and authors—and much more so to artists— are utterly uneconomic.[25]

[23] *BBC Annual* (1936), 160 ff.
[24] PRS Archives, Leslie Boosey to Reith, 21 May 1935. Reith to Boosey, 22 May 1935.
[25] *Stage*, 25 June 1935.

This was special pleading, of course, by the acting profession's trade journal. *Rhythm* had similarly strong opinions, demanding entertainment, instead of education, a threefold increase in the PRS fees, and a seat on the BBC's board for a representative from the Society.[26] Equally pungent, but less prejudiced, support came from the widely read journalist Collie Knox. Fees for broadcast performance, he reported, were 'rapidly becoming a first-class issue', and it was well known that 'broadcasting had caught the music trade, authors and composers a blinding whack in the eye'. The BBC were prepared to pay more, but the Government 'gets five and threepence out of every ten-shilling licence'. It could therefore 'only afford to pay to the Performing Right Society £100,000 a year. It should pay at least £400,000. But what will it use for money?'[27]

Ullswater replied with unexampled munificence. Relevant clauses of his Report recommended both that the Corporation's share of licence revenue should be substantially increased, and that 'payments to authors and composers should be generous':

Broadcasting has opened a new market for musical and literary work at a time when the demand in other quarters may be fluctuating or falling. It brings the artist's works to a very wide audience, without necessarily stimulating the distribution of copies of those works or the demand for their performance elsewhere.

The Committee therefore recommended a 'liberal treatment of creative artists' and, in the event of failure to agree upon terms, submission to arbitration. Neither of these recommendations was explicitly mentioned in the Government's White Paper on the Report, but it did accept the proposed increases in BBC revenue.[28]

The way was at last open for the Society to press its claims.

'A continuous census of . . . music'

The Society which demanded a better deal from the BBC was stronger than it had ever been. In 1936 it represented 1,333 author- and composer-members, 134 publisher-members, and 21 affiliated foreign societies. Its control of copyright music was now virtually complete because, ten years after the return of the popular publishers, the last plank of unification had been put in place, with the election of the remaining 'serious' firms and their composers. Edward Arnold,

[26] *Rhythm,* June 1935.

[27] *Daily Mail,* 17 July 1935.

[28] *Report of the Broadcasting Committee, 1935. The Ullswater Report* (Cmnd. 5091, 1936), paras. 66/67/71/72. *Broadcasting: Memorandum by the Postmaster General on the Report* (Cmd. 5207, 1936).

Novello, Oxford University Press, and Stainer and Bell were the most familiar names, but there were ten others, including R. Smith and Co. who published an extensive repertoire of brass-band music. Some had expressed interest in joining in 1926, but decided to stay out because so much of their business was connected with amateur choral performances. Doubtless, the steady decline of that activity and the increasing importance and complexity of performance fees, particularly from broadcasting, persuaded them to come in.[29] For composers and authors the advantages were unequivocal. In addition to the benefits gained by new members, such as Walton, there were substantial advantages to those composers and authors, or their successors, who were already members and had works published by incoming firms: Bliss, Delius, Elgar, Holst, and Vaughan Williams were distinguished examples. The position of one young member was greatly eased by this turn of events. Benjamin Britten had joined the Society in 1934, and immediately encountered difficulties with Oxford University Press, to whom he had submitted the twelve songs later known as 'Friday Afternoons'. Hubert Foss accepted the songs, but refused to relinquish rights, suggesting that it 'would be unwise to stress too much at this stage, the importance of having your performing rights managed by only one central body'. On the advice of his teacher, Frank Bridge, Britten consulted the Society and then backed down on the immediate issue. But his reply to Foss contains the following remarkable affirmation: 'What I have come to the conclusion is, that I must make up my mind about the principle of performing rights at an early age. I have cast my lot with the PRS, and I feel it right to stick to them'. Then, after ceding the 'Friday Afternoons' rights, he adds, 'In future, however, I must have all my works controlled by the PRS as a matter of principle'.[30]

A touchstone of the Society's success was its increasing ability to cope with the administrative task which was most onerous and most vulnerable to criticism by members. It was attempting to conduct, as a friendly newspaper article exclaimed, 'a continuous census of all the music that is being performed from hour to hour all over the country', and then to pay out appropriately.[31] As the number and range of its activities increased, the difficulties of analysing programme information and distributing fees became ever more burdensome. Accuracy and speed could only be achieved, in limited fashion, by taking

[29] PRS Archives, Novello file, Memorandum, 11 Mar. 1926; PRS to Novello, 13 Dec. 1935.

[30] I am indebted to Donald Mitchell for allowing me to see these letters: Britten to Hatchman, 7 Oct. 1934 and 1 Jan. 1935; Foss to Britten, 20 Dec. 1934; Britten to Foss, 8 Jan. 1935.

[31] *Evening News*, quoted in *Performing Right Gazette*, Jan. 1935, 49.

on more staff, who needed more office space, adding to costs which had to be deducted from fees. A possible escape from this vicious circle was proposed in 1931. In order to deal with 'the present influx of programmes', the Distribution Committee was told, there would have to be considerable new recruitment of staff, 'thereby reaching the limit of available accommodation'. As an alternative to increasing the wage bill and renting more offices C. F. James, therefore, proposed an experiment with 'mechanizing the department' by installing Powers-Sames or Hollerith machines, initially in the hotel section of the programme department, at a cost for six months of £600.[32]

Since machines of this type had been used in the 1890 United States census and the 1911 UK census, it was hardly a revolutionary suggestion; and it took another four years before the Board recommended more extensive use of the Hollerith punch-card system. Yet among performing right societies the PRS was a pioneer in this crucial area of administration. The tradition-bound and labour-intensive procedures of SACEM, which was generally regarded as the societies' exemplar, provided no stimulus to experiment: the French society did not install its first machines until 1937, when its new premises were inaugurated with great pomp by the President of the Republic. There were some experiments by the Swedish society, but information about the practical use of data-analysis systems was hard to come by, and costs were high. Electric data processing, though often fast and technically efficient, was still very expensive in England, at a time when clerical wages, even in central London, were still low. The Board's decision to extend 'mechanization' was eventually taken after comparing costs with the 'present manual system'.[33] Nearly one hundred clerks had been coping manfully, if the phrase be permitted for the staff photographed on pl. 5, with enormous quantities of information, with no assistance save an elaborate division of tasks reminiscent of Adam Smith's description of eighteenth-century pin-making. In 1934 there were over 350,000 'returns' from licensees, and the number of 'points' recorded for the distribution of fees exceeded 111 million. Yet, in place of the old delays and annual payments, members now enjoyed the benefit of four distributions a year. Broadcasting fees from Britain, Ireland, and Australia were distributed in April and November, and there was a 'general' distribution in June. The latter included not only British fees, but also general and broadcasting fees from some thirty foreign countries and numerous parts of the British Empire. Nor did the work

---

[32] PRS Archives, Distribution Committee minutes, 2 July 1931.
[33] PRS Archives, Board minutes, 12 Oct. 1935.

of each distribution end when every member was paid what was due to him from all these sources. Every foreign affiliated society also had to be sent a statement listing which of its works had been performed in British territories, and the payments due.

There were still 'GIGO' problems of course, although their extent was hard to judge. In 1937 The *Melody Maker* reported a new version of an all-too-familiar problem, with some authority, for it was widely read by popular musicians. 'All over England', it complained, 'semi-pro band leaders' were expected to prepare returns under conditions which precluded accuracy: late at night, after long sessions, which included unanticipated request items. As a result 'incorrect PRS returns have been a joke in the profession for years'. The writer offered what he considered to be a simple remedy: the establishment of a coded catalogue, in which 'all the popular tunes of the day' and their publishers would be listed with numbers for rapid identification of what had been played. It was, as C. F. James attempted to explain, a naïve suggestion, blithely ignorant of the size and complexity of the real task. Nevertheless, the problem remained, even if proposed solutions were impracticable. Many returns were 'grossly inaccurate'.[34] Despite these doubts the Society took justifiable pride in its data processing, and its 'electrical accounting machines' were a showpiece for visitors, including several journalists and a few Members of Parliament.[35]

After Ullswater

To coincide with the publication of the Ullswater Report the Society published a nicely produced booklet, under the impressive title: *Radio and the Composer: The Economics of Modern Music*. Its brief foreword was signed, only a few months before his death, by the grand old man of English light music, Sir Edward German. He had joined the PRS in 1915 and served on the Board in 1925 and 1926. The booklet was compiled in the Society's office and 'put into literary shape', as the process was described in response to a disgruntled query about its authorship, by an author-director who had joined in 1914 and was also near the end of his career. Captain Harry Graham had written 'Ruthless Rhymes for Heartless Homes' and the English lyrics of several well-known musical comedies, including 'The Maid of the Mountains' and 'Land of Smiles'. *Radio and the Composer* set out to demonstrate that composers and publishers had recently endured

---

[34] *Melody Maker*, 14 and 28 Aug. 1937; 11 Sept. 1937.

[35] *Sphere*, 31 Oct. 1937. A visit by MPs on 16 Dec. 1936 is reported in *Performing Right Gazette*, Jan 1937, 248.

hard times, which few would dispute, and that radio was responsible, which needed proof. Neither complaint was pressed home, presumably because, quite apart from incompetent drafting, secretiveness and anonymity were regarded as more important, in a *published* document, than convincing argument. Thus, a handful of uncategorized figures from 'nine representative publishers' purport to illustrate sheet music sales, recording, and performance royalties in 1925, 1929, and 1933. Their reliability as indicators has to be taken on faith because 'complete statistics are, of course, impossible to obtain'. A chapter on 'what the composer earns' is similarly vague and inconclusive, sketching in barest outline the woeful experience of five anonymous 'leading composers'. One phrase sticks in the mind, from Edward German's foreword; the composer has been 'deprived by science'. But even the sympathetic reader is left only with a general impression of distress, few facts, and no proof that radio was *responsible* for what had gone wrong.[36] Its unattributed authorship was criticized by the Australian Solicitor-General as 'diminishing its authority'.[37]

If this ill-conceived document was intended to excite public comment and sympathy it failed to do so. A few letters, orchestrated by C. F. James, appeared in newspapers, but failed to arouse discussion. No major journal gave it notice.[38] Its interest lies elsewhere: as a sign of indifference towards public relations, and of dangerously negative attitudes towards change. The former is self-evident, for *Radio and the Composer* was clearly unrepresentative of the best talents available to the Society. The latter is perhaps to be understood as part of the general Ullswater hullabaloo in 1936. As several historians have explained, the Committee provided a last opportunity for representatives of all the weakest and most obsolete elements in English musical life to draw together in a final outpouring of resentment against the BBC. Their absurd pretence that all had been well with music in England before the advent of broadcasting, and their futile attempts to exert control over the BBC, were impotent gestures by yesterday's men.[39] Since some of them were members of the Society they were bound to be heard, but their rhetoric of frustration had little place in a vital institution committed to the future. The strength of the alliance lay in its ability to adapt to unavoidable change. Its immediate complaints and needs were quite

[36] *Radio and the Composer: The Economics of Modern Music, with a foreword by Sir Edward German* (1935).

[37] PRS Archives, Correspondence with Australasian Performing Right Association, 21 Nov. 1935; 18 Mar. and 14 Apr. 1936.

[38] See *Birmingham Post*, 29 Apr. 1936; *Performing Right Gazette*, Apr. 1936, 172.

[39] See Briggs, *Golden Age*, 490–2; Nicholas Kenyon, *The BBC Symphony Orchestra: The First Fifty Years 1930–1980* (1981), 110–15; Ehrlich, *Music Profession*, 221–3.

specific, and not to be confused with mindless antagonism to the BBC. Broadcasting was an unequivocally good thing for the PRS—provided its members were appropriately paid when their work was required. This simple message, which had been obscured rather than elucidated by *Radio and the Composer*, needed pressing home, with abundant, relevant information and cogent argument, sufficient to persuade sceptical holders of purse-strings.

The next step was to propose terms for the BBC licence which was due to be renewed at the end of 1936. It was suggested that this should be based on the extent of 'user' (use of the Society's repertoire) and on audience size. In addition to the familiar increase in both factors, there were two further reasons for increasing the fee. Music published by the 1936 recruits, for which the BBC had hitherto made separate payment, would now be available under the PRS agreement. Secondly the BBC was expanding its schedules, including extensions of broadcasts from 11.15 to midnight. On all these grounds the Society proposed that its annual fee should be set at one shilling per wireless licence.[40] It is unlikely that the BBC were surprised at the size of this demand. Fifteen months had passed since Boosey had visited Reith to tell him that the general view was that BBC payments should be doubled. A Board minute in May 1935 originally read that the licence would have to be 'at least doubled', and was then revised to read 'increased very considerably'.[41] The ground had been further prepared by evidence to Ullswater, which had clearly been received with sympathy. But the Corporation's officials were in no hurry to conclude negotiations. Enjoying a leisurely summer vacation, they took three months before sending a reply. It was remonstrative in tone, and replete with technical arguments about audience size and 'user'. It also demonstrated a readiness to employ jejune arguments and statistics to match those of *Radio and the Composer*, but with opposite conclusions: 'the reaction of broadcasting on other forms of entertainment has, if anything, been *advantageous* as, for instance, is shown by the improvement in the sale of pianos'.[42]

After juggling with figures, but without accepting that conditions had changed since the last agreement in 1933, the Corporation offered 5*d.* per licence.[43] 'We are poles apart', wrote James to Boosey, and concluded that the BBC wanted arbitration and had framed their response accordingly.[44] The Executive Committee was outraged by

[40] PRS Archives, PRS to BBC, 27 July 1936.

[41] PRS Archives, Board minutes, 17 May 1935.

[42] On the limited significance of the 1930s piano 'boom', see Ehrlich, *The Piano: A History* (1976), 184–193.

[43] PRS Archives, BBC to PRS, 19 Oct. 1936.

[44] PRS Archives, James to Leslie Boosey, 21 Oct. 1936.

the offer, expressing 'the unanimous and emphatic view' that it 'could not be entertained'.[45] Noting its disappointment that the BBC's proposal made no attempt to reflect the spirit of the Ullswater recommendations, the Society suggested arbitration by a tribunal consisting of a barrister, a chartered accountant, and a nominee of the Board of Trade. The PRS would be represented by leading Counsel, and each institution would pay its own costs.[46] These arrangements were accepted by the BBC, and a draft licence was prepared before discussions began about the level of fee. At that point there was a last-minute hitch which threatened to destroy the entire bargaining process. Demanding preliminary agreement about technical matters of indemnity, and about television rights, the Corporation peremptorily broke off negotiations.[47]

Not for the first time, but never so strategically, a crisis brought the personal relationship between Boosey and Reith into play. As 'a last attempt to rescue the negotiations from disaster' Boosey drafted a letter, 'an entirely personal and unofficial one from me to yourself', explicitly without consulting legal advisers. He did not send it, visiting Sir John instead, but it needs to be quoted, for its insight into Boosey's thinking at this turning point in the Society's history, and because it obviously formed the basis of their discussions. The latest fracas, he argued, was 'insincere', an attempt to prove that the PRS was being 'unreasonable' and to provoke Government action 'to clip the Society's wings once and for all'. The indemnity complaint was a quibble; the question of television rights had not been altered in any way. Arbitration was now necessary, and welcome because it delegated the still unavoidable task of finding a yardstick:

I should be loath to take upon my shoulders the responsibility of settling what should be paid. If I came to an agreement which you considered fair, they [members of the PRS] might accuse me of having sold their birthright for a mess of pottage. If I insisted on your paying what the authors and composers considered they were entitled to, you might be perfectly justified in going to the P.M.G. and saying our demands were exorbitant.

The two leaders met a week later; the BBC removed its objections, and the arbitration began. It was Leslie Boosey's finest hour.[48]

The arbitration was successful for the Society. Having asked for one

[45] PRS Archives, Executive Committee minutes, 27 Oct. 1936; approved by Board, 12 Nov. 1936.

[46] PRS Archives, PRS to BBC, 16 Nov. 1936; Executive Committee minutes, 27 Oct. 1936; Board minutes, 12 Nov. 1936.

[47] PRS Archives, Memorandum of conference, 30 Dec. 1936; Executive Committee minutes, 1 and 5 Jan. 1937.

[48] PRS Archives, Leslie Boosey to Reith, drafted 6 Jan. 1937; James to Syrett, 13 Jan. 1937.

shilling per wireless licence it got sevenpence, with no more
decreasing scales, plus 10 per cent for Empire broadcasts. Effectively
this amounted to nearly double the previous rate; and in the following
year fees distributed to members from broadcast performances were
actually more than doubled. Despite the significance of these events
they were barely noticed in the press. The *Musical Opinion*, noting a
general tendency towards 'reticence on all matters connected with the
performance of copyright music', commented that 'the magnitude of
the increase . . . should have shown the most harassed sub-editor that
something had been lacking in the previous attitude of the BBC'.[49]
The proceedings had taken thirteen days, with heavy expenditure on
lawyers by both sides. Their interest lies less in niceties of pleading,
and arcane arguments about possible 'yardsticks', than in their
unique assemblage of evidence about what had been happening to
music and musicians in a decade of tumultuous change. In order to
document its case the Society persuaded a variety of publishers to
provide information of a kind which had always been jealously
guarded in the past. Similar at first glance to the gobbets of fact which
had been dropped into *Radio and the Composer*, this documentation is
much more informative: specific, fairly detailed, and probably
reliable, since it was produced for the quasi-legal circumstances of a
tribunal and subjected to sceptical examination.

A Decade of Travail

Each witness set out to illustrate the effect of collapsing sheet-music
sales on individuals and firms, and to blame radio for this. As we have
repeatedly explained, the real causes were far too complex to be
attributed solely to the BBC, and the latter's counsel had no difficulty
in demolishing simplistic arguments, particularly when dealing with
the more obvious cases of obsolescence. Thus, with reference to
Coleridge-Taylor's ballad 'Unmindful of the Roses', he asked whether
'this is the kind of thing which the modern young lady, fresh from the
pillion seat of a motor bicycle, would be likely to sing' to her
boyfriend? Without wishing to ridicule either the song or modern life,
he argued that broadcasting was merely 'one of many allied
phenomena which partly reflect and partly cause changed habits and
changed modes of thought'. With or without broadcasting these
changes would necessarily have affected the sheet-music sales of
'Unmindful of the Roses'.[50] In similar fashion the declining sheet

49 *Musical Opinion*, July 1937.
50 PRS Archives, BBC Arbitration 1937, vol. x. 54–6.

sales of Fraser-Simson and Archibald Joyce could be ascribed, at least in part, to changing tastes. Simson, best known for the Christopher Robin songs, earned over £1,500 from sheet-music royalties in 1921, and £128 in 1935. His total income from composition fell to a quarter of its former level. Comparable figures for Joyce, the 'English waltz king', fell from £499 to £6 (sheet music) and £527 to £183 (composition income). Even Ivor Novello received only £5 from sales of sheet music in 1935, though his total income of seventy-six pounds from composing was presumably well supplemented from earnings elsewhere.[51] And that was the crux of the matter. Musicians had always been forced to piece together a living, and very few composers could expect to survive from composition alone. Had there been any fundamental change in conditions within these limits?

Ralph Hawkes reported the experience of five composers between 1921 and 1935. The copyright earnings of Wilfred Sanderson, who had written such once famous songs as 'Up from Somerset', and whom Leslie Boosey described as 'probably the most successful writer of songs over a period of years that there has been', fell from £4,567 to £372. Those of the redoubtable march composer F. J. Ricketts fell from £520 to £36, and of Roger Quilter from £484 to £95. A pathetic case was T. C. Sterndale Bennett, who had netted £12 in 1921, £82 in 1929, and £10 in 1935. A few of these men were compensated to some extent by performing fees, but only one of them had been reasonably successful in coping with the decade of transformation. Herman Finck's sheet-music royalties fell from £96 to £20. In 1929 his income from gramophone records had reached £815, only to fall to £37 in 1935; but by then his general performing fees were £394, and broadcast fees £299. Such were the expectations of musicians in those days, and the condescension of more successful professions, that these modest figures were sufficient for Finck to be awarded the accolade of 'the Bobby Jones of broadcasting', by a lawyer who was being paid £100 a day.[52]

Similar information was provided by Augener for the composers Frank Bridge, S. Coleridge-Taylor, and John Ireland. Bridge's income from composition was £112 in 1921, £248 in 1929, and £142 in 1935. Out of this grand total his sheet-music royalties had been £60, £112, and £45; his general performing fees had fallen from £36 to £22, and broadcasting fees risen to £73. The heirs to the composer of *Hiawatha* had netted sheet-music royalties of £50 in 1921, and nothing in 1935; but broadcasting and performance had swollen the aggregate

---

[51] Ibid., 'Prove' of Ascherberg, Hopwood and Crew.
[52] Ibid., vol. v., 46–50, and 'Prove' of R. Hawkes.

figure to £52. Ireland was making £162 from composition, £80 less than in 1921. His sheet-music income had fallen from £220 to £68; performing and broadcast fees brought in £92.[53] While these examples had been chosen to make the Society's case, they were broadly representative of many members. Their feelings were well-expressed in a letter from Thomas Dunhill, a composer-director since 1929, to Leslie Boosey, urging him to explain to the arbitrators that composers, though absent from the proceedings, were just as concerned as the publishers with their outcome. 'The more people listen in the less they wish to perform themselves' was Dunhill's simple belief, 'and so, although the composer has a larger audience than he has ever had before, he has never had such small remuneration for his work'.[54]

The popular publishers spoke of trends and titles, rather than the experience of individuals, giving sheet-music sales and mechanical royalties for their six most successful numbers in each of the chosen years. In 1921 'I'm For Ever Blowing Bubbles' earned over £7,000 and £600 from sheets and records respectively; 'Let the Rest of the World Go By' approximately £5,000 and £500; and 'Avalon' £1,500 from the combined sources. In 1929 three leading titles barely exceeded £1,000 from sheet sales, plus a few hundred pounds from records. By 1935 only 'Lullaby of Broadway' earned more than £1,200 from sheets and £600 from records, though 'The Man on the Flying Trapeze' brought in £949 from sheets and £812 from records.[55] John Abbott, of Francis, Day and Hunter, illustrated similar but more extreme trends. In 1921 his firm had published 215 titles, and distributed £24,000 in royalties from all sources. In 1929 the comparable figures were 143 and £49,000. By 1935 they had fallen to 89 and £12,000. In 1921 Francis, Day and Hunter's top six numbers had earned over £27,000 from sheet sales and £6,000 from records, the leader, 'Peggy O'Neil', netting £10,590 and £1,985 respectively. Their 1929 list has some titles which are still familiar, and illustrate the growing influence of Hollywood. 'Pagan Love Song' earned over £5,000 and £3,000; 'Broadway Melody' nearly £5,000 and over £7,000; 'Singing in the Rain' £2,000 and £2,280. Another two titles earned more than £1,000 each from sheets and £2,000 from records. By 1935, with a single exception, no Francis, Day and Hunter song earned more than £800 from sheets or a few hundred pounds from records. The exception was 'When I Grow Too Old To Dream' which netted an astonishing £5,976 from sheets and £1,967 from records.

---

[53] Ibid., 'Prove' of J. W. Woodman.
[54] PRS Archives, Dunhill to Leslie Boosey, 26 Feb. 1937.
[55] PRS Archives, BBC Arbitration 1937, 'Prove' of F. Slevin.

Sentimental, easy to play, and doubling as ballad and waltz, it was, said Abbott, 'the kind of thing that happens only once in five years'. But generally experience had been bleak, and the decline was attributable 'almost entirely to broadcasting'.[56]

The arbitrators were not required to indicate the extent to which they accepted the arguments and evidence put before them. Nor were they required to explain the logic of their decision: they provided no yardstick. But the level of their award was cause for celebration in the Society. The way ahead looked bright and prosperous.

[56] Ibid., 'Prove' of John Abbott, and vol. viii. 41–2.

5

WAR WORK

In June 1939 the Society celebrated its quarter century with the mild euphoria and self-congratulation appropriate to such an occasion, clouded only by reference to contingency plans 'in the event of an emergency'. A few months later apprehension had become reality and the immediate need was to devise tactics for survival. The network of communications and administration, collections and payment, which had been painfully assembled since 1914, was badly mauled, and it never ceased to be vulnerable for the next six years. Those parts which could be protected or salvaged had to be constantly adjusted to the capricious requirements of war. New administrative machinery also had to be improvised, with insufficient resources, particularly staff, to deal with new kinds of performance and location.

Emergency Bulletins

On the home front an immediate cause for alarm was the virtual cessation of public entertainment; an official shut-down which was so extensive that even military bands were silenced. Expecting sudden devastation from the air, the Government imposed a 6 p.m. curfew on cinemas, theatres, and concert halls. Broadcasting was reduced to a single dispiriting channel of public announcements, gramophone records, and organ interludes by Sandy Macpherson. Among many protests G. B. Shaw described the action as 'a masterstroke of unimaginative stupidity'; Sir Henry Wood warned of the 'dreadful poverty' threatening unemployed performing musicians,[1] and Leslie Boosey drew special attention to the plight of composers. Although they were 'prepared to suffer with the rest of us', their livelihood was peculiarly at risk because of its virtually complete dependence on performances, reinstatement of which was a matter of survival for them, and could also serve to 'lighten our darkness'.[2] After a few weeks of disruption, the shut-down ended as arbitrarily as it had begun, the Government relaxing its stranglehold as a result of public outcry and the non-arrival of Hitler's bombers.

[1] *The Times*, 7 Sept. 1939.
[2] Leslie Boosey, letter to press, in *PRS Emergency Bulletin*, Oct. 1939, 4.

A long boom in entertainment began, undeterred when the 'phoney war' became a real one. The BBC launched its immensely popular Forces Programme, films played to packed audiences, and the public's thirst for music became unquenchable. As R. A. Butler later reminded the Society on the occasion of its thirtieth anniversary:

The experiences of the war must have brought real encouragement to your members . . . We have realised as never before what music can mean in everyday life. Music in air raid shelters, rest centres, in factory canteens, workers' hostels, village halls and public parks, and in camps, and on remote battery sites, has inspired and refreshed in times of hard work and strain.[3]

Some observers detected signs of a renaissance, their cultural euphoria fed by images of rapt, uniformed audiences listening to Myra Hess in the National Gallery. Others saw only an undiscriminating 'morass of musical inflation', with ceaseless repetition of a few hackneyed works.[4] But everyone agreed that music of every kind had never been so much in demand. Moreover, people were able and prepared to pay for it. As in World War I, but, ultimately with even greater force, economic conditions stimulated the demand for leisure services. Full employment, rising wages, rationing, and an ever-worsening shortage of consumer goods left plenty of cash to be spent on anything available, including music. There were opportunities here for an expansion of the Society's activities, and substantial improvements in returns to its members, if administration could be organized, payments secured, and public goodwill maintained.

The reawakening of public entertainment soon after the outbreak of war ended fears of complete disruption and severe cuts in the Society's income, but it exacerbated the immediate difficulties of maintaining a skeleton administration. Churchill House, at Horsell in Surrey, which had just been acquired as a rest home for aged or infirm members, was converted to emergency offices and 'billets' for a staff of thirty. The London offices were temporarily closed, while basements were converted into air-raid shelters. As if in a story by Gerard Hoffnung, this work put the electric generators out of action, stopping the calculating machines on which the whole distribution system depended. Eventually, about fifty staff were reinstated in London and began to pick up the threads of programme analysis. The irreplaceable repertory index of several hundred thousand cards was microfilmed and lodged for safe keeping at Woking. The *Performing Right Gazette* was discontinued, and replaced by occasional issues of an exiguous,

[3] R. A. Butler, 'Message to the Performing Right Society', 20 July 1944, in *PRS Emergency Bulletin*, Aug. 1944, 87.

[4] Boyd Neel, *The Story of an Orchestra* (1950), 50–2.

but reasonably informative, *PRS Emergency Bulletin*, starting in October 1939. This brief summary of ceaseless administrative adjustment does scant justice to prolonged feats of improvisation and loyal service. If such actions were common enough among London office-workers in those heroic days, they deserve, none the less, to be recorded and marvelled at in our pampered age. A measure of their early success was the fact that, despite every impediment, the staff managed to complete the 1940 distributions of fees at the appointed times. It was a notable achievement, warmly appreciated throughout the Society.[5]

For the rest of the war, despite setbacks and temporary crises, the office continued to improvise and provide a basic service which kept the PRS afloat. Men were called up, and women drafted into industrial employment, reducing the staff to a third of its pre-war strength. Use of the Hollerith machines was extended to save labour. Distribution procedures were simplified, sometimes makeshift, and subject to delay, but somehow maintained. The administration of licences was extraordinarily difficult because many premises were closed or destroyed, and a great deal of music was being performed in new, unconventional locations and scattered camps. Many of these places were remote and inaccessible, with impossible communications. Delegation to the official bureaucracy was a rational, though unlucrative, solution. The Council for Encouragement of Music and the Arts and the Entertainments National Service Association were given global licences. Ernest Ford, the Society's head of licensing, joined the staff of ENSA to administer its agreement and, doing both jobs, would happily write letters of encouragement or admonishment to himself. Government departments made similar arrangements, including the War Office, Admiralty, and Ministry of Information. Even the Ministry of Food dabbled in music, attempting to make its 'British Restaurants' more tolerable. A highly significant initiative was the licensing of music in factories. Eventually organized through the Ministry of Supply, it gave rise to a multitude of troubles, as will be explained below. Another novel form of licence was granted to the London Philharmonic Orchestra, authorizing performances in places not normally covered for serious music. All of these exercises in 'make do and mend' were carried out in conditions of discomfort and danger, with constant need to anticipate contingencies. In March 1944, for example, an option was taken on rooms near the Wigmore Hall, in case of air-raid damage, with permission to assemble in the Hall itself in an emergency.[6]

[5] *PRS Emergency Bulletin*, Nov. 1940, 25.
[6] PRS Archives, Executive Committee minutes, 7 Mar. 1944.

International arrangements raised a host of administrative, political, and humanitarian problems. In some cases there was complete dislocation, as when Japan's entry into the war closed down the Society's agencies in Hong Kong and Singapore. But the basic framework for future co-operation was preserved to a surprising extent, even among belligerent nations. PRS control of enemy repertories was safeguarded by special legislation, on condition that the relevant fees were handed over to the Custodian of Enemy Property for eventual settlement after the war. There were similar arrangements in Axis countries, for British music was still being performed on the Continent. Before the fall of France an office of CISAC was opened in Berne, largely through the efforts of Leslie Boosey. In co-operation with the International Copyright Union it acted as a registry of accounts and centre of information, maintaining tenuous contacts with the member societies throughout the war. Thus, in 1941 PRS members were given news from most of Europe. SACEM's revenue had been halved, but was now recovering. The Dutch, Danish, and Norwegian Societies were still functioning, but no remittances were possible in either direction, whereas reciprocal payments with Sweden were operating normally. The Polish Society had ceased to exist, losing its records in the bombardment of Warsaw, but its officials were reported safe.[7] A year later there was news from Greece, where the Italian Society had taken over an agency formerly controlled by the French; and from Tangier, where the Spanish Society had similarly supplanted SACEM.[8] In 1943 the Italians were reported to be still collecting fees for performances of English music, but they had fallen to a third of pre-war levels.[9]

There were renewed opportunities to help victims of oppression. The exodus of composers, writers, and publishers, predominantly, but not solely, Jewish, had raised intractable problems since the mid-thirties. Unable to extract their rights from the German and Austrian organizations, or, frequently, even to provide relevant documents of title, they were dependent upon the Society's ability and willingness to temper its international obligations with humanity; allowing these hapless people to transfer their membership to London, in defiance of Nazi wishes. Complexities of nationality and statelessness were now, with the outbreak of war, further confused by the claims of the Custodian of Enemy Property. In October 1939, for example, the Executive Committee scrutinized the definition of an 'enemy' in the Trading with the Enemy Act, and noted that it excluded 'persons of

[7] *PRS Emergency Bulletin*, July 1941, 39.
[8] Ibid., Oct. 1939, 5; July 1942, 49.
[9] Ibid., Aug. 1943, 76.

Austrian, German, or Czechoslovakian nationality who were not resident in enemy territory'. It then authorized payments to 'members of the Society who had previously been members of Societies operating in countries now enemy territory, and who had not acquired British nationality, but were no longer resident in enemy territory'.[10] Concealed beneath the verbiage was solace for people whose lives had been torn apart. The exemplary behaviour of the PRS, and particularly of its harassed officials, in dealing with these tragic events, ultimately brought handsome rewards to the Society. A large and important repertoire of foreign works accrued to its lists. The following illustrious names appear among newly enrolled members during this period: Béla Bartók, Hans Gál, Walter Goehr, Berthold Goldschmidt, Zoltán Kodály, Franz Reizenstein, Miklós Rózsa, Mátyás Seiber, Robert Stolz, Richard Tauber, and Egon Wellesz. Immigrant publishers included Kurt Eulenburg, Erwin Stein, Ernst Roth, who became a Director (representing Boosey and Hawkes) in 1958, and Alfred Kalmus, who joined the Council in 1966.

Calling All Workers

The idea that background music can improve the productivity of labour was promulgated by industrial sociologists, mostly in America, during the late 1930s. It was said to provide an antidote to fatigue and boredom, and there were theories about the appropriateness of different kinds of music to various categories of worker and task: military bands for heavy industry and older workers, dance bands for light industry, repetitive jobs, women, and the young.[11] The appropriateness of such ideas to a war economy appeared to be self-evident, and rapidly gained powerful support. Lord Beaverbrook, at the Ministry of Aircraft Production, and Ernest Bevin, Minister of Labour, were ardent advocates. The BBC began to broadcast 'Music While You Work' on 23 June 1940, to 'lessen strain, relieve monotony and thereby increase efficiency'.[12] By October, broadcast daily at 10.30 a.m., the programme's audience was estimated at 3,500,000, and its later extensions included broadcasts on the Forces Network. In 1943 nearly 7,000 large factories and innumerable small workshops were relaying three half-hour programmes a day to their employees, rising to 9,000 by the end of the war, with, perhaps, five million people hearing the programme. A BBC report listed its attributes as a

[10] PRS Archives, Executive Committee minutes, 19 Oct. 1939.
[11] Examples of the technical literature are cited in Asa Briggs, *The History of Broadcasting in the United Kingdom*, vol. iii. *The War of Words* (1970), 576.
[12] Quoted by Asa Briggs in *The BBC: The First First Fifty Years* (1985), 193.

universal elixir. Used 'wisely and intelligently', music was said to increase production by 'stimulating the tired worker; acting as a mental tonic; relieving boredom; increasing happiness; improving health; minimising unnecessary conversation; relieving nervous strain; and cutting down absenteeism'.[13] Many pundits, pressure groups, and committees, such as the Industrial Health Research Board and Industrial Welfare Society, shared and promoted the general enthusiasm.

The broadcasts of 'Music While You Work', beginning and ending with Eric Coates's jaunty march, 'Calling All Workers', were a turning-point in the history of music in Britain. Using music as a pleasing sound, to be overheard, rather than listened to, was not a new idea; but its systematic exploitation to influence states of mind and human activity, in this case labour productivity, was something quite different: a momentous leap forward towards incessant, inescapable background (and often foreground) noise, wherever people congregate, which the next generation would learn to accept as part of its natural environment. In the 1940s the sound was generally kept quiet, and its ubiquity was limited by an expensive and cumbersome technology; but broadcasts, gramophone records, and Tannoy installations reached large numbers of people. Here was an entirely new and rapidly growing use of music to which the Society, representing its producers, had to respond, sometimes with reluctance on the part of sensitive musicians. Their legal rights were apparently clear. Relays of broadcasts were unequivocally public performances, as had been established in the courts during the past decade. Since the attested benefits of background music were so universally acclaimed, it might have been expected that performing right would be acknowledged by its purveyors, and that copyright owners would be promptly remunerated. This was not to be.

By June 1940 the PRS was receiving urgent enquiries about permission to use broadcast music in factories. Since the need for an immediate response left no time to work out detailed tariffs, the nominal annual fee of one guinea per factory was set as a temporary expedient. Hoping for 'a reasonable measure of co-operation', Executive Committee intended this arrangement to serve two purposes: as a stopgap until adequate scales appropriate to different sizes of factory could be devised, and as a reminder that payment for performing right was legal and necessary.[14] Despite the negligible cost of these temporary licences, hopes of concurrence were soon dashed, as the Society's requests were ignored or rejected. Manufacturers who had

[13] 'Findings of the BBC on "Music While You Work"', quoted in PRS pamphlet *Music in Industry*, 1946.

[14] PRS Archives, Executive Committee minutes, 15 June 1940.

become accustomed to paying inflated prices for materials and labour, the burden of which was cushioned in most cases by remunerative 'cost-plus' contracts with government departments, nevertheless drew the line at paying for the music which eased their production lines. Their opposition hardened when the licences were rationalized, still at minuscule levels. For factories employing up to 252 workers the annual fee was kept at one guinea. Larger factories were asked to pay an extra penny for each additional worker. Many agreed, but a few firms were intransigent, forcing the PRS into court.

It was a reluctant move, hedged by nervousness about public reaction in wartime, and therefore designed to exert minimal force. Seeking neither an injunction nor damages, but only a declaration of its rights, the Society brought a test case against Gillette Industries Ltd. for unauthorized rediffusion, by a receiving set and thirty-three loudspeakers, of copyright musical works. At that time, the summer of 1942, the firm employed about 1,100 workers, most of whom heard 'Music While You Work', though one room muted its three loudspeakers in deference to staff who, in those unenlightened days, preferred silence. The defendants, admitting use of the programmes 'for the purposes of their business and with a view to lessening the industrial fatigue of their employees and of increasing the amenity of their employment', pleaded exemption from payment on two grounds. In the first place their factory was, in wartime parlance, a 'protected place', subject to the Essential Works Orders. In the second place, and this plea can only be reported, without attempting to explain its logic, the existence of a quiet zone meant that their workers were not forced to listen to the programme. The High Court Judge dismissed both pleas and cited several precedents, including the *Hammonds Bradford Brewery* case. Concluding that performances had undoubtedly taken place, he granted the declaration of its rights which the PRS had requested, with costs to be met by the defendants. A few weeks later a similar action was heard by the same judge. In this instance the factory owners sought a declaration that they were not infringing copyright by rediffusing broadcasts, as often as they pleased, to 560 people. Again the Society won the case, with such ease that its counsel was not even called upon to present arguments.[15]

As Leslie Boosey and his colleagues had feared, there was a great deal of press comment, some of it hostile and wildly inaccurate. One report alleged that the licence fee was one penny per worker per hour of music, an absurd exaggeration. Another suggested that the PRS was trying to stop music being played in factories. Two newspapers,

[15] *PRS* v. *Ernest Turner Electrical Instruments Ltd.* See *PRS Emergency Bulletin*, Feb. 1943, 53–8.

however, spelled out old truths which evidently needed frequent restatement. 'It should not have been necessary to take the matter to court', said the *Manchester Guardian,*

but there are still many people, impeccably upright in other business dealings, who are ready to deprive the composer of his due, and even wax indignant when called upon to pay him for services rendered. Composers, after all, must eat. They are worthy of their hire if only as lubricators of the wheels of industry. It cannot be pretended that [the fee] is an excessive charge for a daily hour of stimulating rhythm. To the factory it is an inconsiderable trifle, but it may well add up to the difference between penury and comfort for the composer.

The *Yorkshire Post* was also supportive:

it is right that the copyright of composers should be protected. The payments asked by the Performing Right Society . . . hardly lay a crippling burden on even a very large factory. The man in the street will probably feel that since 'Music While You Work' is clearly fulfilling a function of national value at the present time, an agreement might well have been reached without bringing the matter laboriously into court.

Despite these expressions of goodwill from the North, there was still scope for confusion and malevolence elsewhere. In the House of Commons an attack worthy of Tuppenny days began quietly with a Member of Parliament asking the Minister of Production to make comprehensive arrangements for the rediffusion of 'Music While You Work' so that factories 'might not be inhibited from using this means of increasing production'. Inhibition was a strange response to the request for a small fee, but the attack gathered force when another gallant member added untruth to misconception, with a dash of bad grammar, to produce the following rhetorical question:

Is my right hon. Friend aware that this Performing Right Society are [sic] receiving from the BBC a licence fee, that they are also drawing a similar fee from the artists who sing these songs, and that they are now to receive a similar fee from the factories? Is it not time that this was stopped?

A civilian, but none the less bellicose, MP then demanded that 'the Performing Right Society be informed that the BBC will cease to perform this music if they insist on these blackmailing fees'. Finally, it was alleged that the Society was capable of charging 'an unspecified fee' not three but *four* times for the same performance, and that curbing legislation was therefore urgently required. These ridiculous assertions were eventually refuted in careful detail by the Minister to whom they were addressed. It was explained that PRS fees were reasonable, and always clearly specified, that multiple charges were non-existent, and that curbing legislation would not be required. Unfortunately, this clean bill of health for the Society took time to prepare, for the Minister, unlike his interlocuters, checked facts before giving utterance. A written answer was eventually printed in *Hansard*, and ignored by the press.[16]

Meanwhile, the judiciary was doing something to redress the balance. Both companies had taken their cases to the Court of Appeal, and both were again defeated with costs. The Master of the Rolls delivered a lengthy judgement, not only on music in factories but also on the general interpretation of the 1911 Copyright Act. It gave no succour to the Society's enemies and explicitly refuted sanctimonious appeals to the national interest. 'The owner of the copyright is entitled to be paid for the use of his property unless and until the Legislature otherwise determines, and he is entitled to be paid for it even if the use that is made of it is a use which concerns the public welfare to a very considerable extent'. In the course of the proceedings the judge also demolished several hackneyed arguments which had been given yet another airing. Thus, it had been asserted, for the umpteenth time, that composers should be satisfied with the advertisement value of a performance. And this was particularly so in the case of 'Music While You Work', it was argued, gnomically, because no titles were announced during the programme. The Master of the Rolls dismissed these contentions with contempt: 'It is a novel conception, is it not, that you can take another man's property from him without paying for it, and then excuse yourself by saying: "The mere fact that I am using this fountain pen" or whatever it is, "is a good advertisement for the manufacturer?" ' A request for leave to appeal to the House of Lords was flatly refused: 'In our opinion this is a very clear case. There has been complete unanimity of judicial opinion upon it'. So determined were the Society's antagonists that even this did not deter one of the appellants, who petitioned the House for leave to appeal, and was yet again rejected.[17]

Renewed press comment did something to allay the damage from a previous spate of reports on the malicious questions in Parliament. The *Birmingham Post*, well located to know about factories, was clear and forthright:

To industrial establishments the music has a value actually measurable in terms of output, which is to say in terms of pounds, shillings and pence; and

---

[16] *Parliamentary Debates*, 10 Feb. 1943, vol. 386, 1314–15. The Minister's written reply was published on 17 Feb. 1943, vol. 386, p. 1743. See also *PRS Emergency Bulletin*, 8 Apr. 1943, 67–8.

[17] *PRS* v. *Gilllette Industries Ltd. Ernest Turner Electrical Industries Ltd.* v. *PRS*. See *PRS Emergency Bulletin*, Feb. 1943, 53–8; and Apr. 1943, 61–7.

in comparison with that advantage to themselves—we say nothing for the moment of simultaneous advantage to the nation which requires maximum production for war purposes—the cost of doing justice to composers may be regarded as negligible. The composer is as much entitled to the reward of his ability as the entertainer who appears upon the platform in person. In so far as the general principle is concerned the composer's case is so strong that one almost wonders it should ever have been seriously disputed.

Even the *Scotsman*, reporting from an area where the Society had often encountered opposition, acknowledged that its legal right had been established; but added a sour codicil, hoping that it would 'show a disposition to reach an amicable arrangement so that these adjuncts to the industrial war effort may continue'.

The attitudes of both the Society's functionaries and its critics throughout this long conflict are difficult to explain, even allowing for the stresses and sentiments of war. It is hard to conceive, for example, how the PRS could possibly have been more 'amicable', short of abdicating all responsibility to its members. Its leaders seemed desperately anxious to please, and willing to make unlimited allowances for the inability of its opponents to understand, or their refusal to acknowledge, the law. A few days after winning the Gillette case, Executive Committee was still determined to make only 'nominal charges' and to do nothing 'detrimental to the national effort': sentiments which were expressed, not as public gestures of patriotism, but in the privacy of a committee room, where rhetoric was unnecessary.[18] Throughout the affair the PRS had behaved with a gentle diplomacy which verged upon the supine, even when the opposition played rough and showed no appreciation of courtesy and soft bargaining. An attempt to educate attacking MPs by inviting them to Copyright House was well-intentioned, if largely unproductive. At the Society's twenty-ninth Annual General Meeting Boosey explained, or rather excused, the manufacturers' behaviour in the following terms: 'some of them, perhaps naturally, took alarm. Anyone setting up against others an apparently nebulous claim immediately assumes in the eyes of those others a sinister and unscrupulous appearance'.[19] Typically sensitive towards the other man's point of view, it was an accommodating statement, in the light of recent events, and the intense efforts which had been made, ever since the Society's inception, to establish its rights and educate its customers. Equally surprising, by contrast, is the inflexibility of the

[18] PRS Archives, Executive Committee minutes, 4 Feb. 1943.
[19] *PRS Emergency Bulletin*, Aug. 1943, 70.

recalcitrant factory owners. The sums they were being asked to pay were negligible and easily passed on to the taxpayer; and there were no great principles at stake. Yet they were prepared to fight on, ignoring precedents and high judicial rulings. And they found support, from politicians whose public statements betrayed a blithe ignorance of the subject, despite its frequent public airings in recent times, and from journalists, including some practising above the level of the gutter press, who were slightly better informed, but equally indifferent to the welfare of composers.

An amicable arrangement was achieved by government initiative. The Ministry of Production agreed to pay £25,000 a year to cover, for the duration of the war, 'all premises used for work necessary in the interests of the defence of the realm or the efficient prosecution of the war or for maintaining supplies and services essential to the life of the community', including canteens and hostels attached to such premises. For the Society it was not much of a bargain, considering the number of locations and hours of music being used, and recent massive confirmation of its legal rights. Application of even the previous modest formula would certainly have brought in far more. On the other hand, it would probably have met continued opposition and required extra work by staff who were in scarce supply. In the Board's view 'the Government offer was a reasonable one and should be accepted'.[20] The eighty members listening to this announcement apparently voiced no disagreement, but again a low tariff had been underpinned, storing up trouble for the future.

It was left to A. P. Herbert to press home the essential lesson 'in a 'conversation piece':

'In this particular case—after all, there's a war on—there are all these people making munitions—and 'Music While You Work' is intended to help them along. I should have thought they might stretch a point.'
'And let their work be performed for nothing?'
'Well, in the circumstances, yes.'
'Has there been any proposal to waive the fees due to holders of patents in use in munitions factories?'
'Not that I know of. No I suppose not.'
'Are newspapers and cigarettes distributed gratis in the munitions factories?'
'Probably not'
'Very well then.'[21]

[20] PRS Archives, Executive Committee minutes, 19 Apr. 1943. *PRS Emergency Bulletin*, Aug. 1943, 71.
[21] A. P. Herbert, 'Little Talks', *Punch*, 10 Mar. 1943.

Working Musician

The principal 'lubricator of industry' was a composer whose career was intimately linked to the PRS from the start of both. In contrast to later career patterns of popular success, Eric Coates succeeded only after a solidly conventional training and long experience. He studied viola with Tertis, becoming an accomplished quartet and orchestral player, and served an arduous apprenticeship as a practical and versatile composer, in the tradition of Monckton, Finck, and Ketèlbey. He began writing sentimental ballads before joining the Society in 1914, and scored occasional modest successes: 'I Pitch my Lonely Caravan' (1921), and 'Bird Songs at Eventide' (1926). He experimented with current fashions, sometimes using a *nom de plume*. A 'foxtrot song' for example, entitled 'You Keep Haunting Me' was attributed to 'Ciré' and then, when his publisher, William Boosey, disapproved, to 'Jack Arnold'.[22] By 1928 he was a prominent member, interviewed at length in the *Gazette* with emphasis upon the 'Three Bears' suite, a 'serious work in syncopated vein' which had been premièred at the Proms, and played by Jack Hilton.[23] Then, broadcasting and performing right lifted him into quite a different category of sustained earning power.

'By the Sleepy Lagoon' was written in 1930, 'took off' a decade later, and achieved a kind of immortality with 'Desert Island Discs'. The 'London Suite'(1933) earned a similar permanence when 'Knightsbridge' was chosen as the signature tune for 'In Town Tonight'. The BBC received 20,000 letters in two weeks, requesting the title and composer's name, which became familiar throughout the English-speaking world. This concentrated exposure boosted sales of sheet music and records, commissions for more marches, and many performances, at home and abroad, particularly in the Common-wealth. Constant repetition of 'Calling All Workers' (1940) added to the steady stream of income, with a final influx from the enormously successful march for the 'Dam Busters' film. Thus, Coates became the first 'media success' among English composers, and the Society's highest earner, but his income and life style never rose above modest affluence: a level reached by many energetic or lucky men in other walks of life. Moreover, he was a solitary example, for the dozen or so successful English composers who trailed behind him in earning power received no more than the income of a securely pensioned

[22] PRS Archives, Eric Coates file, 24 Apr. and 14 June 1924.
[23] *Performing Right Gazette*, Jan. 1928, 269–272.

senior civil servant, or a moderately energetic lawyer. Music was not yet capable of breeding millionaires in Britain.[24]

Behind the front echelon of PRS members there was a group of composers, obscure or even unknown, who were still capable of benefiting from performing right and the Society's organization; capturing the public's fickle ear, if not its eye, by close attention to its changing requirements. An early representative of this twentieth-century breed of 'journeyman musician', a sobriquet to which he would not have objected, was Montague Ewing. Ignored by *Grove* and pop charts alike, Ewing was never prominent enough to be much noticed, but his alertness to changing fashion, his superficial versatilility, and ability to write music by the yard enabled him to survive changes in taste and technology which reduced less flexible musicians to penury. Born in 1890, he joined the Society in 1925, listing more than 100 compositions, most of which were light orchestral, 'novelty', and 'educational' pieces. A variety of pseudo-nyms were employed in a bid to enhance what economists call 'product differentiation': Herbert Carrington, Auguste Cons, Stennet George, Theodore Graham, Martin Hart, Paul Hoffman, Brian Hope, Kennedy Thague, Hilary Vaughan. In 1925 SACEM reported that four of Ewing's pieces, including 'Wrigle [sic] Rag', were being performed as 'free works' in France because they had been assigned to a publisher who was not a member of the PRS. Next year therefore he was delighted 'in common with most composers', when many publishers joined or rejoined the Society, bringing 'many of my works under control'. More pieces and pseudonyms were dispatched to cafés and cinemas: Eric O'Neil and Richard Dane, delivering 'legitimate works', and Sherman Myers dance music. The latter name, as he later explained, was adopted at his publisher's suggestion, because it sounded American, and there was a 'prejudice' against British dance music. Between 1925 and 1929 his annual PRS earnings rose from £67 to £134, reflecting the silent movie boom; for he was adept at 'fitting' film numbers, for trifling rewards. Several series of 'Filmelodies' were published under his real name, in orchestral parts and a piano solo edition 'for relief pianists'.[25]

Surviving the crash and depression, Ewing claimed to number himself 'among the Charing X Road dance writers nowadays', though he refused to be associated with their rumblings of discontent at the Annual General Meeting in 1933 (a dispute of which no record appears to have survived). He also developed several new lines:

[24] Guy Routh, *Occupation and Pay in Great Britain 1906–60* (1965), 64–70. Eric Coates, *Suite in Four Movements: An Autobiography* (1953).

[25] PRS Archives, Montague Ewing file, 1925–29.

'Impressions' of Russia, Spain, and so on, each ending with the appropriate national anthem; arrangements for the popular 'loud and soft' pianist, Charlie Kunz; 'Plenty of Time for Play', a vaguely specified advertising jingle, 'for soap or a vacuum cleaner, I think'. The use of his 'Policeman's Holiday' in a Pathé news film brought him in fifteen shillings and twopence. In 1934 he listed over sixty works and eighteen publishers. Thus, with relentless energy Ewing kept a a wary, unblinking eye to the main chance, 'anxious to see from whence the best fees come, and from what type of material results are best'.[26] Throughout the thirties, his earnings fluctuating between about three and four hundred pounds a year, he scrutinized his distribution cheques and challenged alleged deficiencies in genial letters which were scrupulously answered by the staff. Thus, in 1936 he complained of a drop in income though 'asked for more material than I can turn out', and was answered with explanatory accounts of a French slump and delays in German remittances, and an invitation to visit the office for a complete analysis of his distributions. In 1937 he was greatly relieved to hear about the BBC licence increase, but did not complain about the ensuing years of inflation and eroded income. A modestly successful working life ended on a happy upbeat because, adaptable to the end, his music succeeded in tapping a new source of income; beyond the time-period of this chapter, but appropriate to the chronicle of a journeyman composer. In 1953 he expressed 'pleasant surprise' at receiving £628, over half of which was derived from American radio and television. He died in 1957.

The majority of members, less talented, adaptable, or fortunate than Montague Ewing, earned fees which could never amount to a living wage. For those without sufficient alternative sources of income the Society could do very little. In 1932 it set up a 'Members' Assistance Fund' of about £100, to make payments in case of urgent need only to members of ten years' standing, or their dependants. The initial stake was drawn from interest on PRS investments, but in 1933 a Benevolent Fund was established, to be financed by deducting, annually, 0.5 per cent of the fees distributed to members. This proportion was subsequently increased to 1 per cent in 1935, and 2 per cent in 1938. Publishers contributed, but were not allowed to benefit. Between 1939 and 1944 the Fund's income increased from £3,142 to £8,806, and capital from £1,500 to £12,000. There were between two and three hundred applicants, many of whom received small grants or loans.[27] An improvement in these modest levels of

---

[26] Ibid., Ewing to Walters, 19 June 1938.
[27] *Performing Right*, Sept. 1959, 175.

pecuniary achievement and beneficence would depend upon two things: the composers' continuing ability to satisfy public needs, and the Society's success in securing higher levels of payment for their work.

Names and Images

One effect of the 'Music While You Work' fracas was to reawaken concern for the Society's image. A few days after the Commons questions the 'Gazette and Propaganda Committee', defunct since 1927, reassembled as a 'Public Relations Committee' and discussed the proposition that more should be done 'to place the Society's rights and functions before the *general public*', as distinct from clients. It was an important initiative, for, except in moments of crisis, such as the Tuppenny debate, communications with the outside world had generally been neglected, and were sometimes inept. In 1932 the editor of the *Melody Maker* attempted to persuade the Directors that a serious and, above all, *sustained* 'publicity campaign' was a matter of urgency. No one on the Board took him seriously. A press liason officer was appointed a year later, but there was little attempt to supervise and encourage his activities at a high enough level to reflect and influence major issues of policy.[28] Even communications with Westminster were poor, for Woodhouse's earlier initiatives with a parliamentary agent never led to an active and continuous input of information and ideas. Apart from rare and adventitious personal contacts with politicians, there were only the important, but narrowly defined, messages to the Board of Trade about licensing. Whether this general neglect of public relations and politics stemmed from indifference, a wish to economize, or a more positive desire to maintain a low profile, is unclear. The question does not appear to have aroused much interest among the Directors and, like most aspects of policy, was not discussed with the members.

Whatever its causes or justification, the cost of inactivity was now plain for all to see. In press and Parliament the latest display of ignorance and antagonism suggested that ground gained by past successes—in the courts, in the Tuppenny debate, and in the BBC arbitration—had not been consolidated. Indeed, thanks to the efforts of ill-wishers and the more ignorant, but no less influential, communicators, much had been lost. It was an indication of concern that the belated inaugural meeting of the Public Relations Committee mustered a weighty gathering: Leslie Boosey, John Abbott, Ralph

[28] PRS Archives, Board minutes, Jan. 1932 and 13 July 1933.

Hawkes, and Eric Coates, along with the three senior officials and the press officer, who initiated most of the discussion. With one significant exception, it was sadly inconsequential, demonstrating how little thought had yet been given to these matters. Regular advertising was one of the options put forward. Avoided in the past, it was now thought to be a possible means of appealing directly to the public, and, perhaps, gaining sympathy from some journalists. Such benefits might, however, be outweighed by antagonism from those papers which had not been allocated advertisements. Best begin, then, with the trade papers; but that would miss the general public who were supposed to be the prime target. So the argument came full circle to swallow its tail. On balance it might be better to leave contacts with the press to individual initiatives by members. A more important, indeed, a 'primary object of the Society' should be to encourage 'sympathetic understanding' of its work by the House of Commons; but here again there were to be no professional and sustained initiatives, not even a corporative effort. Prominent members might write to their MPs, or friends in the House of Lords. Another naïve suggestion was that 'a simple and interesting explanation of PRS operations' could be printed on the back of sheet music. Since few members of the general public looked at sheet music any more, the impact would have been slight at the best of times but, as publishers on the Committee patiently explained, wartime paper shortages left no space for explanatory messages.

There were two sensible propositions. One was slight; the other would become a hardy perennial, and neither bore quick fruit. It was suggested that the BBC should be asked to broadcast a statement, or an interview with the PRS chairman; and that the Society should attempt to change its name. The existing one, it was thought, encouraged people to regard the PRS as an ordinary business, acquiring and exploiting performing rights solely for the profit of its shareholders. In fact, it had always been a rare kind of corporate animal, a company limited by guarantee; and, as such, it had neither share capital nor shareholders. Would it be possible and sensible, the Committee was now asking, to adopt a new name which was both legally acceptable and more appropriate to the Society's true functions? Would the Board of Trade allow the PRS to rename itself something like 'The British Association of Composers, Authors and Publishers of Music'? Could 'Limited' be dropped, with its misleading connotations of mercenary capital and rich dividends? Sensitivity to these matters was not entirely new. In 1939 James had asked for legal advice about the deletion of 'Limited', and was assured that it had to be used. In 1941 the revised Articles of Association substituted the

word 'Society' for 'Company' wherever it appeared, to 'assist in
dispelling the erroneous idea, which still persists in some quarters,
that the Society is a Company trading for its own profit'.[29] Now it
seemed that these tentative cosmetic gestures might develop into a
serious quest for an appropriate corporate image, less bleak and
commercial, and more attuned to the Society's membership and
activities. Expert opinion was sought from lawyers and the Chartered
Institute of Secretaries, but their response was unencouraging. It was
thought that success with officialdom was unlikely, and failure would
be 'a bad advertisement'. The idea was quietly dropped, for a time.[30]

At the annual meeting and luncheon in July 1945, a few months
after VE day and one month before the defeat of Japan, the mood was
one of quiet celebration and gratitude. There was particular
acclamation for the Chairman's tribute to his colleagues. James,
Hatchman, Walter, and their staff had striven unremittingly, refusing
to be shaken by bombs, flying bombs, rockets, privation, and stress. It
was, indeed, a splendid achievement. Leslie Boosey then went on to to
express satisfaction with the Society's financial record. Not only had
income been maintained, he claimed, 'but, to my still intense wonder,
the revenue actually increased and continued increasing, last year
being a record despite the absence of the greater part of our
continental income [*Applause*]'.[31] It was an occasion when breast-
beating or objective self-appraisal could hardly have been expected.
Nevertheless the statement, and its enthusiastic reception, were
extraordinarily complacent when measured against the actual record.
The Society's cash income had indeed risen, about 44 per cent since
1939, but that takes no account of inflation. In the economy as a
whole, the general level of incomes had approximately doubled, and
there had been a substantial increase in the cost of living. Precise
measurement is impossible, given the distorting effects of wartime
controls, but on the most favourable estimate PRS earnings could
barely be said to have maintained their pre-war level, in real terms;
and this despite the huge increase in the use of music. Nor was the loss
of continental income an adequate explanation, for in peacetime it
had never accounted for a substantial proportion of total revenue. So
poor a return could only be explained by the low level of tariffs. Their
revision, long overdue, was now an imperative task.

[29] *PRS Emergency Bulletin*, July 1941, 37.
[30] PRS Archives, Public Relations Committee minutes, 16 Feb. 1943. Correspondence with
Syrett, 6 and 8 Dec. 1939; 19 and 23 Feb. 1943, and 11 Mar. 1943. Correspondence with
Chartered Institute of Secretaries, 22 and 23 Feb. 1943.
[31] *PRS Bulletin*, Aug. 1945, 95.

6

PEACE WITHOUT PROSPERITY

For the music industry the immediate post-war years seemed to promise a return to the status quo, despite the election of a Labour government, and the persistence of chronic austerity. Neither the relevant technology nor public tastes in entertainment and music were much changed since the 1930s. Wireless sets were still bulky objects, made in England, and plugged into a wall socket. Television, which had been abandoned during the war, began again in 1946, but was only watched in a few thousand homes, and absorbed a small proportion of the BBC's energies and budget. In the same year cinema attendances reached a peak. There was no commercial broadcasting. Gramophone records were still expensive shellac 78s in plain paper covers, requiring two turntables or a cumbersome 'autochanger' to provide more than four minutes of continuous music. Wire and tape recorders were confined to a few studios, offices, and workshops; nobody made recordings at home. The procedures of music makers and the preferences of listeners were, similarly, unchanged, except for a steady growth of background music. The latter was usually quiet and rather jolly. Ordinary music was used, not a specially manufactured noise: 'muzak' and its kind had not yet emerged. Guitars and pianos were 'acoustic', and electronic instruments, except for cinema organs, were confined to the laboratory. With obvious exceptions among jazz and 'folk' artists, the ability to read 'dots' continued to be an indispensible qualification for professional musicians, serious and popular. Composers wrote, or employed someone to write, notes on a page; publishers published them and performers played from them.

The predominant taste, middle-aged and middle of the road, was reflected at practically every level of music making. Serious composition was, indeed, entering a new golden age, the like of which had not been experienced in England since Purcell's day. But the concert-going public and the musical establishment—critics, academics, and impresarios—were overwhelmingly conservative and middlebrow, impervious or allergic to twelve-note rows, or even to Mahler, and preferring contemporary music to be anything but modern.[1] Most

[1] See Donald Mitchell and Hans Keller (eds.), *Music Survey: 1949–52* (1981), particularly their 'Preface in the form of a dialogue'.

'popular' music, was similarly, orthodox, well-schooled, and 'professional'. The dominant idiom was American, brimming with innate vitality and self-confidence, but also enjoying the enormous marketing benefits of Hollywood. British popular music was generally at a low ebb; sometimes donning transatlantic chromium-plate; often persisting with tired ballad and 'novelty' routines. But indigenous 'light music' was still very successful. No one could agree about its scope and functions, as the BBC discovered when they asked for a report from Eric Coates; but it was generally acknowledged that he was its most celebrated practioner.[2] Less familiar was the fact that he was also the country's most successful composer, in the commercial sense, earning more than any 'popular' musician and, of course, far outpacing his 'serious' colleagues. Nothing better illustrates the prevailing musical scene, and its distance from our own, than this fact. Neither popular nor light music, from any source, made particular concessions to adolescent preoccupations. If young people had spare cash for entertainment, and few had much, they shopped in markets dominated by adults.

Unchanging musical taste was reflected in the Society's membership and hierarchy. Most of the composer-members of an ageing Board of Directors in 1945 were men whose musicianship and outlook had been formed before the First World War: Bantock (b. 1868), Bax (1883), Coates (1886), Dunhill (1877), Squire (1871), Haydn Wood (1882). Only Harry Parr-Davies (1914), accompanist and song writer for Gracie Fields, broke the pattern, which was reinforced by the Chairman, Boosey (1887), Vice-Chairman, Clutsam (1866), and Consulting Director, Woodhouse (1861). Most of the author- and publisher-directors were of comparable vintage, and few members of the Board, in all three categories, had not been in place since the 1920s or earlier. Nor was their retention, as was the case in many other institutions, merely a result of the younger men being at war. Gerontocracy was the prevailing pattern, but it was not a temporary aberration, nor did it necessarily fail to represent the Society's general membership.

Perhaps the most characteristic features of the PRS, and of its governing body, at least after the consolidation of 1926, and reinforced by the turmoil of 1930, were a desire for continuity and profound respect for 'experience'. Unlikely traits in an organization dependent upon the most volatile of industries, they posed few difficulties in times of equipoise. There were disadvantages, of course,

[2] Asa Briggs, *The History of Broadcasting in the United Kingdom*, vol. iii, *The War of Words* (1970), 590–2.

but whatever the Board might lack in vitality and initiative, through natural enfeeblement, self-selection, and the debilitations of war, it was not yet seriously out of touch with the members it was required to represent, or the music market they needed to serve. By 1946 there were 1,205 full members and 899 associate members. Qualifications for membership had been slightly relaxed over the years. For a long period applicants were required to have at least six compositions in the catalogues of publisher-members, and acceptance was at the discretion of the Board. Later the criterion was eased to work 'published or unpublished, performed in public at premises licensed by the Society to a sufficient extent' to ensure 'more than a negligible sum' in fees. Before 1933 there had been only one category of membership. Novice applicants were deferred until they had enough works and performances to pass the 'negligible' test. The introduction of associate membership was intended to meet the need for 'a sort of probationary' status enabling newcomers to draw fees, without 'privileges, including voting rights' until they were well enough established to become full members. By 1949, the year in which Michael Tippett was elected to full membership, the threshold was £30 a year, earned in each of three consecutive years. A year later the figure was raised to £50. Clearly, neither youth nor affluence were common attributes among PRS members; unless, of course, the latter derived from some other source than the composition of music or lyrics.[3]

Reconstruction and Restraint

As soon as the war ended there was a flurry of activity to re-establish contacts with foreign societies, reinstate administrative procedures, analyse accumulated statements of accounts, and settle delayed payments—tasks whose intrinsic difficulties were exacerbated by widespread damage, disruption, and the cumbersome machinery of exchange control. In a few cases the latter encumbrance delayed final settlement for ten years. The Society took a lead in all this reconstruction. Like many British institutions in 1945, it enjoyed the prestige which was attached to the nation's great victory of liberation and temporarily acknowledged leadership of Europe. It was also a repository of much-needed expertise. When the Foreign Office, for example, required advice and help with the administration of performing rights in Germany, it naturally consulted PRS officials. A Nazi organization, STAGMA, had replaced the legitimate society

[3] *Performing Right Gazette,* July 1933, 174.

GEMA, and was now destroyed; its premises in ruins and most of its records lost. Gerald Hatchman was asked to visit Germany and report on the competence and acceptability of a disinterred GEMA, which was speedily and efficiently reinstated.[4]

Much of Leslie Boosey's time and energy was devoted to the revival of the International Confederation (CISAC). He had been an active member of its Council since 1936, engaged in such tasks as a deputation to Goebbels about German copyright, and became Vice-President in 1938. Largely responsible for the survival of CISAC at the beginning of the war, he was now uniquely placed to breathe new life into its co-ordinated efforts for the protection of intellectual and artistic property on an international scale. In twelve months between 1945 and 1946 he travelled some 30,000 miles on its behalf, visiting Buenos Aires, Rio de Janeiro, Ottawa, New York, and several European countries; an arduous itinerary at that time. Recognition of this work came with his election as President of CISAC, the first Englishman and the first publisher to be so honoured, the distinction usually being awarded to a prominent writer or composer; Richard Strauss had been his immediate predecessor (1938–46). The first post war congress of CISAC was held in Washington, in October 1946, with Boosey in the chair. Hatchman, James, A. P. Herbert, Eric Coates, and William Walton also travelled as PRS delegates. In June 1947 the Society acted as host in London for the fourteenth congress, when 150 delegates represented 42 authors' societies from 24 countries, and Boosey was re-elected President. Next year they were in Buenos Aires, hoping to give a lead to the protection of authors' rights in Latin America. The Congress was formally opened by the Argentine dictator, complete with claque chanting 'Peron! Peron!' When the PRS President rose to reply, Walton, no mean hand at clamour, led an antiphonal chant: 'Boosey! Boosey! Boosey!' The Congress was also notable for introducing Walton to Susana Gil, the Argentinian lady who became his wife.

On home ground Boosey's most memorable achievement was the rescue of Covent Garden Opera House. Its wartime use as a dance-hall might have continued for at least another five years but for his active intervention. Procuring its lease for Boosey and Hawkes he asked the newly formed Arts Council to consider returning the great house to its proper purpose. Kenneth Clark received his deputation, in the absence of Keynes, but secured the latter's vital and enthusiastic assent. In Clark's words, Boosey 'behaved with great public spirit and made the take over as easy as possible'.[5] It is

---

[4] *PRS Bulletin*, Aug. 1946, 102.
[5] Kenneth Clark, *The Other Half: A Self-Portrait* (1977), 130–1.

important testimony because a subsequent dispute over repair costs at the opera house led to Boosey's firm being sued by the Ministry of Works. The fault could in no way be attributed to him (he was abroad at the time), but with typical punctiliousness he felt obliged to refuse a CBE which, with unerring bad timing, had just been offered. Thus, like the aborted DSO, another tangled but innocent incident was added to what Leslie Boosey later wrily described as his 'long story of near misses'.[6] Having refused an honour, he was never offered another by his own country, although France had made him a Chevalier of the Légion d'Honneur in 1932.

Administratively, there was a great deal of catching up to do. The large foreign repertoire which had been acquired with the admission of refugee members now had to be properly registered, along with the necessary documentation of affiliated societies. This was a huge project, requiring the reading of hundreds of contracts and associated papers, in half a dozen languages. Liberation of accumulated fees from custodians of enemy property in belligerent countries was another laborious and complex task, which was delayed by the slow completion of peace treaties. Final settlements were often a nightmare of accountancy because many claimants and their heirs had been forced into the most elaborate international peregrinations. Royce Whale deserves most of the credit for completing these tiresome but rewarding operations, which ground on until nearly ten years after the end of the war, the files, as he recalls, growing 'like sunflowers during a hot summer'. His unique ability to disentangle the business affairs of distinguished German and Austrian composers and publishers brought great credit, and practical benefits to the Society. Whale was the first of a new breed of post-war administrators. Educated at Merchant Taylors' School, but very much an autodidact, he was fluent in French and competent in German, Italian, and Spanish. After some experience in printing and publishing, and war service which included Dunkirk and bomb disposal, he joined the Society's staff and rose rapidly, becoming Assistant Secretary, Secretary, Assistant General Manager, and finally General Manager in 1964. *En route* he taught himself to be a leading authority on copyright, author of a standard textbook.[7]

Licensing required extensive adjustment to peacetime conditions. Quite apart from any new initiatives, it was necessary to renegotiate many tariffs, as the paraphernalia of wartime regulations and

[6] PRS Archives, Leslie Boosey to Michael Freegard, 30 July 1976.
[7] R. F. Whale, *Copyright: Evolution, Theory, and Practice* (1971). R. F. Whale and Jeremy J. Phillips, *Whale on Copyright* (1983). See appreciation of Whale by Vivian Ellis in *Performing Right*, Oct. 1969, 7–8.

government contracts was dismantled, and the economy slowly
lurched back to normality. But there was also a paramount need to
increase tariffs across the board in order to regain ground lost by
inflation. In some cases a doubling of the existing tariff might have
sufficed; in others far more was necessary if the fees earned by
members were to catch up with what most people were getting in
other walks of life. But, although there was a desire to make these
necessary adjustments, it was still dampened by fear of a tribunal.
According to Whale, who inherited, and eventually broke away from,
this timorous tradition

the Society was constrained to operate in the knowledge that its tariffs would
one day come before a tribunal and that equally inevitably the users would
then endeavour to persuade the tribunal that the tariffs, however reasonably
they had been maintained meanwhile, were excessive. This is, indeed,
perhaps the most significant single element in all the Society's operational
history.[8]

Unfortunately, gentleness in business does not necessarily beget
gratitude, and the forbearance which had inflicted only moderate self-
sacrifice in times of stable prices was much more damaging in times of
inflation. Moreover, the very fact that the Society had been patient for
so long now made adjustment difficult. Licensees had become
accustomed to wholly unrealistic payments, and resented disturbance
of an amiable status quo. A typical example of this unwillingness to
come to terms with change was a long, unresolved dispute about one
of the earliest tariffs to have been issued by the PRS, which affected
the use of music throughout the country. The licensing of places
owned or controlled by local government authorities, and used for
diverse entertainments, had last been agreed in 1921, with minor
adjustments in 1935. It was levied as a proportion of the users'
expenditure on music, a procedure which, if it had been simply
applied, would have compensated for inflation. But, in practice, the
licensees were granted an elaborate system of discounts with the
unintended effect of wiping out this automatic adjustment. The
Society's attempt to catch up with inflation by levying a flat rate, in
the hope of securing adequate payments in future, came to nothing.

Another quaint example of obsolescence was the music-hall tariff,
which reaped a little over £3,000 from 57 halls in 1945, almost exactly
the same sum as had been gleaned in 1931. Labyrinthine in the
complexity of its administrative details, but essentially unchanged
since 1929, it was based upon the seating capacity of theatres. It
therefore took no account of nearly two decades of increased business

[8] Whale, in *Performing Right*, May 1974, 3.

and diversification. Music-halls, broadly defined as they must be in this context, had diversified and changed their bills of fare, from Marie Lloyd to Windmill Girls, but had not yet gone into terminal decline. In matters concerning performing right there had been fundamental changes in programming. 'Proprietary songs', for example, which reserved singing rights to individual artists, had long been displaced by material from the Society's repertoire; and the latter was more comprehensive and useful to managements than in 1929. The idea that performances stimulated sales of sheet music, which had once been used to justify low tariffs, was now quite obsolete and inapplicable. The precise burden of the tariff on individual theatres in 1945 defies simple measurement, but it was considerably less than the modest 1 per cent of 'money holding capacity' which was now asked. By comparison, SACEM charged French music halls 6 per cent of their takings, and was prone to complain that it was 'embarrassed' in its own negotiations by the absurdly low PRS fee. All of these arguments, with a plethora of statistical backing, were presented to the two music-hall Associations, and shown to the Board of Trade, in accordance with the Society's pre-war pledge to keep that government department informed about tariff revisions. Anticipating 'some political reaction', the PRS was prepared, in the absence of agreement, to submit the case to arbitration, and even to contribute to its adversaries' costs. The offer was rejected, but protracted negotiations eventually led to a slight increase in the tariff, a few years before music hall ceased to be of any importance.[9]

The cinema tariff was similarly overripe for revision, no less than fifteen years after its last significant adjustment. In 1938 the Society, complaining about a 'very low return' from cinemas in relation to their greatly increased use of music, had presented detailed assessments, and reminded the Exhibitors' Association that comparable continental tariffs were very much higher. Receiving a 'discourteous' reply, the PRS Board decided that further negotiations would be futile and that the matter should be referred to arbitration. But a few weeks later the Chairman, conciliatory as always, had to explain 'at length' to his colleagues that he had offered a renewal of the existing contract, at the old rate, for a further two years, because of their pleas that business was poor. He now suggested that the Society might seek an arbitrator if cinema owners continued to reject an increase after this concessionary period elapsed, in 1941.[10] These promises of future

---

[9] *PRS Bulletin*, Aug. 1946, 101, and Aug. 1947, 128. PRS Archives, 'Memorandum: History of Contracts, EPA and PEPMA', 23 Aug. 1945; Music Hall Tariff Committee, 30 Aug. 1945; Memorandum of interview at Board of Trade, 3 Sept. 1945.

[10] PRS Archives, PRS to CEA, 20 Oct. 1938.

firmness came to nothing during the war, of course, although cinemas enjoyed prodigious business: admissions increased from 1,027 million in 1940 to an all-time peak of 1,635 million in 1946. Then the sparring was resumed, in much the same fashion as before the war, but with frequent reference by both parties to the Board of Trade. When the PRS informed that government department that it was willing to go to arbitration, the cinema owners tried evasive action, with several adroit manœuvres. They made the customary complaint against 'monopoly abuse', and played the patriotic card, suggesting that Americans would be the sole beneficiaries of an increased licence fee. Reminding the Board of Trade that the Cinematograph Exhibitors' Association had protested a willingness to arbitrate ever since 1930, the PRS refused to be cowed by nationalistic prejudice, and gave a timely reminder that it was 'entirely neutral and impartial in its distribution of fees, irrespective of the country of origin of the music performed'. The CEA at last backed down and accepted a doubling of the pre-war fee, without arbitration. This was a sensible decision on their part, for an outsider might well have awarded more. But it was unfortunate for the Society that in this case, as in others, its offer to arbitrate was refused by users who would later complain that new tariffs had been imposed by diktat.[11]

A younger, but similarly modest, agreement was the 1943 factory music contract with the Government, which expired in 1946. It was replaced by individual licences charged at an annual rate of one penny per worker for half an hour of daily relays. Under the new arrangement a factory with 300 employees was charged five guineas a year for two hours of music a day. An attractive and lucid pamphlet, *Music in Industry*, with an excerpt from Coates' march, 'Calling all Workers', was published by the Society to explain its background, *raison d'être*, and new procedures. This improvement in publicity was not matched by any serious attempt to secure better returns from factory music. Reporting on the accounts for 1946, Boosey expressed satisfaction with proceeds from the new arrangement, and encountered no criticism, despite the fact that their total was less than what had been earned under the previous government scheme. There were no further complaints from industry, of course, but goodwill, if such it was, had been bought at a high price.[12]

Since fees from broadcasting still accounted for about half of the

---

[11] PRS Archives, Memorandum by Hatchman of interview at Board of Trade, 15 May 1946. Memorandum of telephone call from Board of Trade, 3 June 1946. On cinema attendances, see James Curran and Vincent Porter, *British Cinema History* (1983), 24–30.

[12] PRS Archives, Executive Committee minutes, 6 Dec. 1945. PRS pamphlet, *Music in Industry* (1946). *PRS Bulletin*, Aug. 1947, 127.

Society's income, the renegotiation of the BBC's contract was of prime importance. The Society's case for raising its fee was based on three factors. Not only had costs greatly increased since 1937, but the BBC's ability to pay had been substantially improved. The charge for wireless licences had just been doubled, from ten shillings to one pound. There was also a considerable increase in the Corporation's use of PRS material, arising from general expansion and from the launching of the Third Programme, which was strongly committed to modern music. The Executive Committee therefore considered, with customary caution, that there was a 'prima-facie case' for doubling the 1937 award rate of sevenpence per wireless licence, and some reason to charge an extra increment for additional use.[13] In the outcome the Society got one shilling per licence, precisely the amount, in monetary terms, which had been requested in 1937, but now halved in value. Satisfaction was expressed at this result, again apparently without comment by members, at the Annual General Meeting in July 1947.[14]

Such acquiescence was ill-advised because it overlooked two fundamental weaknesses in the Society's most important transaction. As has already been noted, the new tariff's value was lower, in real terms, than in 1937, despite the BBC's increased wealth, prestige, and use of repertoire. Even more serious, in the longer run, was the fact that the agreement carried no potential for future growth in income without thorough renegotiation. Previous increases in the Society's earnings from broadcasting had depended, essentially, on the rapid and continuous growth of radio licensing. That expansion had slowed down during the war and would shortly stop. Once again the Board was storing up trouble for future dealings with a licensee, and in this case it was with the Society's principal source of income. The BBC's historian suggests that, because it was a source of livelihood for the PRS, there was an ideal relationship between the two organizations. In contrast to the Corporation's experience with some other bodies, 'it was possible for public corporation and private association to be on excellent terms'.[15] That cordiality was, as we have repeatedly observed, largely the achievement of Leslie Boosey, and it had brought rich rewards. But there were also costs, in modest and belated cash settlements and, more subtly, in habits of caution, reticence, even deference which, by 1949, had become deeply ingrained. When the Beveridge Committee began its investigation of

[13] PRS Archives, Executive Committee minutes, 1 Oct. 1946.
[14] *PRS Bulletin*, Aug. 1947, 129.
[15] Asa Briggs, *The History of Broadcasting in the United Kingdom*, vol.iv, *Sound and Vision* (1979), 346.

the BBC, receiving 223 memoranda and innumerable letters from every kind of interested party, the PRS Executive Committee decided that there were 'no representations the Society could usefully make'.[16] When the next opportunity for renewal came at the end of 1951, Executive Committee minuted that, 'having regard to all the circumstances of the present time, an offer should be made to renew the contract on the present terms for a further period of two years'.[17]

Mild Disturbances

Placid waters were mildly ruffled by two groups of composers who were dissatisfied with the status and remuneration of their music. The Composers' Guild, inaugurated in 1944 under the chairmanship of Thomas Dunhill, was descended from the long-standing, but ineffectual, Composers' Section of the Society of Authors, Playwrights and Composers. By 1947 its 180 members included many familiar names, ranging from Vaughan Williams to Noel Coward, and it contained a particularly active sub-committee of film composers, concerned about serious deficiencies in the safeguarding of their contractual rights.[18] The Songwriters' Guild represented British popular musicians; but some people joined both organizations, including Coward and Richard Addinsell, the composer of much theatre and film music, notably the immensely successful 'Warsaw' Concerto. The Songwriters, all of whom were members or associate members of the PRS, were presided over by Bruce Sievier, composer of such numbers as 'Love's Last Word is Spoken', and the experienced broadcaster Eric Maschwitz, who had written the words for 'A Nightingale Sang in Berkeley Square'. Their Board included a woman whose long career and association with the PRS merits a footnote in the Society's history. Hero de Rance had appeared on the stage at the age of ten, worked as a plugger for other people's songs, and eventually her own; prospered moderately during the silent cinema boom, and survived the depression as a theatre pianist and composer, with occasional visits to the film studios to sell a song outright for five pounds. Her greatest success, 'You're Mine' was written to words by Bruce Sievier in 1937, and featured by Richard Tauber. Forty years later she was awarded the Guild's Gold Badge of Merit, and a decade after that was playing the piano in a London theatre. She joined the PRS in 1926 and is still (1987) a familiar figure at annual general meetings.

[16] Asa Briggs, The BBC: The First Fifty Years (1985), 257–8. PRS Archives, Executive Committee minutes, 7 July 1949.
[17] PRS Archives, Executive Committee minutes, 15 Nov. 1951.
[18] Report by Alan Bush in the Author, Autumn 1947, 16–18.

Both Guilds were chauvinist, but the Composers' Guild tended to attract less attention for its vaguer and more altruistic sentiments. Avoiding a narrowly defined 'professionalism', it allowed, in Stephen Dodgson's happy phrase, 'the Douanier Rousseaus' to become members. It kept on friendly terms with the BBC, and aspired only to be 'a persuasive force' for British music.[19] The Songwriters were, by contrast, openly and belligerently protectionist from the start. Initially they called themselves the 'British Songwriters' Protective Association', complaining that only 19 per cent of music broadcast by the BBC was British, and setting their case before the Prime Minister.[20] Their target was American popular music, whose appeal they attributed to a variety of causes, unconnected with its vitality and professionalism. The dominance of Hollywood films, which had exerted enormous influence on public taste since the coming of sound movies, had been reinforced in wartime, the Guild protested, by the presence of American troops and the absence of British song writers in uniform, serving overseas. The BBC's increased use of commercial discs, at a time when local material was in short supply, had favoured American recordings. The recent arrival of *Oklahoma* and *Annie Get Your Gun* had caused further damage. London continued to be 'invaded by American publishers' who ensured that American songs were, *horribile dictu*, plugged. But it was the Guild's expressed belief that the public's apparent preferences should not be taken as proof of permanent Americanization. Fundamental loyalties could be more accurately assessed, it argued, by sales of sheet music, where British songs continued to top the lists 'to the extent of 50 per cent'. The mere 19 per cent of 'air time' given to home-grown products did not therefore 'truly represent the taste of the British public'. These opinions were presented in a long letter to the Director-General of the BBC which the historian of the Guild describes as 'impressive, polite and respectful'.[21]

In so far as they were intended to change broadcasting policy, and, ultimately, the nation's taste, the Guild's activities were not very effective; principally for a reason which it touched upon in its first submission: 'one criticism we would make of the BBC itself is that there exists, among the younger and less experienced of its producers, a tendency to favour "transatlantic" entertainment as being more cosmopolitan and less "corny" (if we may be forgiven the term) than the home-grown product'. The admission is revealing, for it was precisely youth, rather than 'experience', which was about to provide

---

[19] Stephen Dodgson, 'The Composers' Guild of Great Britain—Its Nature and Work', *Performing Right*, Sept. 1961, 266–8. Briggs, *Sound and Vision*, 729–30.
[20] *Success Story 1947–68: The Songwriters' Guild of Great Britain* (1968), 12.
[21] Ibid., 24–5.

the key to success in popular music; a success which would depend primarily upon the creation of new, rather than the protection of old, styles of music. Some of the latter would survive, not by quota but on merit: an obvious example being the charming songs of Vivian Ellis, who was a rather undemonstrative member of the Guild. 'Spread a Little Happiness' had been a hit in 1929, as it would be again half a century later; and in 1947 *Bless the Bride* (words by A. P. Herbert) was holding its own against the most powerful form of American competition. It opened a few days before *Oklahoma*, and ran for 836 performances.[22] Forty years later it was revived at Sadler's Wells.

The Guild's campaign continued sporadically for more than a decade, beginning with the announcement of a 'big scale counter-attack', and reaching dizzy heights of rhetoric in its submission to the Beveridge Committee on broadcasting. In common with pressure groups from most of the entertainment professions, including the Composers' Guild, the Songwriters were determined to lambast the BBC:

Failure to give practical encouragement to writers and composers writing in the British style will result in damning up the stream which has flowed throughout the centuries from the first folk song to 'Tipperary' and 'Roses of Picardy'. The popular song of today may become the folk song of tommorrow.[23]

In 1951 the American paper *Variety* reported that Maschwitz, who had been attached to British Intelligence during the war, was master-minding a 'cloak and dagger' operation to 'finger bandleaders and reps of American publishers who are allegedly deliberately supporting the U.S. tunes to the exclusion of native numbers'.[24] Maschwitz then published his complaints against the BBC, claiming that it was employing 'American-minded' band leaders, and 'self-styled "disc jockeys" (horrible term) who are in the main guilty of the same lack of feeling for British music'. He recommended that its officials should attend pantomimes if they wanted to understand true British taste.[25]

Another ardent propagandist for the Guild was Jimmy Kennedy, the Irish writer of many successful songs, including 'Red Sails in the Sunset', 'South of the Border', and 'Washing on the Siegfried Line'. Kennedy had long since improved upon his PRS earnings of £1 in 1930. By the late thirties and early forties he was one of the few prosperous popular composers in the Society with fees which

---

[22] Vivian Ellis, *I'm On a Seesaw* (1974), 234–6.
[23] *Band Wagon*, July 1947. Briggs, *Sound and Vision*, 347.
[24] *Variety*, 1 Aug. 1951.
[25] *Daily Telegraph*, 27 Dec. 1951.

sometimes approached those of Eric Coates, though they were usually closer to half, and far more volatile. He was not indulging in self-pity, therefore, when, in a lengthy statement to the American trade paper, *Variety*, he claimed that out of some 400 Guild members, no more than thirty could earn a living, because of American dominance and the BBC's 'accent' on 'Culture' rather than 'Pop'.[26] And so the campaign continued, with repeated demands that the BBC impose high British quotas, and occasional excursions into the clouds. Thus in 1954 the Board of Trade was asked to establish regulations by which every pop record made in Britain should contain one side of British material, a strange attempt to reincarnate the spirit, and perhaps the letter, of the 'quota quickies' which had brought so much unintended mirth to cinemas in the 1930s.

In its dealings with both Guilds the PRS had to balance diverse pressures and responsibilities. In the first place, as well as representing British composers it also had members who published foreign music, notably the formidable M. E. Ricketts who had succeeded the eighty-two year-old Edwin Goodman as Chappell's representative on the Board in 1949, and became its *éminence grise*, active, highly influential, and almost totally anonymous, until 1972.[27] Chappell published many English composers and writers, including Ivor Novello, Vivian Ellis, and even Maschwitz, but its lists also contained most of the greatest American names, from Gershwin downwards. Secondly, the Society was an undiscriminating (in the best sense) agent for affiliated societies. Thirdly, as always, but particularly during the early 1950s when copyright reform was imminent, it was anxious to avoid too close an association with restrictive policies. Finally, and fundamentally, its survival ultimately depended upon keeping in touch with the public's musical taste, a *sine qua non* which brooked no denial by special pleading. In these circumstances pressure from the Songwriters had to be resisted with tact. Coates and, more significantly, Maschwitz and Sievier were on both the Guild Council and the Society's Board. At the Society's thirty-eighth Annual General Meeting in July 1952 there was a determined effort to push the PRS into more active chauvinism. In addition to its intrinsic importance, the incident is noteworthy because of the way it was handled. For the first time, at least since 1926, conflicting views within the Society were openly discussed and reported to the broad membership, most of whom never attended meetings, and generally received scant information. On at least one previous occasion, in

---

[26] *Variety*, quoted in the *Quarterly Bulletin of the Songwriters' Guild of Great Britain*, no. 17, July 1952.
[27] *Performing Right*, Dec. 1972, 32.

1933, a serious internal dispute had been so effectively muted that, despite several oblique references (by Ewing, for example) the surviving records give no indication that anything untoward ever took place.

The account of the 1952 meeting which appeared in the *Performing Right Bulletin* was brief and euphemistic, but moderately informative. Bruce Sievier was reported as expressing 'grave disquiet among British composers and authors arising from the preponderance of foreign music in this country', and proposing that the Board should devote 'a substantial sum of money annually to propaganda for more British music'. There were several supporters, including Kennedy, who stressed the particular importance of patriotic broadcasting. The Chairman's reply was firm but diplomatic. The Society's income came from fees which were 'collected for foreign as well as British music'. It would therefore be 'improper and contrary to our contracts of affiliation with Societies abroad to spend any of it on propaganda for any particular class of music'. But he agreed, with support from the Vice-Chairman and Maschwitz, to write to the new Director-General of the BBC, as soon as he was appointed: there were hopes, perhaps, of a change in policy following Haley's departure from the Corporation. The PRS would urge 'in the strongest possible terms that the BBC should take immediate and adequate steps to ensure substantially more performances of British music, both in radio and television programmes, particularly in the field where it had been most neglected—namely, popular music'.[28]

Ensuing discussions with senior officials of the BBC confirmed the realities of public taste, as distinct from the alleged significance of sheet-music sales. Any willingness to increase broadcasts of British 'popular' music was tempered by abundant evidence of its current unpopularity. Listener research revealed an overwhelming preference for American sounds. The Executive Committee of the PRS agreed to continue giving general support to the Guild, facilitating its subscription procedures, for example, but to keep its distance from a subject 'not in the Society's province'.[29] Whatever the reasons for this decision, it was fortunate and timely, for the protection of obsolescence was neither desirable nor, as events would shortly prove, necessary, to ensure the prosperity of British popular music. Meanwhile, the Guild's leader continued to retain a fond belief in the BBC's ability, given the will, to turn the tide, steering 'public taste in any desired direction'.[30] The depth of feeling underlying this

---

[28] *Performing Right Bulletin*, Aug. 1952, 207. (The name was changed from *PRS Bulletin* to *PR Bulletin* in Apr. 1948, but some pages still carried the old heading until Aug. 1951.)

[29] PRS Archives, Executive Committee minutes, 2 Oct. 1952.

[30] *Bulletin of the Songwriters' Guild*, Dec. 1952.

antagonism to current trends was most frankly expressed by Eric Maschwitz in his autobiography, published in 1957; but by then there was a significant new emphasis. In place of a generalized Americo-phobia, the indictment centres upon subservience to 'the semi-Americanised "teen-age" listener who in these times of high wages and full employment, has an excess of pocket money to spend upon foolish, often vulgar, musical fads'.[31] It was a prejudiced observation, and slightly premature, for youthful affluence was not yet a dominant force in the market, but its prescience can hardly be denied.

Copyright Reform

In 1951 a Committee was appointed to reappraise the United Kingdom law of copyright, including performing right, in the light of technological developments, since 1911, and the revised Berne Convention. The latter was precisely that revision of the international code which had been expected in 1935, and was ultimately achieved in 1948. Among its provisions was the granting of an exclusive right to writers for the authorization of public performance of their works; but practical details and levels of remuneration, in the absence of agreement, were left to be determined by individual governments. In accepting the Convention, the British Government attached to the appropriate articles a reassertion of its freedom to legislate in order 'to prevent or deal with any abuse' of monopoly. This reiteration of the Damoclean threat was accompanied by renewed attempts to reassure the PRS. The cordiality of a long-established official correspondence was reinforced by a remarkable public statement. In a lengthy speech at the Society's annual lunch, which, by the insistence of its language, was presumably intended to carry more weight than is common on such occasions, the President of the Board of Trade, Harold Wilson, explained that there was 'not a jot of evidence' of need for the imposition of legislative constraints. Nor was there any suggestion that the 'work your Society is doing is the kind of work which ought to be referred to the Monopoly Commission'. Following

a policy for the past twenty years or more which has been, in my view, of the very highest national interest; you have sought to maximise our earnings from abroad, which is a most important national consideration at the present time; you have sought to protect the rightful interests of those . . . who have the right to get the earnings from their work, but you have not abused the position of monopoly which you hold.

The rhetorical equivalent of a blank cheque, this might be taken as a

---

[31] Eric Maschwitz, *No Chip on My Shoulder* (1957), 157.

significant endorsement, coming from a future Prime Minister who was currently head of the relevant Government department.[32]

Equanimity was somewhat disturbed when the composition of the Copyright Committee was announced. Its predecessor, which had prepared the way for the 1911 Act, had numbered three publishers, a painter, and a writer, as well as several copyright lawyers, among its members.[33] The 1951 group included an eminent copyright specialist, F. E. Skone James, editor of Copinger's standard work on the subject since 1927; but otherwise it was strangely lacking in people with relevant experience. As Leslie Boosey pointed out, in a letter to its Chairman, Lord Reading, none of the members was versed in a range of intricate problems arising from the performance, publication, and recording of music.[34] Similar complaints, with a broader context, were addressed to the Board of Trade in a joint letter from the Society of Authors, the Publishers' Association, the Music Publishers' Association, and the PRS. In reply they were assured that the Government's intention was to provide a review by 'a small body of substantially independent character which could consider objectively the views and evidence of the many interested organizations and persons'.[35] Clearly, in the light of the Society's past experience, it would be necessary to monitor and lobby at every stage of the Committee's work, from the taking of evidence to the enactment of legislation.

Subsequent events were, in many respects, like a replay of the Tuppenny game, with post-war variants and without benefit of Low and Herbert. Users of music, including an Association of Ballrooms, and representatives of theatres, cinemas, restaurants, and caterers complained about monopoly power, the allegedly arbitrary imposition and hiking-up of tariffs, and failure to provide complete lists of protected works. No one called up the ghost of Harry Wall, but otherwise the proceedings must all have been very familiar to veterans of the 1930 campaign. Apparently much of the chorus of rebuke made little impression on the Committee, so far as can be judged from its Report. Thus, it patiently attempts, yet again, to explain that the PRS cannot provide lists of a vast and constantly changing repertoire.[36]

---

[32] Wilson speech in PRS Bulletin, Aug. 1948, 144–7. See, also C. F. James, Story of the PRS (1951), 117–8; A. Peacock and R. Weir, The Composer in the Market Place (1975), 129–31.

[33] The 1909 (Gorell) Committee included G. R. Askwith and T. E. Scrutton; William Boosey, Henry Cust, and Frederick Macmillan; Alma Tadema, H. Granville Barker, Anthony Hope Hawkins, and Walter Raleigh.

[34] PRS Archives, Leslie Boosey to Marquess of Reading, 17 May 1951.

[35] PRS Archives, President of Board of Trade to Arthur Bliss, 21 May, 1951. Performing Right Bulletin, Aug. 1951, 188–9.

[36] Report of the Copyright Committee (Gregory Report, 1952, Cmnd. 8662), para. 137.

Referring to the existence of monopoly power, with the implication that users of music could generally not escape the need for a PRS licence, it does not accuse the Society of abusing that power. Indeed, the Report notes that two major users of music, the BBC and the National Council of Social Services, had expressly stated that they had no complaint against the PRS. On the other hand, the Committee did not attempt to check allegations by other users against the historical record of tariff negotiations and inflation. Considering such investigations beyond its terms of reference, it managed to obscure what should have been a much less equivocal verdict on the Society's tariff policy. On balance, however, the image of the PRS which emerges from the Report is benign, in marked contrast to its comments upon a quite separate and distinct licensing organization, which was all too easily confused with the PRS in the minds of everybody except a handful of specialists. During the Committee's proceedings, Phonographic Performance Ltd., who had controlled the public use of gramophone records since 1934, was bitterly attacked by the NCSS, on behalf of many voluntary organizations, for allegedly arrogant behaviour, which extended to the wilful refusal of licences. The Committee denounced its 'arbitrary and autocratic manner' and advocated statutory limitation of its 'opportunities of exploitation'.[37] Close reading of the Report confirms, as an expert commentator points out, that the Committee placed 'PRS and PPL in different categories because, while the former never refused licences to prospective licensees, PPL frequently did'.[38] But, since the general public and, for that matter, most journalists and politicians were not close readers of blue books, there was every likelihood that the two licensing organizations would be tarred with the same brush.

It should be said, in parenthesis, that PPL's occasional displays of intransigence could be explained in terms of apprehension and conflicting interests, within the music industry, and in relation to the general public. Every technical improvement in recorded music increased the machine's threat to live music, and these improvements were now beginning to come thick and fast. Their exploitation in public was, therefore, feared and opposed by performers and their associations, such as the Musicians' Union, but not necessarily by representatives of composers and lyricists, who stood to benefit from both live and mechanical performance. Nevertheless, the PPL had been attacked by the Copyright Committee, and there was considerable apprehension that the PRS would suffer as a result. Among the available palliatives, the Board pinned great hopes on a change of

[37] Ibid., para. 150.
[38] Gavin McFarlane, *Copyright: The Development and Exercise of the Performing Right* (1980), 134.

name, which might help to distance guilt by association, in addition to giving a fairer indication of the Society's interests and functions. The idea which had been dormant since 1943 was once again eagerly canvassed, with such urgency and confident expectation that existing stocks of headed notepaper were allowed to run down.[39] Ten alternative new names were circulated to the Directors, one of which, 'The Society of Composers, Authors, and Publishers of Music Ltd.', was said to have been 'verbally approved' by the Board of Trade.[40] A resolution to change the Society's name was set out in the notice of the thirty-ninth Annual General Meeting. Then the Board changed its mind, apparently because it could not, at the last moment, secure approval for its favoured name from the Board of Trade. A final touch of absurdity was added by the rigours of the Companies Act, which required the now unwanted resolution to be formally put, without amendment, by a chairman who simultaneously pleaded that it be rejected, which the meeting did, unanimously. Thus ended the Society's last attempt to change its name.[41]

The Copyright Committee's Report was published in 1952 and, in preparation for legislation, the PRS led a tenacious campaign, efficiently organized by Royce Whale, to protect the rights of copyright holders. Representations were made to the Board of Trade and at every stage of the ensuing Bill's progress through Parliament, culminating in a petition. A British Joint Copyright Council was formed, with Whale as its Honorary Secretary and the Society as its 'animator, scribe and executant'.[42] Much of the argument was highly technical, and the *PR Bulletin*, which had been rechristened *Performing Right* with a new format in September 1955, began to look like a law journal, in an attempt to keep members informed. Amid the plethora of legalisms there were several key issues affecting their future welfare. One of the Committee's proposals which the Society managed to get changed, would, in its original form, have greatly harmed composers of commissioned film music, effectively vesting copyright in the film's producer. This had been a bone of contention ever since the beginnings of sound film and was, as we have noted, of vital interest to the Composers' Guild. The reform was of immediate benefit to composers of film music, the most successful of whom became leading earners. It had equal significance for future television commissions.

[39] PRS Archives, General Manager to staff, 20 Feb. 1953. General Manager to Board of Trade, 11 Mar. 1953. Secretary to all Directors, 24 Apr. 1953. General Manager to all full members and overseas agents, 29 Jun. 1953.
[40] PRS Archives, Secretary to William Walton, 24 and 29 Apr. 1953.
[41] PRS Archives, Executive Committee, 5 Feb. 1953. General Manager to Manager, Australasian Performing Right Association, 4 Aug. 1953. *Performing Right Bulletin*, Aug. 1953, 225–6.
[42] *Performing Right*, Mar. 1957, 68.

Another potentially damaging proposal arose, with seeming inno-cence, from complaints by the National Council of Social Services. Without amendment, it would have allowed exemptions from performance fees to a group of organizations so loosely defined that it might have been interpreted as including the BBC! After vigorous protests, and a letter to the *The Times* from the President and many prominent musicians and writers, the Government amended that clause.[43] There were also lengthy and complex arguments about recording and diffusion rights. The apprehensions of composers about these matters were set out in another letter to *The Times* signed by a remarkably eclectic group which included Bliss, Vaughan Williams, Britten, Coates, Vivian Ellis, A. P. Herbert, Maschwitz, and Sydney Torch.[44] The Bill became law in 1956, having been improved, in Whale's words, 'at every point where success could reasonably be hoped for'.[45] But the Damoclean sword which had overhung every licensing negotiation since 1930 was now given a new edge. A Tribunal was appointed 'to protect the general public against the abuse of performing right'.[46]

The extra burden of work imposed by copyright alarms and excursions had to be carried at a time of acute crisis in the administration of the Society. The General Manager, Charles James, who had served the Society since 1919, retired at the end of 1951 and was appointed as a Consultant Director. His successor, Gerald Hatchman, was able and experienced. He had joined the staff in 1922, became Secretary in 1929, and acted as both Assistant General Manager and Secretary between 1935 and 1938, when he relinquished the latter post. Since then he had continued to serve as an excellent administrator. Apart from ill health he seemed ideally qualified for the tasks at hand. An acknowledged expert, witness his report on Germany, he was a good linguist with a rare and highly relevant ability to reduce complex verbiage to lucid prose. He died thirty days after taking over as General Manager. In his place the Board appointed Leonard Walter, temporarily at first, and then perma-nently. A member of staff since 1929, Assistant Secretary since 1932, and Secretary since 1938, Walter was thus the third person to become chief executive within a month. Highly conscientious, a pillar of integrity, and a stickler for detail, he is also remembered as being 'blunt and direct in personal relations', though there is no record of

[43] *The Times*, 7 Sept. 1955.

[44] Ibid., 16 Oct. 1956.

[45] *Performing Right*, 1957, 71.

[46] President of the Board of Trade, introducing the second reading of the Copyright Bill in the House of Commons, 4 June 1956 *(Parliamentary Debates*, vol. 553, p. 719). For further discussion, see Peacock and Weir, *op. cit.*, 128–37; McFarlane, *op. cit.*, 133–5; and *Performing Right*, 1957 and 1958.

his attempting to rival Woodhouse in this respect. The Secretary's chair, vacated by Walter, was occupied by William Grice, who had taken care of the Members' Fund for many years, and was Leslie Boosey's personal assistant. Throughout this game of musical chairs there was apparently no attempt to recruit senior management from outside.

The work of this reshuffled and hastily assembled team of administrators was gradually becoming even more difficult, because of shifting frontiers of responsibility. The old high-handed manner of running the Society, initiated by William Boosey and Woodhouse, had been modified by Leslie Boosey and his associates, but procedures continued to be essentially informal and paternalistic. Day by day, and over the long term, the effectiveness of policy and administration depended upon the willingness and ability of the Chairman to devote unlimited time, and share loosely defined authority with an inner circle of directors and senior staff. It also depended upon the existence of an acquiescent Board, and a docile membership, most of whom never attended meetings. The time was not yet ripe for a thorough overhaul of this system, but it was beginning to show signs of strain, as the business of the Society grew in scope and complexity. Leslie Boosey continued to make it work without too much friction, despite an occasional decision to take unilateral action, or such rare mishaps as the name-changing farce. He was conscious of the need to try for a better balance between old blood and new, devising, for example, means which allowed 'certain Directors, whose services the General Council would be most reluctant to lose, to retire without completely severing their connection with the direction of the Society'. New Articles of Association provided for the appointment of a President of Honour and Honorary Members of the General Council who would be allowed to attend Board meetings without a vote.[47] There was also a change in nomenclature. The Board was renamed General Council, and the former Chairman rechristened President. This, it was argued, would 'add dignity' to the Society's governing body. The change was not merely cosmetic, for it was rooted in a practical need to emphasize 'the trustee nature of the Society as an organization operating not for its own profit but solely in the interests of its members'.[48]

At the Society's fortieth Annual General Meeting Leslie Boosey handed over the Presidency to Sir Arthur Bliss and was himself appointed 'President of Honour for his incomparable service'. His new position was no sinecure, for he continued to be Chairman of the

[47] *Performing Right Bulletin*, Aug. 1953, 227.
[48] Ibid.

Executive Council, but the arrangement was a symbolic break with the past because, for the first time, the titular head of the Society was a composer, not a publisher. Bliss was a contemporary of Boosey, educated at Rugby and Cambridge, and a Guards officer during World War I. A musician of wide and cosmopolitan experience, almost unique among his English contemporaries, he had achieved a reputation as an *enfant terrible*, written film music, taught in America, and been director of music at the BBC. His practical musicianship was widely admired, by knowledgeable contemporaries, and he had recently become an active and acclaimed Master of the Queen's Music. In addition to his international reputation as a composer, his wide range of social and musical contacts was new to the Society, and of inestimable benefit. For a time, the Council over which he presided was possibly the most distinguished in the Society's history, including Britten and Walton, as well as Coates and William Alwyn. It could not last because, as with any institution which represents creative people, and the occasional genius, the most productive members could spare little time for committees. The earlier case of Frank Bridge is remarkable in this respect. There was no doubting the Society's status in the worlds of serious and light music by the mid–1950s. Only popular music was a backwater. As Boosey sadly admitted, in his last speech as President, 'The vast majority of the hits come from the other side of the Atlantic . . . it is becoming ever harder to make British music popular'.[49]

[49] *Performing Right Bulletin*, Aug. 1953, 229–30.

7

LIFT OFF

The late fifties and early sixties were years of unexampled prosperity for most people in Britain', 'ignorantly blissful' perhaps, but blissful none the less.[1] There was full employment; and rationing ended, of most foodstuffs in 1954, of meat in 1956. Motor cars, refrigerators, and the washing machines which liberated half the population became widely accessible for the first time, though it would take another decade before their ownership was widespread. Living on credit became a way of life as hire purchase, which had been pioneered in the previous century by a branch of the music industry, financed the new durables.[2] And there was the 'youthquake', detonated by a sudden accession of spare cash to a segment of the population which had never before had much to spend. The group's size was an inevitable consequence of the post-war baby boom. Its combined purchasing power was tempting to marketers of fashion, not only through sheer magnitude but also because, with limited family responsibilities at that stage in their lives, adolescents were easily persuaded to become avid buyers of ephemera. Conditions were ripe for the creation of a market and 'image', the new cult word, which first repelled, then bemused, and finally took over, the adult world.[3]

Since almost everybody paid obeisance to 'pop', it would be an understatement to say that entertainment in general, and music in particular, had a share in the new affluence and life-style. The industry's frontiers were redrawn, more suddenly and irrevocably than at any time in the past. Practically every aspect which had appeared stable in the previous decade was transformed within a few years. People stopped going to the cinema. Annual admissions dropped from 1,182 million to 327 million between 1955 and 1965, and then halved again in the next five years. Dead cinemas which had once housed Rogers and Astaire became depositories of cheap furniture and bingo: not every cultural change was linked to youth. Over the same period the number of television licences increased from

---

[1] The phrase is T. W. Hutchison's. See Vernon Bogdanor, and Robert Skidelsky, *The Age of Affluence 1951–1964* (1970), 8.

[2] Cyril Ehrlich, *The Piano: A History* (1976), 98–104.

[3] See, *inter alia*, Christopher Booker, *The Neophiliacs* (1969) and Colin MacInnes, *Absolute Beginners* (1957).

4.6 million to 13.5 million, and then to 15 million. The music-hall finally abandoned its old haunts, but turned up again in the newly prosperous working men's clubs of the still industrial Midlands and North. Along similar lines, a relaxation of licensing laws brought more entertainment and noise into the pubs. Cheaply imported transistor sets transformed the use of radio. Family listening was no longer determined by the single, immobile, wireless, and young people were liberated from the tastes of their elders. As television took over the living room, radios and record players retreated to the adolescent bedroom. Sounds became increasingly a preoccupation of youth, particularly when 'disc jockeys' began to broadcast on 'pirate' radio. The quality, cost, and convenience of recorded sound were changed out of recognition by cumulative improvements in technology: long-playing discs; the radiogram's defeat by the domestication and mass manufacture of 'hi-fi'; stereo sound; reel-to-reel tape; cassette recorders. Torrents of music were one result; and another was that copying and piracy of copyright material, in sound recordings and on paper, became easy and, eventually, very cheap. Its practitioners, domestic and international, appeared to be as immune to control as were the earlier pirates, while the law again failed to keep pace with technology and human ingenuity.

Musical tastes, attitudes, and patterns of consumption were all subjected to upheaval. Technology took such firm control that live, natural music, without benefit of electronics, steadily retreated beyond the everyday experience or concern of most people. Background sound became inescapable and ever louder, although some of it was specially manufactured in order to eliminate those points of interest which might deflect attention from foreground pursuits, like shopping. But whatever the provenance of the sound—and incongruousness became imperceptible as music lost its roots—it was only really necessary that it always be available for indiscriminate continual use, in every public meeting place, at negligible monetary cost, and virtually without need of human agency. Portable transistor radios and cassette players were primarily responsible for cheapening and spreading what had been expensive and inconvenient in the recent past.

The shape, context, and perception of what might be termed 'foreground' music could not escape these influences. People's capacity to listen, rather than overhear, began to atrophy and, for an easy social life was perhaps best not cultivated. With a few notable exceptions, particularly among leading English composers, serious contemporary music continued its retreat into an intellectual ghetto. It received some support from non-market patronage, but little encouragement to widen its appeal, in a prevailing aesthetic which rejected hierarchies of taste. The age of 'musical appreciation' and Reithian improvement, which had reached its peak in wartime, was now dead, inside and outside the broadcasting studios; 'élitist' becoming a term of reproach. This did not prevent 'standard classics', some of which were still in copyright, from tapping new markets. A massive increase in recorded material was geared to several inter-linked demands: for active listening, for background 'wallpaper', and for mood associations. Thus, excerpts from Holst's *The Planets* became indispensible for dramatized space fiction, and Elgar's Cello Concerto or *Introduction and Allegro* for Edwardian nostalgia. If such adventitious use of music was not new, having obvious roots in the theatre and cinema, its potential for commercial exploitation was now enormously increased, and could bring unexpected benefits. Music which had earned a few hundred pounds from performances in the late 1920s was commanding several thousands a generation later. In 1966 Imogen Holst attributed the renewed interest in her father's music to a recording of his *Choral Fantasia*. It was an unworldly belief, but who would begrudge the belated flow of funds, whatever their *raison d'être*, to worthy recipients?[4]

Light music began to lose its former prominence, though it continued to provide employment for those who, unconsciously emulating Montague Ewing, monitored trends and tailored their product accordingly. Surviving forms included material for 'easy listening', background sound in locations requiring something decorous and, above all, 'theme' music for film, and later, television. Skilled practitioners in the latter market became high earners, some remaining practically anonymous, without need of the outmoded use of *noms de plume*.[5] Popular music was transformed into 'pop', an entirely technological artifact, though a few individual talents of near genius were still capable of creating works of art from its clatter. Its hegemony transcended the world of music. Its words, much concerned with the alienation and suffering of youth, were distanced from the preoccupations of earlier lyricists, in tone and sentiment; abandoning patriotism for international accord, and adding 'protest' to hackneyed themes of love. Its principal instruments were electric guitars and keyboards, and it was played and sung with rudimentary techniques which rarely needed formal training or the ability to read

---

[4] 'PRS Profile: Imogen Holst', by Ursula Vaughan Williams, *Performing Right*, Apr. 1966, 12–13.

[5] The use of pseudonyms was formally restricted to one in 1959, conforming to a recommendation of the International Confederation of Authors' and Composers' Societies. This rule was subsequently relaxed to a limited extent.

notes. Musicians skilled in the traditional disciplines were only occasionally employed, at better rates than they could earn elsewhere, to provide 'backing' for a 'group'. Finally, in this remapping of frontiers, since most music now depended increasingly upon manipulation of tape rather than print, the role of the publisher had to be redefined.

At the epicentre of this cultural earthquake stood the PRS, trying to interpret and adjust to the flow of seismograms. An account of the Society's subsequent evolution as simply a record of continuous growth and success would, therefore, be unjust to its members, directors, and, most particularly, its indefatigable managers and staff. Their achievement of a new found prosperity was hard won, and never peaceful.

Tapping New Markets

In 1965 Ernest Ford, who had been in charge of licensing since 1928, looked back at the expansion of a market which he had done so much to define and build up. When he joined the Society in 1926 less than 6,000 users of music held its licenses. During the early 1930s he calculated, by analysing 'intensely worked specimen districts' and estimating new prospects, that the 'saturation point' for the British Isles would be about 50,000. By 1939 the total exceeded 40,000 and Ford thought he could see the end of the road. After wartime setbacks there was a slow recovery, followed by accelerating growth until the mid-fifties when the numbers approached 60,000. The Society was then issuing about 5,000 new licences every year, a rate of growth which was only slightly offset by cancellations, when a business changed hands or the owner stopped using music. As Ford neared retirement, with 100,000 licences on the list in 1965, he was no longer prepared to predict a level of saturation. The growth of business which he depicted did not emerge by gentle evolution along predetermined and unwavering lines. Lurching between the contraction of old markets and the expansion of new ones, it required an active and responsive licensing policy, making constant adjustments to the geographical and functional relocation of music which accompanied the cultural revolution. If Ford and his colleagues had continued along well-trod paths, acquiescing in the loss of traditional outlets without seeking new opportunities, they would have been behaving like many of their contemporaries in declining British industries. Instead they were resourceful and successful, but only by relentlessly slogging through the territory, familiar and unknown.

There were occasional reports from the front:

I had to spend several weeks in convalescence, but, being impatient to get back to work, I set out one morning with a large piece of adhesive tape across my jaw and looking very much the worse for wear. I entered a public house about 11 a.m. and gave my card to what appeared even to me (I am over six feet tall) a giant of a man. He immediately tore up the card and threw it on the counter. Unabashed, I gave him another and suggested that he did not know his own strength. This was fatal. He said that 'If you don't get out of my pub I'll put my !?--!=!! fist down your !=?-!+=! throat'. Bravely . . . I suggested that if he did I would take great pleasure in biting it off at the wrist. His reaction was most unexpected. He said 'Well done, lad. How much do I owe you? and let me know if you have any trouble with any of the others' . . . I had only to quote this gentleman's name to other licensees and they were most co-operative.

Persistence was sometimes as rewarding as bravery. Finding a bar piano which the publican refused to licence, a representative stayed on. First a lady was dissuaded from playing it by a drink 'on the house'. Then another customer had to be silenced in similar fashion.

Then two sailors came in, rather merrily, and loudly enquired whether anyone there could play the piano. They too got free drinks. Finally, another customer also made for the piano, and the landlord, evidently calculating that free drinks were going to cost him more than our licence, came over and whispered 'All right, you win!'[6]

New potential outlets were created by legislation and technology. Reform of the drink laws encouraged large brewers to install music in thousands of pubs until, by 1963, over 30,000 held PRS licences. The 1963 Betting, Gaming and Lotteries Act led to the establishment of places which needed background music, from bingo-halls to casinos. Juke-boxes, which had been common in pre-war America, came late to Britain. In the 1930s there was merely 'an experimental handful', and only 500 were licensed in 1955. By 1960 upwards of 10,000 had been identified, 8,000 of which were licensed by the Society, and between 20,000 and 25,000 were thought to exist. Many were sited, often with exasperating impermanence, in cafés and small clubs which had previously never used music, making their 'policing' difficult and costly, but bringing in fresh revenue. Across the whole field of mechanized music it was cassettes which universalized the use of tape. They were simple enough to operate for the provision of continuous music, and managements were further encouraged to install them by the activities of companies which supplied complete background sound systems and pre-selected tapes. Between 1959 and 1964 the largest of these businesses increased its subscribers from

---

[6] 'Front Line Communiqués', *Performing Right*, May 1969, 10–12.

3,000 to over 10,000. The Society made bulk agreements with such firms at first, but it increasingly negotiated individual tariffs with multifarious organizations for 'amenity music'. Large gatherings were charged twopence-halfpenny per hundred spectators at football matches in 1963, one penny per hundred at greyhound races. Bingo sessions in cinemas and ballrooms paid ninepence per hundred seats, with a minimum annual fee of three guineas a year; 266 cinemas were so licensed, not without protest. The music was 'quite inessential to the playing of the game' complained their counsel before the Performing Right Tribunal. But this was merely a bargaining ploy, for the truth was that it had become as indispensible to bingo as to most other businesses seeking to provide people with what they had come to regard as a congenial environment. As another lawyer explained, with the air of pained condescension still common among men of his calling: 'unquestionably there are a very large number of people who require music as a background rather like the smoking habit. This is a comparatively recent development—the musical background people require for almost everything and even in their own houses'.[7] Thus, the market was reassembled and developed, licensing music for:

dance halls, cinemas and theatres, concert halls, hotels, restaurants, cafés, clubs, public houses, circuses, town and village halls, factories, offices, shops, skating rinks, fairgrounds, amusement arcades, football grounds, exhibitions, greyhound racing tracks, swimming pools, bowling alleys, coaches and buses, ships, railway trains, and aircraft, in parks and on promenades, and at bingo sessions.[8]

Capricious Adjudications

The Society's tariff policy was now being conducted in a new and unpredictable climate, created by the Performing Right Tribunal. Out of seven PRS tariffs referred to this body in its first decade of work, two were confirmed—juke-boxes and bingo-halls—and five reduced. The choice of yardsticks was capricious and indeterminate. Among the available selection, comparisons with foreign tariffs were certainly ignored, for all of the rejected proposals were at levels far below what was commonly being paid on the continent. If any element of consistency could be deduced from the Tribunal's

[7] Performing Right Tribunal, 7/62; *The Times*, 22 Jan. 1963.

[8] On the expansion of the market, see Ernest C. Ford, 'Where the Money Comes From', *Performing Right*, Sept. 1955, 16–19, and 'The Composer's Expanding Market', *Performing Right*, Oct. 1965, 25–6. *Board of Trade Journal*, 11 Oct. 1960. Performing Right Tribunal 6/60. Letter from Royce Whale to the *Financial Times*, 14 Sept. 1961. On Ford's work, see L. Walter, 'Ernest C. Ford: An Appreciation', *Performing Right*, Oct. 1968, 6–7.

deliberations, it was the idea that a 'fair' rate should be based on what a 'willing buyer and willing seller' might agree upon. Simple and reasonable enough at first glance, this rule of thumb led in practice to the imposition of tariffs which were based upon settlements made *in the past*. Since the Society had almost invariably conducted its negotiations, as we have repeatedly demonstrated, under various forms of constraint, and with the utmost complaisance, this was an approach which could hardly have been bettered as a means of dispensing injustice. A good example was the local government tariff, without major revision since 1921, obsolescent since 1935, unreformed after World War II, yet still regarded by the Tribunal as a fair base for negotiation in 1963.[9] Among several other maladroit adjudications, by far the most important, because so much money was at stake, was the Tribunal's handling of the BBC tariff.

Since 1947 BBC payments to the Society, which continued to be linked to the number of radio and television licences, had slowly risen from 1s. to 1s.5d. per licence in 1957, and 1s.6½d. for the period 1962–6; an arrangement which failed even the elementary test of keeping pace with inflation. Low tariffs had persisted until 1962 for reasons already explained. Then the Society accepted another poor bargain because it was starting negotiations with the commercial television companies, and thought that a simultaneous dispute with the BBC would strain its resources. It was also confident that the Corporation's finances, which were currently under strain, would soon be improved by an increase in the price of radio and television licences. After this long period of reticence, the PRS at last attempted to catch up, in 1966, by proposing an increase in the tariff of 40 per cent for the next four-year period. Such a settlement would have added £500,000 to the current annual payment of £1,250,000. The BBC flatly refused, and appealed to the Tribunal, with a counter-claim that its aggregate payments should in future be *reduced*. This extraordinary reaction was based on an attempt to show that it was now reaching a smaller audience for music: because of the swing from radio to television; and through the effect on its external broadcasts of decolonization and cultural change in the Third World. The latter assertion had some validity, for Empire broadcasting had long been replaced by the Overseas service—sitar and tabla began to displace marches by Alford or Eric Coates; but in other respects there was little substance in the BBC's case.

In response, the Society agreed that conditions had changed since 1937, undermining the validity of the old formula, but it then went on

[9] See analysis by Denis de Freitas in 'The PRS and The Performing Right Tribunal', (*Performing Right Supplement no. 1*. Oct. 1968, 17–18.

to draw very different conclusions from these facts. In the first place, it was no longer sensible to estimate the size of the listening public from sales of receiving licences. Dodging payment was common at that time, possibly to the extent of two million unlicensed sets. Even more important was the enormous increase in sales of transistor radios, from 1.3 million in 1956 to 3.5 million in 1965. These new acquisitions were not reflected in the licence figures because only one licence was required for each household. It would therefore be more realistic henceforth to assess the potential audience for broadcast music in terms of the whole population. If demand had increased, so had supply, for the BBC's use of music was far greater than it was prepared to admit, both retrospectively and in the Corporation's immediate plans for the future. There had been considerable programme extensions in 1964, and the use of pop was about to be transformed by the introduction of Radio One, in response to the now disbanded 'pirate' stations. Pirate broadcasts had started in 1961, and 'Radio Caroline', beginning in 1964, claimed seven million listeners within a few months. The new BBC programme, providing continuous pop and starring four ex-pirate disc jockeys, was boosted by the Corporation as providing a specialized service to the new youth audience.[10] These facts and plans were either known to the Tribunal or could easily have been elicited. They were not convincingly presented by the PRS, but no detached, informed observer could have failed to take them into account.

The Society's second argument was that in an age of inflation the cost of living must be taken into account, both retrospectively and in anticipating the period of agreement. Particularly serious, though it was not argued on this occasion, was the fact that Tribunal hearings themselves added a further element of delay to negotiations. With inflation necessitating frequent tariff revisions, every delay meant further losses to the Society's members. Finally, it was submitted that the 'true economic value' of television had recently been established, with the onset of commercial competition. If foreign tariffs were not acceptable as a yardstick (*autre pays autre mœurs*, as William Boosey had said long ago), then here was an alternative, directly British comparison. By all these standards the BBC were getting their music 'dirt cheap', and their payments were so low as to be 'contemptuous'.[11]

The Tribunal's decision, delivered at the end of 1967, after a

[10] Asa Briggs, *The BBC: The First Fifty Years* (1985), 344–5.

[11] See analysis by Royce Whale and Denis de Freitas in 'The PRS and The Performing Right Tribunal', op. cit.; and by de Freitas in 'The Performing Right Tribunal in the United Kingdom', *Journal of the Copyright Society of the USA*, Jan. 1987, 166–92. For press comment on the BBC adjudication see *The Times*, 6 June and 15 Aug. 1967; *Financial Times*, 14 Jan. and 17 Aug. 1967.

hearing which lasted for eleven expensive days, was a shocking surprise for the Society. Having asked for an extra ninepence per receiving licence, it got threepence, without any retrospective payment. The Tribunal disregarded arguments from both sides, assimilating none of the implications of change since 1937 except for an inflation adjustment; and even that was less generous than what had previously been agreed by the contesting parties! The 'award' was fixed until 1971, so the PRS drew no benefit from extensions of BBC programmes in 1968, and the substantial increase in broadcasting licence revenue which financed them. That infliction exacerbated resentment against injustice.[12] Among the chorus of protest was a notable link with the past. Eric Fenby, who had been amanuensis to Delius and was currently Chairman of the Composers' Guild, spoke for most composers when he expressed their 'bitter disappointment' at the rejection of proposals which had been 'reasonable by standards accepted in advanced countries generally'.[13] Royce Whale, who was approaching retirement, after valiant attempts to make the Society's bargaining more resolute and effective, summed up his view of the past and advice for the future in letters to Leslie Boosey and the Directors. The Tribunal, he confided to Boosey, would probably 'have compromised anyway, but it has once more been demonstrated that the Council's policy in the past of extreme moderation is always misconstrued, and has benefited only the users'.[14] To Directors he proposed a campaign to improve and inform the Tribunal, starting with open criticism of its decisions, for the first time. Escape from 'the economic strait-jacket' which it had imposed would only be possible through resolute efforts to change its viewpoint, assisted, perhaps, by changes in its personnel.[15]

Similar arguments were put more forcibly and publicly by a member speaking from the floor (as distinct from the platform) at the Society's fifty-fourth Annual General Meeting. Angered by a foolish and uninformed Tribunal decision from which there was no appeal, F. Jackson deplored the Society's lack of toughness in negotiation, and demanded action. It was a most unusual expression of grass-roots frustration, and a fresh sign of more open debate, which could be said to have arrived a quarter of a century too late. The Chairman did not accept the criticism, and the meeting was persuaded not to press a resolution on Jackson's speech because 'representations' had already been made to the Government.[16] These consisted of a letter of

[12] *Performing Right*, 1968, 2–3.
[13] Ibid., 4.
[14] PRS Archives, Whale to Leslie Boosey, 20 Dec. 1967.
[15] PRS Archives, Whale to Leslie Boosey, 25 Apr. 1968. *Performing Right*, Apr. 1968, 2–3.
[16] *Performing Right*, Oct. 1968, 15–19.

complaint to the President and officials of the Board of Trade, with a
resumé of events and arguments; submissions to the Lord Chancellor's
Department; and proposals for the amendment of the Copyright Act.
The Society's 'grave plight', it was argued, stemmed essentially from the
Tribunal's terms of reference, which were incompatible with the
Berne Convention. They gave every appearance of failing to limit it to
the remedying of abuse; and the resulting damage was increased by its
unwillingness to consider evidence of comparable tariffs elsewhere. A
highly illuminating pamphlet was written by Whale and his formidable new lawyer colleague, Denis de Freitas, setting out the Society's
case with unprecedented detail, professional assurance, and frankness. First reactions from the Government were curt and dismissive,
but Whale was not to be put down. Expressing 'astonishment that
such detailed and circumstantial representations concerning matters
touching the livelihood of one of the creative sections of the
community have been so summarily dismissed', he elucidated a few
points of law, and rebuked the Minister, Anthony Crosland, for
adding to 'the catalogue of misconceptions which threaten perma-
nently to deny justice in our country to the music creators of the
world. This is a situation which the Society cannot accept'.[17] In tone
and content this correspondence, and its associated papers, mark a
distinct break with the past. Reticence, forbearance, and deference
were no longer conditioned reflexes when the Society was under
attack.

By the time that the next chance came to negotiate, in 1971, there
had been changes in the chairmanship of the Tribunal, and in the
Society's management. The BBC wanted only minor adjustments for
inflation, but the PRS now set out the case for a completely new
approach. It argued that substantially increased payments were
required, and that they should be based upon a rejection of the
ancient formula for deciding fees according to the number of receiving
licences. Instead there should be a simple percentage levy, on either
the BBC's revenue or its expenditure. Again the dispute was referred
to the Tribunal, but this time the Society's case was received with
sympathetic understanding, and without equivocation. The 1971
Tribunal's adjudication amounted to a complete dismantling of its
predecessor's procedure and findings. First, it acknowledged the
ravages of inflation: 'the effect of the 1967 decision was to maintain
the royalty at a level which was substantially below the level which it
would have reached if full account had been taken of the rise in the
cost of living since 1957'. There was a similarly frank acceptance, by

[17] PRS Archives, Crosland to Whale, 19 July 1968; Whale to Crosland, 22 July, 1968.

the Tribunal and the BBC, that the latter's use of PRS music, far from waning, had increased by some eighty per cent since 1957. As most of this increase had taken place, or been anticipated by the BBC's programme planners, before 1968, the Tribunal concluded that its predecessor's threepenny award had dealt inadequately with use, as it had with inflation. Moreover, the BBC had opened about twenty local radio stations since 1967, using some 11,000 hours a year of PRS music, selected from a greatly extended repertoire. The Society's membership had increased from 2,996 in 1957 to 4,042 in 1967 and 5,309 in 1971. There was also a vast increase in the number of composers and publishers belonging to foreign affiliated societies: a factor which must also be brought into the calculation. The Tribunal, therefore, saw 'no reason to doubt that the value of the PRS repertoire has increased substantially over recent years'. Next, the adjudication turned to comparability. The Society had recently negotiated a three-year agreement with the commercial television companies for £936,000 a year, indexed against inflation and with safeguards against their increased use of copyright music. The Tribunal agreed that this was a relevant yardstick. Accepting that it was better to introduce a formula, which could be used or adapted for future negotiations, rather than merely imposing a simple lump-sum royalty, the Tribunal explored the four methods which had been submitted. It selected the Society's formula: a simple percentage levy on the BBC's licence revenue and grant-in-aid, with only two modifications. The proposed 2.75 per cent was reduced to 2 per cent, and ceiling payments of £2,350,000 and £2,550,000 were imposed for the first two years. This outcome was a triumph for the PRS after years of underpayment. If it reflected a more judicious Tribunal, prepared to examine complex evidence with the thoroughness appropriate to decisions affecting people's livelihood, no less could it be attributed to superb document-ation and presentation by the Society's new team of officials.[18]

Queen's Award

On 13 February 1963 Dick James wrote to the Society to recommend two young men who wished to become members. His own back-ground in popular music made him a shrewd judge of new talent. A cockney in his forties, he had sung with dance bands since he was sixteen, worked with Henry Hall and Geraldo, broadcast from Radio Luxembourg, and made successful records including 'Robin Hood'

---

[18] *Performing Right Tribunal*, 24/71. *Performing Right*, May 1972, 2–10. de Freitas, 'The PRS and the Performing Right Tribunal', loc. cit.

which sold over 300,000 and was used as a television sound-track. In 1953 he had joined a publishing firm and scored twenty-eight hits in eight years before forming Dick James Music Ltd. in 1961. A year later he was introduced by his former recording manager, George Martin, to a Liverpool business man who was promoting a local group. James now wrote about two of its members, whose songs 'Love Me Do' and 'Please Please Me' were being released abroad and were already successful 'in juke-boxes throughout the country which, of course, will necessitate the PRS collecting general fees on behalf of these writers'. He then added, with marvellous understatement, 'I would like to mention that these two boys have written many, many more songs which will very shortly be recorded by artists other than themselves and I feel sure that they are more than justified in applying for membership'.[19] Thus, J. Lennon and P. McCartney were introduced to the PRS.

A mountain of print has described, and attempted to explain, the musical and social significance of what followed. Beatle-mania provoked anguished political debate, and the group's work was subjected to learned sociological discussion and earnest musical analysis.[20] 'Love Me Do', which Dick James had submitted as a credential for PRS membership, was later depicted as 'the culmination of an era and the beginning of a fundamental change in a generation's life style'.[21] Problems of adjustment were not confined to the Beatles' impact on England. In September 1965 the Rolling Stones, two of whom had become associate members of the Society in the previous October, performed in Munich, where music was exempt from tax. The city authorities claimed £1,270 from the group, on the grounds that they were not musicians, but mere purveyors of noise whose essential function was to trigger demonstrations by fans. During nine months of legal hearings, which amounted to a German inquest on pop, four judges were prevailed upon to attend a Beatles concert in Munich, and the Stones' lawyers quoted Leonard Bernstein on the elemental purity of the Mersey sound. They won their case.[22]

The letter from Dick James was a turning point in the history of the PRS. In their own right, and as trend- and pace-setters, the Beatles initiated profound changes in the scale of the Society's operations, in

[19] PRS Archives, J. Lennon file 1, Dick James to PRS, 13 Feb. 1963.
[20] One book is indispensable: George Martin, *All You Need is Ears* (1979). See also report of a House of Lords debate on 'The Beatles Cult' in *The Times*, 14 May 1964; W. Mellers, *Twilight of the Gods: the Beatles in Retrospect* (1973); D. Harker, *One for the Money* (1980); Ian Whitcomb, *Rock Odyssey: a Chronicle of the Sixties* (1983).
[21] Peter Gammond and Raymond Horricks, *The Music Goes Round and Round: A Cool Look at the Record Industry* (1980), 56.
[22] *Performing Right*, Oct. 1966, 8.

its prosperity, and eventually in its fundamental structure and organization. Individual and aggregate income levels reached unprecedented heights. The adverse balance of international payments was reversed: no longer was it necessary for British popular music to demand protection from foreign competition. New publishers emerged; and pop groups began to take a hand in their own publishing and promotion, sharing risks and proceeds, and changing the old clear-cut division between publisher and composer. 'Northern Songs' was the outstanding example, formed by Dick James with Brian Epstein, John Lennon, and Paul McCartney, but there were many others. It was a sign of the times that the financial press began to feature long articles on the pop business. 'One of the first things a star does when he steps on the ladder to the charts', explained one of these essays, 'is to establish his own music publishing company'.[23] It was a trend fraught with significance for the PRS.

The suddennesss of this transformation was breath-taking. In May 1960 Sir Arthur Bliss, opening the Society's new offices in Berners Street, was still deploring the neglect of British 'entertainment' music.[24] A year later the alleged need for protective quotas was eagerly discussed at the Annual General Meeting; and even in the spring of 1963 there were complaints against American 'dumping'.[25] By autumn that year, as Leslie Boosey later explained to a more contented AGM, 'the beat groups began to invade the United States and other foreign countries'.[26] Individual earning power 'lifted off' with equal suddenness, as a result of the high productivity of the new technology (much more output per unit of input), and the profits which could be tapped from appearing, if only to mime, in front of huge adolescent audiences in every affluent society. Eighteen months before Dick James's letter, the General Manager had challenged figures in a *Financial Times* article which claimed that an exceptionally popular song might earn its writer £1,000 a month from broadcasting royalties. 'I can say with some certainty that it has never been achieved and is unlikely ever to be achieved', wrote Whale; the biggest hits in recent years had earned less than £1,000 in *six months*. The article's claim that 'fortunes for songwriters are rare', should be amended to read 'fortunes for British songwriters are non-existent'.[27] Lennon and McCartney changed all that, earning rather more than enough to qualify as full members in 1966, and going on to make 'fortunes' beyond the wildest dreams of their predecessors.

[23] *Financial Times*, 6 Feb. 1965.
[24] *The Times*, 31 May 1960.
[25] *Performing Right*, Sept. 1961, 259–61.
[26] *Performing Right*, Oct. 1965, 3.
[27] *Financial Times*, 9 Sept. 1961, General Manager to *Financial Times*, 14 Sept. 1961.

The impact of these changes on the size and structure of the Society's income can be seen in Table 2. (p. 160) Total income almost trebled between 1965 and 1975, more than keeping pace with the general level of prices, which approximately doubled. This ability to keep ahead of inflation, throughout a most difficult decade, stood in notable contrast to the Society's previous record. Equally remarkable was the changing direction from which funds flowed in. Practically since the BBC began, broadcasting had been the main source of revenue, sometimes paying more than half the total fees. Now, for a time, the contribution of radio and television was exceeded by 'affiliated societies', which is to say overseas earnings. To some extent the new emphasis was due to poor returns from the BBC, until the Tribunal's 1971 adjudication; but, essentially, it reflected the enormous success of British music in foreign markets. It was not solely a trade in pop. The work of Britten, Malcolm Arnold, Miklós Rózsa, William Alwyn, Elgar, Walton, and a diversity of less familiar composers all contributed to the country's great new 'invisible' export. The net inflow of funds, after allowing for remittances abroad to pay for foreign works played in Britain, amounted to some two million pounds. London had temporarily become the world's musical capital, and Berners Street could claim to be one of its principal centres. On 24 June 1971 the Society received the Queen's Award to Industry for export achievement.[28]

Revolt and Reform

Continued success required new kinds of management and participation, appropriate to the Society's growth and transmutation. As it attempted to come to terms with these imperatives, it discovered that administrative improvement was more easily achieved than constitutional reform, though in practice the two were not easily separated. Efficient administration required 'only' a loyal and energetic team of professionals, capable of working together, with clearly defined goals. Some of its members, such as Gordon Jones, were recruited through the traditional channels of internal promotion; others, like Denis de Freitas, from outside. Their leader was Michael Freegard. Joining the staff in 1964, he became Secretary two years later, and General Manager in 1969 while still in his thirties. This was a period of decisive change in the structure of policy making and administration. In 1966 Leslie Boosey announced his intention to relinquish Chairmanship of the General and Executive Councils, although

[28] *Performing Right*, Nov. 1971, 8–12.

continuing to be President of Honour. His retirement in 1967 was, of course, the end of an era. Its administrative significance was enhanced by the fact that his successor as Chairman was not a publisher, a man of business, but the song writer, J. G. O. ('Paddy') Roberts.[29] The new managers were, thus, endowed not only with abundant experience and increased professional expertise but with more autonomy than their predecessors. In conditions of continuous growth and transformation, their task was complicated by the need to design rules and procedures which assimilated the new membership without swamping, or alienating, the old. During the decade leading up to the Queen's award, the membership had increased from less than 3,400 to more than 5,400, and showed no signs of abating. Changes in its structure were even more remarkable, for the total of *full* members had actually *fallen*, from 1,259 to 1,138. Associate membership had increased from 2,097 to 2,592, and the number of provisional associate members had risen, astonishingly, from 36 to 1,730. The latter category had been set up in 1958, primarily to deal with the new evanescent breed of pop 'publishers'.[30] The same pattern was accentuated throughout the seventies. By 1976 there were 1,176 full, 2,970 associate, and 5,312 provisional members. In that year the Society was at last beginning to make headway with the slow process of constitutional review. At about the same time one of the provisional associate members launched an attack which provoked more upheaval than in the worst days of the Tuppenny Bill.

Trevor Lyttleton was a Cambridge graduate, solicitor, administrator, publisher and composer of background music, and, not least, heroic writer of letters. At an early stage of his dealings with the Society he may have contemplated entering its employment, but by 1975 he was mainly familiar to its management as a prodigious generator of correspondence. Frequent enquiries about the level of his performing fees, though never abandoned, were increasingly outweighed by constitutional inquisitions and peremptory demands for reform. All members, he argued, regardless of their status in the Society, should have equal rights to attend annual general meetings, and vote for the directors. The former privilege had, in fact, been granted to associate members in recent years; the latter raised more fundamental problems, which were patiently expounded by various members of staff up to, and including, Michael Freegard. Since it was very easy to become a provisional member, they reminded their interlocutor, by recording or publishing a solitary work, it would be inequitable to allow such novices an equal voice with long-established professional composers, or major publishing houses.[31] Such explanations were ignored, and he went on to insist, with similar, but more subtle, implications, upon better access to information. Existing procedures were condemned as unnecessarily secretive, and there was a demand that information should be both more detailed and more widely available. These opinions were forcefully expressed, with great stress upon their allegedly firm base in morality and law, by means of a continuous stream of letters, each answer prompting more enquiry and comment. This first stage of what had become a campaign of harassment culminated in an ultimatum, presented as a resolution for the Annual General Meeting in June 1976. At this point, but only for a short time, Lyttleton was still receiving guarded support from several people who were, or would soon become, prominent in the Society, including Tim Rice, an authority on pop, and future director, and Roger Greenaway, a future chairman. The Council's response to attack was a reassurance that it was already reviewing the constitution, with particular reference to categories of membership and election procedures.[32]

The campaign entered its next stage, building up a head of steam with great energy and resourcefulness. A press report of an interview demanding that the Society be 'run properly, honestly and openly'[33] led straight to court, and was followed by a twelve-page questionnaire to every member of Council. The correspondence with Berners Street piled up until, by the Spring, more than 150 communications had been received, quite apart from Lyttelton's continuing enquiries about his own works. The tide was not stemmed by a suggestion that its propagator should meet servicing costs. Public comment also began to develop. Praise for the reform movement in one magazine was followed by a demand for an 'independent review' in another, implying that the Council had utterly lost members' confidence.[34] There was another tortuous and expensive excursion through the courts, decisions being reversed at each stage up to the Court of Appeal, in an attempt to extract the list of full, voting members from Council. It did not resist disclosure, as was alleged, in contempt of democratic rights, but because such action would have breached confidence by revealing information about individuals' incomes. Meanwhile Parliament was engaged, with demands that the Society should be investigated by the Department (successor to the Board) of

[31] PRS Archives, Freegard to Lyttleton, 14 May 1976.
[32] *PRS Yearbook* (1977), 26.
[33] *Music Week*, 10 July 1976.
[34] *Time Out*, 7 Apr. 1977; *Music Week*, 18 June 1977.

Trade. Established members now began to express their concern. Letters poured in, from musicians famous and obscure, old and young, commercial and academic. Tim Rice withdrew his support for the campaign, recording 'total satisfaction' with the Society's ten years of work on his behalf. Others who were entitled to speak for English music commented in tones of gentle remonstrance or magisterial outrage. Imogen Holst wrote to express heartfelt thanks to 'you and your Committee and staff for all that you are doing for musicians'. Walton sent a handwritten letter to Freegard which will grace some archive long after these events are forgotten:

I have received communications from a Mr Lyttleton about the way the PRS is run. I am sure I speak for all serious composers when I say that I continue to have the greatest admiration for the way the PRS is run—fairly and efficiently. I think it would be utterly pointless to have an independent enquiry as Mr Lyttleton seems to want. Can he be persuaded not to interfere with a first-class organization? I do hope so.[35]

The stage was set for an eventful sixty-third Annual General Meeting.

It was a gathering of 284 members, including ninety associates, and was chaired by Alan Frank, head of the music department of Oxford University Press since 1954, a PRS director since 1950, and husband of the composer, Phyllis Tate. An additional informal meeting, to discuss the 'Lyttleton Resolutions', allowed full and free debate, in a variety of styles which reflected both the diversity of membership and their unanimous sense of outrage. The Chairman gave a résumé of recent events, and read letters of support for the Council and management, including Walton's. There was spirited comment from the floor, one member of thirty-nine years' standing, suggesting, to amused applause, that the complainant 'should spend more time writing music and less time writing letters'. Another man, in his seventies, used demotic language to express what must have been in the minds of many of the older writers and publishers. Picturing himself addressing the Law Society, he declared:

I am a song writer. I want to get in on this law racket. Do me a favour, I am only a part-time chappy, but I think I can teach you law makers a lot about the game. Furthermore, don't you think that what you have been administering as law for the past five or six hundred years is a lot of rubbish? Don't you think we should reorganize the whole lot.

A major publisher addressed one of the basic issues with simple directness: 'each member's voting power must reflect his financial stake in the Society'. For many this was almost insignificant, but

[35] PRS Archives, Walton to Freegard, 5 Apr. 1977.

others, like his company, depended for their very livelihood on PRS revenue. The debate's outcome, as reported in an American trade paper, was 'total defeat' for Lyttleton, who secured only 1 vote; 10 abstained and 183 were opposed. Several members called for his expulsion, a suggestion which was 'greeted with prolonged applause'.[36]

These opinions and feelings were reiterated at an open forum and Extraordinary General Meeting in November. Several members suggested that ridicule could be the Society's best defence, though no one recalled its devastating effect in 1930. What was sorely needed was an image of disparagement, but there were no successors to David Low and A. P. Herbert at hand. Useful discussion was addressed to the Council's new constitutional proposals. Associate members were to be given one vote; full members an extra ten in polls of importance; and those with two years of very high earnings, or more than twenty years of earnings at a professional level, would be allowed a further addition of ten votes. As the Chairman explained, the scheme was designed to open up voting rights while ensuring that the Society remained in the hands of full-time professionals. Lyttleton's criticisms of these reforms met a 'hostile reception', and there were renewed calls for his resignation. Donald Mitchell, a Council member representing Faber Music, suggested that a record of the meeting should be sent to MPs who had been criticizing the Society in the Press.[37] It was significant advice for, having failed within the Society, the campaign was now raging outside.

As so often in the past, and again without reference to the historical record, Parliament and the press were used as baiting arenas. A letter attacking secrecy and oligarchy was signed by several members of both Houses, and patiently answered by the harassed Alan Frank.[38] The level and allocation of administrative expenses were challenged in the Commons.[39] Unsuccessful attempts were made to get the Society's activities referred to the Monopolies Commission; there were dark allusions to 'proxy votes' and it was described as exhibiting 'some characteristics of a self-perpetuating oligarchy'.[40] An 'announcement' was placed in *The Times* explaining, no doubt to a bewildered public, that the Society's successful appeal against revealing the members' list would not be contested. Thus, the announcement continued, 'a Monopoly collecting £21 million (which practically all

[36] *Performing Right News*, Supplement, Oct. 1977; *Billboard*, 16 July 1977.
[37] *The Times*, 25 Nov. 1977; *Performing Right News*, Supplements 1 and 2, 1978.
[38] *The Times*, 29 Oct. and 2 Nov. 1977.
[39] *Hansard*, fifth Ser. vol. 939, 12 Aug. 1977.
[40] Ibid., vol. 934, 28 Jun. 1977, 128; vol. 940, 29 Nov. 1977, 154; 5 Dec. 1977, 992.

British composers have to join) will continue to be run by a self-perpetuating Council with sole access to the voting members'.[41] And so the barrage continued. By June 1978 the *New Statesman* was noting that 'the documentation would make even the most copious historian blanch'.[42]

At the Annual General Meeting in July another massive vote of confidence, and condemnation of 'destructive, mischievous and misleading criticism' had no effect on the campaign.[43] Throughout the summer and autumn of 1978, gobbets of coloured information and gossip, letters of accusation and refutation, found their way into the the trade and national press. We list a sample, for the record and to demonstrate its profusion: the *Guardian*, 20 June, 7 July; the *Daily Telegraph*, (with a scrupulous apology for inadvertent misreporting), 21 June, 4 July, 7 July; *The Sunday Times*, 11 and 25 June; *The Financial Times*, 7 July; *Billboard*, 1 July, 19 August; *Classical Music Weekly*, 15 July; *Record Business*, 10 July; and, inevitably, *Private Eye*, 23 June, 4 August. *Music Week* devoted so much space, mainly to letters from obscure correspondents, that it eventually cried halt, the matter having been 'fully, exhaustively and fairly debated in our columns' (15 July, 22 July, 5 August, 7 October, 11 November, 25 November, 2 December, 16 December).

There was a lull in 1979, and a brief revival in 1980 when the *Guardian* published a lament for Lyttleton's legal costs, and old contests were refought.[44] The worst was over, though in 1981 there was a forlorn attempt to reopen wounds. An MP asked for an official investigation into 'one of Britain's most secretive monopolies'.[45] Attempts to associate this initiative with altruistic reform could not conceal its essential roots: the old familiar desire for free music, with complaints against 'arbitrary' demands for cash. It was left to Nicholas Maw, Chairman of the Association of Professional Composers, to expose the cant of reformers 'attached to the principle rather than the practice of copyright'.[46]

Muck-raking is a time-honoured means of reform. What had been achieved by these years of agitation? The sanest contemporary comment appeared long before the campaign was finally abandoned. In March 1978 the *Investors' Chronicle* concluded a long, balanced résumé by acknowledging Lyttleton's achievement. He had 'almost certainly nudged the society into reviewing and updating its

[41] *The Times*, 21 Sept. 1977.
[42] *New Statesman*, 23 June, 1978.
[43] The *Guardian*, 7 July, 1978.
[44] Ibid., 28, 29, 31 Jan. and 5 Feb. 1980.
[45] *The Sunday Times*, 15 Mar. 1981. The *Guardian*, 16 Mar. 1981.
[46] The *Guardian*, 4 and 18 Apr. and 9 May 1981.

constitution more rapidly than corporate bodies, by their nature, are wont to do'. But now 'a sensible compromise' had been reached. The 'PRS functions efficiently. Its higher executives live well, but they are not alone in that among decision makers in large corporate enterprises'. The time had come to stop rocking the boat.[47] To ignore this advice was foolhardy in several ways. It entailed association with a strangely assorted company of allies. Some were genuinely concerned with what they considered to be serious problems of equity and public accountability. Some were outraged by the extravagant success of pop, and wanted to bring it to heel, while a very different group desired greater rewards and recognition for its latest practitioners. A few were mere busybodies looking for a cause. Strangest of all was the temporary presence in the same camp of two mutually exclusive groups. Attacks and demands for reform were coming indiscriminately from the Society's traditional opponents—users who wanted free music—and from some of its hungriest new members, who wanted their fees increased and more rigorously enforced. There was no future in such an alliance.

For broader consideration, de Tocqueville is a guide: 'The most dangerous moment for a bad government is generally that in which it sets about reform'. Not that the Society's government was 'bad' in the sense of malevolent or corrupt. Nor was it in acute danger; for renewed political intervention was never seriously contemplated, and there were few signs that internal dissent would lead to a repeat of the 1919 breakup. But the PRS had been slow in discarding many of the characteristics of an *ancien régime*, and these had become untenable, because of fundamental changes in its membership and in society at large. Inbred and overburdened with obsolete procedures, it had loyally attempted to retain stifling commitments to people and ideas from the past. Secretiveness, which stemmed originally from creditable motives, had become obsessive, leaving members poorly informed, and outsiders suspicious, without real cause. A deep-rooted preference for low profiles and decent obscurity, which had long been in conflict with the need to establish an image, inform and educate public opinion, was now quite impossible to sustain, in a modern, ungentlemanly age of frankness, hype, and investigative journalism.

Reform had begun slowly in the mid-sixties, largely initiated by Royce Whale, but encouraged by Leslie Boosey. There was increasing awareness of the need to distinguish, as far as possible, between general policy and administration, and to establish more formal procedures, in place of the cosy, paternalistic informality of the past.

[47] *Investors' Chronicle*, 17 Mar. 1978.

Far more delegation was required as agendas became overladen. This implied giving a freer hand to the General Manager, and redefining the functions and responsibilities of the Directors. It is a remarkable fact that Leslie Boosey, who had built up the old system, was still capable of responding with acuity to the need for change.[48] Like the hero of a novel by Ford Maddox Ford finding himself in a play by Harold Pinter, he was eccentrically cast, but intelligence, open-mindedness, and utter dedication to his Society outweighed any inclination to cling to old ways. There was, however, little sense of urgency. Thus, in 1958 concern was expressed about investment policy: the essential but temporary allocation of funds which would eventually be distributed. Five years later this was still guided by the very elderly Ricketts, wedded to traditional procedures in an age of inflation. In 1965 investment was finally taken in hand by profess-ionals.[49]

At about the same time a number of officials who had devoted the greater part of their lives to the Society were handing over to a younger generation. Charles James and Leonard Walter withdrew as Consultant Directors. Other retirements included the Secretary, Victor Tucker, who had begun as an accountant in 1919, and William Long, who joined in 1922 and managed broadcasting distributions for several decades. During the early seventies the pace of change was beginning to accelerate. There was talk of constitutional reform, and unprecedented consultations with the members. Categories of mem-bership were formalized, and the introduction of annual elections effectively reduced the service of directors from eight to four years.[50] By 1976 Freegard was articulating grievances with clarity and force. 'We will have to find ways of extending franchise', he wrote to Boosey, 'because these days there are quite a lot of young writers in the "pop" world who start to earn substantial sums very quickly, and who get impatient at having to wait for five years before being eligible for full membership'.[51] Reforms in the following year included two rules which indicated how much progress had been achieved: retiring directors were no longer eligible for automatic re-election and, except for the President and Deputy President, they were normally expected to retire at the age of seventy.[52] Agitation and criticism, much of it ill-founded or ill-disposed, lent new urgency to these reappraisals, but

---

[48] PRS Archives, Leslie Boosey memorandum, 21 Aug. 1964.

[49] *Performing Right*, Nov. 1967, 28. PRS Archives, Investment subcommittee minutes, 18 June, 1958.

[50] *Performing Right*, May 1973, 3–4; Oct. 1973, 11–12.

[51] PRS Archives, Freegard to Leslie Boosey, 28 June 1976.

[52] *Performing Right News*, Oct. 1977, 2.

there can be no doubt that they were starting before the muck-raking began. Even information services, the Society's Achilles' heel, were slowly but perceptibly improved. The *Directors' Report and Statement of Accounts* became a little less tight-lipped. *Performing Right* abandoned its dour format and style in 1965 to become an attractive and literate magazine, under the editorship of Eric Crozier, who was also on the Council. Its aspirations to be 'more readable, more varied in its contents, and more distinctive in its appearance' were fully realized during the next few years, but it was not much more informative about the Society than its predecessors.[53] Real improvement began in 1974, when Lesley Bray was appointed as Executive Assistant to the General Manager, with responsibility 'in the field of communications between the Society and its licensees on the one hand, and its members on the other'.[54] The launching of *Performing Right News* in 1976 and *The Performing Right Yearbook* in 1977 enormously improved the Society's dissemination of information. Keeping members and the public 'in the picture' had become, at last, a continuous objective of policy.

[53] *Performing Right*, May 1965.
[54] *Performing Right*, Nov. 1974, 35.

8

PROSPERITY

The last decade has been a period of continuous expansion and prosperity for the Society. Between 1975 and 1985 total income increased more than fourfold, keeping well ahead of inflation: the retail price index approximately trebled during the same period. Gross income, from all sources, had risen to £74.5 million. Net income, available for distribution to members and affiliated societies, was just under £60 million. In 1975 the membership totalled 8,697, of whom 1,221 were full members, 2,902 associates, and 4,574 provisional associates. Ten years later the complement had more than doubled, standing at 19,792, (1 July 1985) and consisting of 2,109 full, 7,850 associate, and 9,833 provisional members. Classified by function, 16,171 were living 'writers' (that is, composers and/or lyricists), 2,436 were publishers, and 1,185 were owners of copyrights, and 'successors' to deceased writers.

These spectacular results did not merely flow, spontaneously, from the production and dissemination of music. They were achieved only by ceaseless vigilance in Berners Street. If the phrase seems unduly dramatic, we should remember the damage done by gentle inflation and inflexible tariffs in earlier times, and imagine what might have happened when prices doubled, between 1975 and 1980. Only constant monitoring, 'indexing', and readjustment of licences could protect the Society's membership against such devastation. Nor was inflation the sole hazard, for nothing affecting the PRS stood still, and the pace of change was ever faster and more bewildering. Relevant developments in technology, law, politics, and the use of music all had to be understood, assessed, and assimilated into policy, if the Society was not to be overwhelmed by late twentieth-century upheaval. The efficient administration of performing right still required knowledge and skills which had always been necessary, in music, law, and accountancy; but it also needed a different kind of professional management, familiar with an ever-expanding catalogue of innovations. Several appointments and promotions consolidated this balance of aptitudes among the Society's senior staff. Gordon Jones became Repertoire Controller, bringing an unrivalled knowledge of popular music, gained in a lifetime of service to the PRS. The Secretary, George Neighbour, was a Cambridge graduate and accomplished

P. R. S. LTD.
Recd. 12-SEP-1934
Ansd.

File No. *A798*

Date of Election *13ᵗʰ September 1934.*

APPLICATION FOR MEMBERSHIP.

(For the use of Composers, Authors, Arrangers, Music Publishers or Copyright Owners wishing to join the Society.)

To the DIRECTORS OF THE PERFORMING RIGHT SOCIETY, LTD.,

Chatham House, 13, George Street, Hanover Square, London, W.1.

GENTLEMEN,

I, ...EDWARD.....BENJAMIN.....BRITTEN.........(give real Name in full)*

Being of........BRITISH.....................Nationality, Writing or Trading under the

Name of ..........BENJAMIN...BRITTEN...

.....(E.B.BRITTEN occasionally)..

....*(give all pen Names used)*

beg to apply as a..........COMPOSER..*(State whether*

as Composer, Author, Arranger, Music Publisher or Copyright Owner).

to be admitted a Member of your Society on the terms of its Memorandum and Articles of Association, and, if admitted, I agree to abide thereby and by its rules and regulations, on condition that in the event of the Society being wound up my contribution for the payment of debts and liabilities of the Society and the costs, charges and expenses of winding up is not to exceed £1.

* *(Firms or Companies should write " We," giving Trading Title, and Applicants should state whether " British " or otherwise.)*

Signed ....*Benjamin Britten*...........................

Address ....21. Kirkley Cliff Road,..............

..................................Lowestoft...............................

Date....*September 11ᵗʰ*.....19*34*.....Suffolk

(This form should be filled up and forwarded to the Secretary of the Society, at the above Address).

Direct to Board 13/9/34
Elected Associate Member that day.

C/36 P 1m. 10-29

1 Application for Membership

2 Founders, 1914

3 'Musical Piracy', 1902 (*Punch*)

4 'Tuppence' by David Low, 1929 (*Evening Standard*)

5 Programme analysis, 1934 (General Programme Analysis Dept.)

6 Data preparation, 1984 (The Punch Room)

7 New offices, 1934

8 Offices, 1984
(the Society's
London
headquarters)

9 Frank Bridge (front right) at a meeting of the Council

10 Presentation by Edward German to Leslie and Mrs Boosey, marking the Society's twenty-first anniversary, 1935

11 (Left to right) Leslie Boosey with Zoltán Kodály and Mr and Mrs Eric Coates in London, 1947

12 Fortieth-anniversary luncheon, 1 July 1954

13 A. P. Herbert and Arthur Bliss

14 CISAC Congress, 1964. Left to right: Sir Frederick Wells, Sir Arthur Bliss, Mr Edward Heath, Mr Albert Willemetz (President CISAC), Professor G. Bodenhausen (Director-General of BIRPI), Mr Claude Masouye (BIRPI)

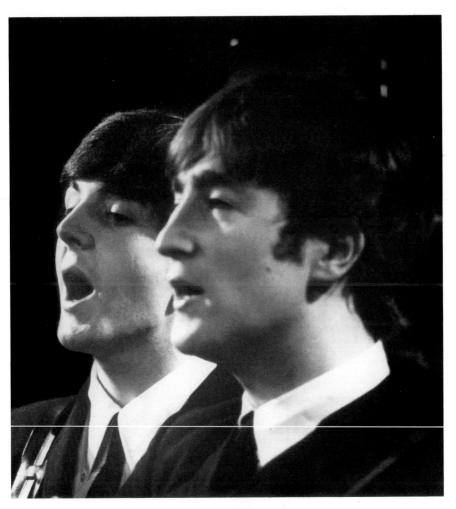

15 Lennon and McCartney, 1964

16 (*above*) Malcolm Arnold,
William Walton, Vivian
Ellis, and Lennox Berkeley,
1975

17 Tune Identification,
1965
(*Daily Mirror*)

"Lucky for you I can't tell
what you're playing."

18 Annual General Meeting, 1978. Background, left to right: George Neighbour, Victor Blake, Michael Freegard, Alan Frank, Lennox Berkeley, Vivian Ellis, Richard Toeman, Steve Race, Bill Ward. Foreground, left to right: Joseph Horovitz, Roger Greenaway, Cyril Simons, Ron White, Tim Rice, John Gardner

19 Roger Greenaway and Vivian Ellis, 1983

20 Eightieth-birthday party for Vivian Ellis, 1984. Back row, left to right: Bill Martin, Andrew Lloyd Webber, John Gardner, Don Black, Howard Blake. Front row, left to right: Roger Greenaway, Vivian Ellis, Mike Batt

21 PRS Members' Fund, 1987. Standing, left to right: Daphne Oram, Michael O'Shea (Assistant Secretary), Brian Willey, Leon Young, Roger Greenaway, Alan Owen, Madeleine Baker (Visitor), Les Britton (Honorary Consultant). Seated, left to right: Hubert W. David, Muriel James (Deputy Chairman), Geoffrey Bush (Chairman), John Logan (Secretary), David Adams. Absent from picture: Geoffrey Brand, Robert Dicker, Gordon Langford, Len Thorpe (appointed October 1987)

22 Members of the General Council and officers, pictured at the General Council Meeting on 21 October 1987. Standing, left to right: Mike Batt, John McCabe, Joseph Horovitz, George Rizza, Christopher Gunning, Peter Barnes, David Dorward, Dennis Collopy, John Brands, Jonson Dyer, Maggie Rodford, Ernest Tomlinson, Michael O'Riordan, Christopher Morris, Brendan Graham, Andrew Potter, Roger Greenaway. Seated, left to right: Anthony Ghilchik (Financial Controller), Brian Wilkinson (Secretary to the General Council), Marshall Lees (Director of Administration), Robert Abrahams (Director of External Affairs), Michael Freegard (Chief Executive), Ron White (Chairman), John Gardner (Joint Deputy Chairman), Donald Mitchell (Joint Deputy Chairman), Cyril Simons, Bill Martin, Wayne Bickerton, Tony Pool. Not present: Vivian Ellis (President), Richard Thomas, Richard Toeman, James Wilson, Ruth Beltram (Secretary of the Society)

choral singer, with immediate recall of any score and every musician. Marshall Lees, an economist and chartered accountant, became Director of Operations, and later Director of Administration, coping, among other things, with the complexities and hectic technical change of data processing. Robert Abrahams was recruited as a special consultant in 1979. A lawyer with a decade of international copyright experience in the record industry, he became Director of External Affairs in 1980. His responsibilities included the Society's relations with major users of music, foreign affiliated societies and, later, with Music Copyright (Overseas) Services Ltd. (described below). He was also in ultimate charge of legal affairs.

Led by Michael Freegard, who was now designated Chief Executive, this team of specialists faced up to a relentless onslaught of necessary preoccupations. The main path of collection and distribution had to be pursued across an obstacle course whose hazards at any time during the 1980s would include some of the following: computers and statistical sampling; cable and satellite television; discos, and the 'demographics' of music use, as adolescent consumption of pop was reinforced by the 'nostalgia market'; piracy and 'bootlegging' at home and abroad; antitrust legislation in the United States; problems arising from developments in the Common Market and the decolonized Third World. Legal complexities and reform greatly increased the burdens of administration. One example was the growing tendency towards 'split copyright': works written by two or more composers, each of whom had contractual relations with a different publisher. Another was a House of Lords decision in 1980 about 'reversionary rights'. This required wholesale revision and redocumentation of the ownership of works by deceased authors. There was also a revision of the Berne Convention in 1971; a new report on copyright law in 1977; several consultative green papers; a white paper, and the prospect of legislation in 1988.[1]

Negotiating such hurdles the team developed policies, to be discussed with a General Council which had, similarly, undergone considerable change. Most of its members were younger and more active than had been common a generation before. Their constituencies, expertise, and life-styles were also far more diverse. Representatives of multinational companies sat with spokesmen for successful pop groups, and leaders of traditional publishing houses. Some writer-directors owed their elevation to pop, others to formal musical education and training. But they still represented the music industry, perhaps more accurately than ever in the past: it was the industry

[1] *Report of the Committee to consider the Law on Copyright and Design* (The Whitford Committee—Cmnd. 6732, 1977). *Intellectual Property and Innovation* (Cmnd.9712, 1986)

which had changed. In the musical world of the late twentieth century, a television jingle could earn far more than a major work, and rival film composers could contest plagiarism in a court where no one, including the composers, was able to read a note of music, with the sole exception of the judge. More than the marvels of technology, perhaps, it was such commonplaces, stemming from its dominance, which would have surprised the Society's founding fathers. Though Charles Volkert would have recalled much conservatory-bred poverty, and Fred Day have remembered Irving Berlin's musical illiteracy (and F sharp piano playing!) they might both have been even more startled by the new, comparatively open, relationship of Council and management to members and the general public. Proceedings and decisions were now subject to scrutiny. Annual General Meetings, to which the press was invited, could no longer be relied upon to be docile and ill attended. Reports and Accounts were detailed and informative. Criticism, comment, and debate were generally spontaneous, and often searching.

Licences, Computers, and Psephology

Licensing continued to be the 'sharp end' of PRS policy. Its victory over inflation has already been noted, and though it would be tedious to enumerate the many renegotiations of tariffs which made this possible their importance is self-evident. There were also several new developments, at home and abroad. A significant break with past practice on the home front was the introduction of licensing for record and music shops in 1976. They had always been exempt because demonstration of records was infrequent, and usually confined to prospective buyers, in sound-proof booths. Now they were played continuously for the entertainment of everyone in the shop, which was licensed accordingly. An attempt to challenge this policy in court was unsuccessful, and the new tariff became a useful source of revenue.[2] Meanwhile, music was spreading throughout retailing. In 1975 fees from shops and stores still amounted to little more than 1 per cent of total British royalties. Ten years later they contributed more than 9 per cent of a total which had increased threefold. As a trade paper advised its readers, 'taped music is an essential part of any shop'.[3]

Since the use of music continued to grow and change apace, Ernest Ford's successors had to follow his example of making continuous checks and reappraisals. Under Bob Strangeways, who retired in 1972

---

[2] *Performing Right Society Ltd.* v. *Harlequin Record Shops,* 17 Jan. 1979.
[3] *Convenience Store,* 14 June, 1985.

after forty-six years on the staff, followed by Marshall Lees, and then Mike Hudson, who took over in 1979, the licensing department continued to expand and monitor new patterns and locations of music use. Operations in Ireland were centralized by establishing a Dublin office in 1977; and an Edinburgh office was opened in 1984. Field staff were doubled in a decade. How effective was their surveillance? In 1965 Ernest Ford, with 100,000 licences on his books, had given up forecasting possible saturation. By 1985 the total number of licences had doubled, and independent surveys suggested further potential. In 1986 the Society initiated a tougher policy towards infringement, charging an additional 50 per cent for the first year of licences where no application had been made. After press announcements of the new rule there were 3,000 immediate applications for new licences.

Licensing in the new Commonwealth was another field of rapid change and reform. Originally this vast area was part of the Imperial copyright system created by the 1911 Act; and the Society's work was carried out by agents who reported directly to the London office. The end of Empire brought a confusing diversity. Some countries enacted their own copyright legislation; others adopted the United Kingdom 1956 Act, and a few kept to the 1911 statute. The PRS encouraged the formation of local societies, as it had done in the old Commonwealth. APRA in Australasia, CAPAC in Canada, and SAMRO in South Africa, had all begun as local agencies of the Society and grown into autonomous institutions. The PRS helped to establish the Indian Performing Right Society in 1969, and later rendered similar assistance in Kenya, Zimbabwe, Trinidad, Nigeria, and Singapore. In 1977 Music Copyright (Overseas) Services Ltd. was set up as an additional way of supporting overseas agencies. It was a small, non-profit-making company, with PRS directors on its board, and administered by Denis de Freitas, who added to his copyright expertise the experience of having been Solicitor General to the West Indies Federation. The activities of MCOS were by no means peripheral to the Society's main concerns, for 'mediaization', and the need to protect intellectual property, knew no barriers of politics or culture.[4]

Continuous processing of information, 'the census of music', remained at the centre of the Society's operations. As the quantity and complexity of data increased, labour costs rose steeply, exacerbated by raging inflation. There were only two ways of controlling this expenditure: by using computers and statistical sampling. But both

---

[4] On 'mediaization', see Roger Wallis and Krister Malm, *Big Sounds from Small Peoples: The Music Industry in Small Countries* (New York, 1984).

were slow and costly exercises, comparable to 'research and development' in other industries. The punched card system continued to give good service until 1966, but in that year it was upstaged by a glamorous newcomer. Few computers can ever have enjoyed so auspicious an investiture as the PRS machine, which was greeted, in front of television cameras, with an ode by the Vice-President, Sir Alan Herbert.[5] It began:

> Welcome, you wonderful, unnatural toy,
> To this august Society's employ!
> Without your like, it seems this Age can't act:
> No Bank can add—though they can still subtract.

and later continued:

> Who else could calculate how much is written,
> How much is won, by Beatle or by Britten?
> Or reckon justly what the earnings are
> of (A) an organ, (B) a group guitar?

Rising to the occasion, the computer replied in seven stanzas, prompted by Vivian Ellis, beginning:

> A computer's supposed to be neuter,
> But I'm not averse to a suitor
> Because sex, nowadays,
> Comes in all sorts of ways
> And I'd love APH as a tutor.
>
> In computing Sir Alan's attractions
> I've credited many good actions
> On divorce, on the stage,
> On librarians who rage
> And on copyright users' transactions.

and admonishing:

> The Council by me stands corrected;
> My copyright must be protected,
> And that reminds me,
> Has the licensing fee
> For performing this work been collected?

After this bright start the newcomer was set to mundane tasks and began to sulk, as computers were then inclined to do. In a gesture typical of its generation, it sent a bill for £34,946 to a Scarborough publican who had been employing a guitarist for a few hours. A drink

---

[5] The complete verses, by A. P. Herbert and Vivian Ellis, are in *Performing Right*, Oct. 1966, 10–11.

trade paper was not amused.[6] But the machine settled down and began to earn its keep, so that by the late sixties it was estimated to be saving the Society more than £15,000 a year in administration expenses. Beginning with the staff pay roll and simple royalty collections, it was gradually programmed to handle distribution procedures, though this entailed the purchase of more 'wonderful toys', including a key-processing system, then the largest of its kind in Central London.[7] The Everest it had still to conquer was programme analysis. At the time of the Queen's award, some three million items were being logged every year, by a staff of 150. The repertoire index contained approximately two million titles, of which 250,000 were 'active'. Programming computers to process this material was a slow, hazardous, and expensive operation. By the early 1980s there was progress in assembling a data base, as a first step to providing all the advantages of storage, immediate accessibility, and rapid manipulation of information which became part of the new environment: at Copyright House, as in society at large. In 1985 a Planet communications network was installed, with 70 terminals, later increased to 400. It gave access to a repertoire of 500,000 active works, and licence fees from 200,000 premises. For the PRS the successful assimilation of this technology was comparable to the 'Big Bang' in City finance.

Statistical sampling was less glamorous and expensive than computing, but also of great potential benefit. A crude experiment had been tried, with ENSA concerts in 1945, when only a proportion of programmes could be analysed because of staff shortages. But serious attention was not given to sampling until the sixties, when BBC local radio began and it soon became apparent that complete logging of the output from twenty stations would cost more than could be earned in revenue. Full analysis was therefore replaced by random sampling after six months.[8] When commercial local radio began, the Society faced an avalanche of information: a vast number of performances over and above the million or so pieces of music and jingles played each year on national radio and television. Since local transmissions paid far less to the Society than national broadcasts, a system of sampling had to be adopted quickly, with as much accuracy as statisticians could devise. An expert study was commissioned, and procedures established to make the sample 'as unbiased and representative of all music played on local radio as is humanly possible within reasonable cost limits'.[9] These necessary models, or

[6] *Morning Advertiser*, 3 Nov. 1967.
[7] *Performing Right*, May 1969, 5–6; Nov. 1970, 21.
[8] *Performing Right*, Nov. 1971, 17; *Supplement*, Oct. 1973.
[9] *Performing Right News*, July 1977, 2.

simulations, of realities which had become too large and complex to handle, were pointers to future imperatives; but they inevitably caused disquiet among some members who feared that performances of their work were not being correctly monitored. Reconciliation to the new procedures came both from their improvement, and from a more general understanding and acceptance of statistical techniques in society at large. Market research, public opinion polls, and most notably, the analysis of voting patterns by 'psephologists' became familiar to the general public.

The link was surely close, for the PRS was very much concerned with the psephology of music, registering a special kind of voting behaviour. But no matter how much technical and statistical ingenuity became available to the Society, there always remained a need for human knowledge and ingenuity; for what kind of machine could interpret a reported 'Kodaly. Buttocks pressing song' as 'Could I but express in song'?[10]

Prosperity, Disparity, and Welfare

It will surprise no one to learn that the benefits of success were unevenly spread. Millionaire pop stars and pauper musicians are the industry's most potent images. Attempts to describe the spread of incomes more accurately run into two difficulties. Familiar is the need to respect privileged information, always a necessary priority in the PRS. Equally important is the fact that most musicians have always had to make their living from a number of different activities.[11] Even the frankest disclosure of individual performing right fees could therefore not be equated with incomes. Nevertheless the Society has been willing in recent years to be a little more explicit about these matters than in the coy days of *Radio and the Composer* (See pp. 80–4).

In 1986 the distribution of fees to writer members was as follows: 72 per cent of them received less than £250; 13 per cent between £250 and £1,000; 9 per cent between £1,000 and £5,000; 2 per cent between £5,000 and £10,000; and 4 per cent more than £10,000. A cursory reading of newspapers, in an age of aggressively inquisitive journalism, will suggest that some of the high earners commanded annual fees far in excess of £10,000. More surprising is the fact that a few serious musicians had joined the front rank, through long-established, wide-ranging eminence, and because their talent had become attached to some particularly remunerative sector of the music

---

[10] Performing Right, Oct. 1968, 22.

[11] On the implications of 'piecing together' a living, see Cyril Ehrlich, *The Music Profession in Britain Since the Eighteenth Century* (1985), 39–42, and 174–6.

industry. Further down the scale there were a number of composers, working in various styles, who earned good fees. Both the fortunate few and the prosperous middle group were new to the industry. This state of affairs was a remarkable improvement, not merely on Crabbe's 'Feed the musician and he's out of tune', but on conditions in Coleridge-Taylor's day, just before the establishment of the PRS. It is one of several yardsticks for measuring the Society's achievement, provided its application is correctly timed. The following statement by McFarlane, for example, is true in substance, but anachronistic: 'the successful composer of popular works could earn a fortune in a matter of months from performing right royalties. Perhaps more important, the composer of serious music could now in a number of cases expect to live by his work'.[12] Everything depends upon the date attached to that judgement. If, as the context suggests, McFarlane believes it to be true by 1939, it cannot be accepted. Prosperity was cause for celebration at the Society's seventy-fifth, not at its twenty-fifth, birthday.

What of the less privileged and the casualties? No calling is more precarious than music, and no organization can do much to alter this; but the Society's recent prosperity has provided more opportunities for cushioning than was ever possible in the past. Some initiatives, like the Members' Fund, were simply and disinterestedly benign in purpose; others were concerned with redistributing income to balance need and fashion, culture and commerce. All were manifestations of the coalition spirit, for how better should the Society justify its existence than by looking after its own? The Members' Fund grew out of the old Benevolent Fund (see p. 101), its purpose to relieve distress, its benevolence constrained, its administration dedicated, scrupulous, and humane. Special mention should be made of Bill Ward, who served on the management committee for twenty-three years, and was Chairman from 1964 until 1981. By 1986 the Fund was able to make grants, mostly in the form of weekly allowances, amounting to more than £40,000; and to allocate more than £18,000 in loans, for temporary emergencies. It established a network of visitors to keep in touch with beneficiaries, and began to make plans for sheltered housing. Part of its income came from the legacies of deceased members, among whom were several figures who have appeared in this narrative, including Ketèlbey and W. H. Squire.[13]

Methods of redistributing income within the Society had been discussed, at least since the 1920s, when there was talk about

---

[12] Gavin McFarlane, *Copyright: The Development and Exercise of the Performing Right* (1980), 145.

[13] See recent copies of *Performing Right Yearbook* and *PRS Members' Fund Report and Accounts*.

compensating 'serious work', as against 'commercial music'. It was also a policy long established by CISAC that societies should give preferential treatment to serious works when distributing royalties, usually by means of paying more per minute for longer works. (It was said that Webern got short shrift!) In Britain the 'points' system worked in this direction, and 'awards' were sometimes made to composers whose financial returns were thought to be incommensurate with their reputation or status. After many experiments, assistance to serious music eventually took two forms. While fees from broadcasting were 'weighted' by the length of a work, live concerts and recitals were subsidized from general revenue. The latter were allocated points, according to a work's duration, its instrumentation, and the seating capacity of the hall where it was played. Thus, in 1985 a thirty-minute work for full orchestra, performed in the Royal Festival Hall, earned £208; and a string quartet of similar length played in the Purcell Room received £91.[14]

Further assistance to serious music came in the form of outside donations, most of which supported its composition, performance, or recording. This was a real break with the past. In 1947 Executive Committee rejected a request for help from the London Contemporary Music Centre, on the grounds that it would be 'unconstitutional', set a bad precedent, and was essentially 'a matter for publishers of serious music'.[15] Thirty years later the Society could afford to be more generous. Some £20,000 was handed out to forty musical organizations; and grants of £1,000 were allocated to four institutions for outstanding young musicians.[16] By 1986 musical donations amounted to nearly £160,000, and the list of recipients filled a double-columned page. There were also several scholarships and awards, including Arthur Bliss and John Lennon Scholarships, and the Vivian Ellis workshop and prize for young writers of musicals, which was inaugurated to celebrate the eightieth birthday of the Society's President.

Redistribution of income was not simply a matter of making minor adjustments between pops and classics. Many of the poorest members of the Society in recent times were composers of outmoded 'popular' music, few of whom had enjoyed consistently good incomes, even at the height of their powers, as Jimmy Kennedy once argued on their behalf (see pp. 116–17). Similar distress was to be found among composers of light music whose style could not be adapted to new requirements. An attempt to bring succour came in 1969, when a system of 'cushioning', later called 'earnings equalization', was

[14] *Performing Right Yearbook* (1987–8), 89–90.
[15] PRS Archives, Executive Committee minutes, 4 Dec. 1947.
[16] For details see *Performing Right Yearbook* (1978), 34–5.

introduced, to be financed from part of the Society's investment income. Its original stated purpose was 'to ensure, *as of right*, the maintenance in future of a certain minimum standard of income for members whose works have contributed substantially to the Society's active repertoire in the past but which, because of changes in musical taste, have ceased to be performed to the same extent'.[17] Elaborate in conception, its high ambitions were vulnerable both to the irrevocable change in popular music, and, like many pension arrangements, to the burdens of inflation and an ageing population. But the Society's burgeoning prosperity kept the scheme afloat. In 1972 an average supplement of £170 was paid to 368 eligible members.[18] By 1978 the total sum being distributed had more than doubled. Publishers' shares of investment income, which had previously been excluded from the scheme, were now added to the fund.[19] By the mid-eighties 'earnings equalization' was demonstrating the benefits to be gained from sustained growth. In 1983 payments were being calculated at 50 per cent of the difference between an individual's past earnings and current earnings, subject to a maximum payment of £1,512. That maximum was received by seventy members. A total of 445 writer-members qualified for the scheme, receiving average payments of £788.[20] In 1986 the maximum payment rose to £1,767 (paid to 78 members) and 468 received an average of £944.[21]

Leslie Boosey died in 1979, departing with a typically quixotic and last-minute failure of public recognition. A petition on his behalf had just been signed by distinguished men of music and the arts, but it was too late.[22] He was mourned by the Society, which still remembered him as its exemplar a decade later, chief architect of an institution which, as it approached a seventy-fifth birthday, continued to serve the general public no less than its members. The former were provided with access to the world's music, easily and cheaply, while giving due reward to its producers. Among the members there was general satisfaction with the Society: an efficient alliance of interests, maintaining a reasonable balance between writers and publishers, serious and popular music. It had begun so in 1914, stumbled in 1919, recovered in 1926, and then survived every upheaval described in these pages, resilient and prosperous.

[17] *Performing Right*, Oct. 1969, 8–9.
[18] *Performing Right*, Oct. 1973, 3.
[19] *Performing Right News*, June 1979, 4.
[20] *Performing Right Yearbook* (1984–5), 25.
[21] *Performing Right Yearbook* (1987–8), 27.
[22] PRS Archives, Letter to Lennox Berkeley, Lord Drogheda, Vivian Ellis, Denis de Freitas, Lord Goodman, Lord Harewood, Anthony Lewis, John Tooley, David Willcocks, and Malcolm Williamson, 6 Sept. 1979.

APPENDIX I

PRS *Membership*

	Year-end No. of members		Year-end No. of members
1915	199	1951	2,493
1916	234	1952	2,576
1917	297	1953	2,657
1918	386	1954	2,753
1919	437	1955	2,835
1920	435	1956	2,934
1921	459	1957	3,030
1922	491	1958	3,100
1923	526	1959	3,239
1924	557	1960	3,370
1925	564	1961	3,392
1926	855	1962	3,442
1927	924	1963	3,504
1928	932	1964	3,564
1929	963	1965	3,715
1930	1,029	1966	3,934
1931	1,061	1967	4,126
1932	1,105	1968	4,442
1933	1,161	1969	4,688
1934	1,205	1970	5,053
1935	1,374	1971	5,460
1936	1,517	1972	6,126
1937	1,633	1973	6,908
1938	1,790	1974	7,788
1939	1,861	1975	8,697
1940	1,894	1976	9,458
1941	1,894	1977	10,536
1942	1,925	1978	11,870
1943	1,961	1979	12,611
1944	2,002	1980	13,462
1945	2,062	1981	14,715
1946	2,104	1982	16,142
1947	2,175	1983	17,919
1948	2,266	1984	19,150
1949	2,338	1985	20,712
1950	2,416	1986	21,085

TABLE 2

Gross and Net Income 1915–1986

Year	Total Gross Income £'000	Domestic General £'000	%	Broadcasting £'000	%	Overseas Agencies £'000	%	Affiliated Societies £'000	%	Interest etc. £'000	%	Total Net Income[a] £'000
1915[b]	4											2
1920[b]	23											14
1925[b]	43											31
1930[b]	173											144
1935	346	153	44	135	39	19	5	32	9	7	2	300
1940	619	175	28	337	54	55	9	34	5	18	3	568
1945	858	316	37	420	49	61	7	40	5	21	2	794
1950	1,495	482	32	636	43	78	5	270	18	29	2	1,332
1955	2,444	584	24	903	37	152	6	747	31	58	2	2,189
1960	3,296	880	27	1,453	44	211	6	661	20	91	3	2,864
1965	5,612	1,527	27	1,961	35	218	4	1,743	31	163	3	4,878
1970	9,127	2,386	26	2,605	29	284	3	3,601	39	251	3	7,927
1975	17,181	3,773	22	5,948	35	447	3	6,379	37	634	4	14,597
1980	39,342	10,520	27	16,374	42	402	1	9,441	24	2,605	7	32,523
1985	74,487	18,031	24	27,862	37	409	1	24,220	33	3,965	5	59,788
1986	85,283	21,115	25	33,099	39	629	1	26,450	31	3,990	5	69,440

[a] Total Net Income is the surplus for the year of Total Gross Income over licensing and administration expenses and tax, after transfers from or to distributable reserves, and deduction of other amounts appropriated.

[b] No breakdown available.

TABLE 3

Gross and Net Income 1915–1986, in 1986 prices[a]

Year	Total Gross Income £'000	Domestic General £'000	%	Broadcasting £'000	%	Overseas Agencies £'000	%	Affiliated Societies £'000	%	Interest etc. £'000	%	Total Net Income[b] £'000
1915[c]	113											56
1920[c]	320											195
1925[c]	847											610
1930[c]	3,793											3,157
1935	8,398	3,713	44	3,277	39	461	5	777	9	170	2	7,281
1940	9,790	2,768	28	5,330	54	870	9	538	5	285	3	8,983
1945	11,300	4,162	37	5,532	49	803	7	527	5	277	2	10,457
1950	16,206	5,225	32	6,894	43	846	5	2,927	18	314	2	14,439
1955	21,385	5,110	24	7,902	37	1,330	6	6,537	31	508	2	19,155
1960	25,905	6,916	27	11,420	44	1,658	6	5,195	20	715	3	22,510
1965	37,083	10,090	27	12,958	35	1,441	4	11,518	31	1,077	3	32,233
1970	48,182	12,596	26	13,752	29	1,499	3	19,010	39	1,325	3	41,847
1975	49,185	10,801	22	17,028	35	1,280	3	18,262	37	1,815	4	41,788
1980	57,573	15,395	27	23,962	42	588	1	13,816	24	3,812	7	47,594
1985	77,042	18,650	24	28,818	37	423	1	25,051	33	4,101	5	61,839
1986	85,283	21,115	25	33,099	39	629	1	26,450	31	3,990	5	69,440

[a] All Figures adjusted by reference to index of retail prices.
[b] As defined in Table 2.
[c] No details available.

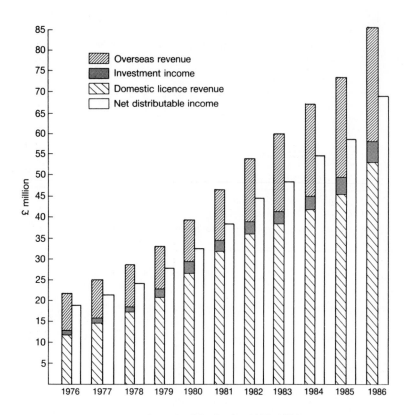

FIGURE I. *Growth of the Society 1976–1986*

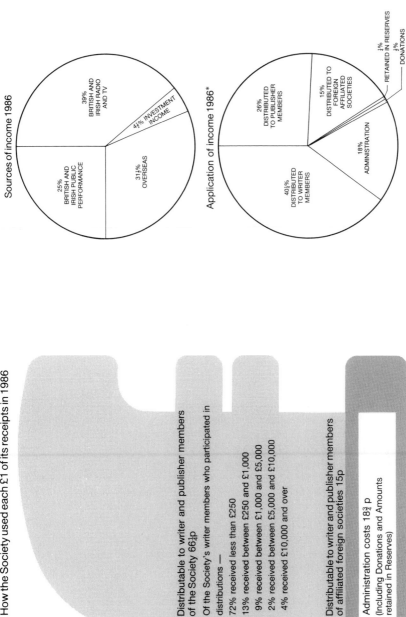

Sources of income 1986

39% BRITISH AND IRISH RADIO AND TV

4¼% INVESTMENT INCOME

25% BRITISH AND IRISH PUBLIC PERFORMANCE

31⅓% OVERSEAS

Application of income 1986*

26% DISTRIBUTED TO PUBLISHER MEMBERS

15% DISTRIBUTED TO FOREIGN AFFILIATED SOCIETIES

⅓% RETAINED IN RESERVES

⅓% DONATIONS

40⅓% DISTRIBUTED TO WRITER MEMBERS

18% ADMINISTRATION

*with split of Distributions as 1985, the latest year available in full

How the Society used each £1 of its receipts in 1986

Distributable to writer and publisher members of the Society 66½p

Of the Society's writer members who participated in distributions —

72% received less than £250
13% received between £250 and £1,000
9% received between £1,000 and £5,000
2% received between £5,000 and £10,000
4% received £10,000 and over

Distributable to writer and publisher members of affiliated foreign societies 15p

Administration costs 18¾ p
(Including Donations and Amounts retained in Reserves)

FIGURE 2. *Sources and Applications of Income*

TABLE 4

Performing Right Earnings of Four Composers (£)

	Frank Bridge	Montague Ewing	Gustav Holst	Arnold Ketèlbey
1927	126	60	31	468
1930	168	223	119	1,630
1935	295	635	407	2,733
1940	605	1,120	648	3,493
1945	476	797	897	2,577
1950	956	1,005	1,704	2,906
1955	781	2,185	6,546	3,641
1960	569	838	4,563	3,168
1965	865	882	8,616	5,221
1970	1,482	1,679	13,027	5,269
1975	3,218	1,256	31,590	7,470
1980	17,220	1,857	58,080	12,061
1985	18,582	4,177	134,035	21,079

Grateful acknowledgement for permission to publish these figures is made to the Musicians' Benevolent Fund, the PRS Members' Fund, and the trustees of Frank Bridge and Gustav Holst. The latter wish to state that 'the substantial increase in royalty earnings in the past twenty years has been primarily due to the incorporation of the company G. and I. Holst Ltd., which made it possible for Imogen Holst, in the last fifteen years of her life, to devote herself mainly to her father's interest'.

APPENDIX II

1851 French performing right society established.

1882 Copyright (Musical Compositions) Act: first attempt to stop Harry Wall's activities.
Italian performing right society established.

1886 International Copyright Conference and Convention at Berne.

1888 Copyright (Musical Compositions) Act: second attempt to stop Wall.

1897 Austrian performing right society established.

1901 Spanish performing right society established.

1902 Musical (Summary Proceedings) Copyright Act: attempt to curb piracy.

1903 German performing right society established.

1906 Musical Copyright Act: curbs piracy.

1908 Berlin Revision of the Berne Convention.

1909 Gorell Committee on Copyright (Cd. 4976): William Boosey a member; Pierre Sarpy gives evidence.

1911 Copyright Act.

1913 23 December: Agreement to establish The Authors', Composers' and Music Publishers' Society.
Netherlands performing right society established.

1914 6 March: The Performing Right Society Ltd. registered as 'a Company limited by guarantee and not having a share capital'.
1 April: First Annual General Meeting of PRS.
ASCAP established (first USA performing right society).

1915 February: Death of Pierre Sarpy.
PRS has 199 members.
Total gross income £4,051.

1916 234 members.

1917 First distribution of fees (nearly £11,000 for the three years ending April 1917).

1918 386 members.
PRS v. *Thompson*: first contested action for infringement (Atkin judgement).
Polish performing right society established.

1919 437 members.
Resignation of 'popular' publishers and their composers.
Czechoslovak and Uruguyan performing right societies established.

1920   Total gross income £22,468.

1921   *Performing Right Society Ltd.* v. *Bradford Corporation* (1917–23 Macg. Cop. Cas. 309): a local authority is liable for performances given on premises in its possession and control.

1922   July: *Performing Right Gazette* begins publication.
        November: BBC begins broadcasting.
        Belgian performing right society established.

1923   526 members.
        18 October: First PRS licence issued to the BBC.
        Swedish and Swiss performing right societies established.

1924   New members include Arnold Bax (Director 1945), Arthur Bliss (Dir. 1947, President 1953), Frank Bridge (Dir. 1926), Frederick Delius, John Ireland (Dir. 1926), Roger Quilter, and Cyril Scott.
        5,487 licences.

1925   562 members.
        Gross income £42,880.
        Agencies opened in South Africa.
        Frank Bridge joins the Committee.
        New members include A. A. Milne and Hamilton Harty.
        Canadian and Portuguese performing right societies established.

1926   'Popular' publishers rejoin the Society.
        855 members.
        Leslie Boosey joins the Board of Directors.
        After successful proceedings against unauthorized performance of copyright music on board an ocean-going liner, sixteen shipping companies take up PRS licences for 125 vessels.
        New members include Gustav Holst.
        CISAC established (Confédération Internationale des Sociétés d'Auteurs et Compositeurs).
        Australian and Danish performing right societies established.
        Reciprocal relations reopened with the Austrian and German performing right societies.

1927   924 members.
        New members include Edward Elgar.

1928   Rome revision of the Berne Convention.
        New members include Julius Harrison and Marjorie Kennedy-Fraser.
        Finnish performing right society established.
        Messager v. *The British Broadcasting Corporation* (1929 AC 151): the broadcasting of a work is a public performance under the Copyright Act 1911.

1929   William Boosey retires as Chairman of the Board of Directors and is succeeded by Leslie Boosey.
        Charles James becomes General Manager.
        1 November: 'Tuppenny Bill' introduced into the House of Commons as

a Private Member's Bill by W. M. Adamson, and supported by five other Labour Members ('A Bill to Amend the Law relating to the Right of Public Representation or Performance of Copyright Music').

4 December: A. P. Herbert publishes 'Why Twopence' in *Punch*.

11 December: Appointment of Select Committee on the Musical Copyright Bill.

New members include Rutland Boughton and Rupert D'Oyly Carte.

Norwegian performing right society established.

1930 July: Report of Select Committee on the Musical Copyright Bill: effectively killing the 'Tuppenny Bill'
1,029 members.
Gross income £173,443.
Greek performing right society established.

1931 Widows, children, and personal representatives of deceased members become eligible for membership of the Society.
SESAC established in the USA to administer performing rights in addition to ASCAP.

1932 Members' Assistance Fund set up (subsequently described as the 'Benevolent Fund', and later as the 'PRS Members' Fund').

1933 New category of Associate Membership created.
New members include Havergal Brian and Bud Flanagan.
Performing Right Society Ltd. v. *Hawthorns Hotel (Bournemouth) Ltd.* (1933 1 Ch. 855): the playing of music in the lobby of a hotel is a public performance.

1934 16 July: The Society's new offices opened by Sir Edward German at Copyright House, 33 Margaret Street, London W1.
New members include Arthur Benjamin, Noel Coward, A. P. Herbert (Vice-President 1966), E. J. Moeran, and Alec Templeton.
Leslie Boosey becomes Chairman of the Members' Fund.
Performing Right Society Ltd. v. *Hammonds Bradford Brewery Ltd.* (1934 Ch. 121): even if there is a performance in a broadcasting studio, there is a separate performance given by the receiving set and loudspeaker in a hotel.

1935 1,374 members.
Gross income £346,329.
New members include Walford Davies, Howard Ferguson, Harry Lauder, and William Walton (Dir. 1946).
Mexican performing right society established.

1936 Several publishers join the Society, including Novello, Oxford University Press, and Stainer and Bell.
Ullswater Report on Broadcasting (Cmd. 5091) recommends more generous treatment of creative artists.
New members include Richard Addinsell (Dir. 1957), William Alwyn (Dir. 1951), Lennox Berkeley (Dir. 1957, President 1975), Benjamin Britten (Dir. 1953), Alan Bush, Hubert Clifford, George Dyson, Eric

Fenby, Gerald Finzi, Imogen Holst, Gordon Jacob, Elizabeth Maconchy, Eric Maschwitz (Dir. 1952), Jack Payne, Alan Rawsthorne, Rabindranath Tagore, Phyllis Tate, and Henry J. Wood.
Argentine and Israeli performing right societies established.
Performing Right Society Ltd. v. *Camelo* (1936 3 All ER 557): a performance in private which can be heard in public premises is a public performance.
Jennings v. *Stephens* (1936 1 All ER 409): even if a performance is shown in the presence only of members of a private club and their guests, it will be a public performance. The criterion for a private performance is whether the audience is of a domestic or quasi-domestic nature.

1937   Arbitration awards PRS large increase in BBC tariff.
First distribution of television fees.
New members include Arnold Dolmetsch, Constant Lambert, Walter de la Mare, Edmund Rubbra, and Mátyás Seiber.

1938   New members include Béla Bartók, Lord Berners, and Zoltán Kodály.

1939   New members include John Gardner (Dir. 1965), Walter Goehr, Berthold Goldschmidt, Elizabeth Lutyens, Hans May, Gregor Piatigorsky, Kurt Roger, Miklós Rózsa, Joseph Szigeti, Robert Stolz, and Egon Wellesz.
Japanese performing right society established.

1940   1,894 members.
Gross income £619,076.
23 June: 'Music While You Work' first broadcast.
BMI established in the USA to administer performing rights in addition to ASCAP and SESAC.

1941   New members include Ronald Binge (Dir. 1969).

1942   Brazilian performing right society established.

1943   New members include Benjamin Frankel, Joyce Grenfell, and Michael Tippett.
Moroccan performing right society established.
Performing Right Society Ltd. v. *Gillette Industries Ltd.* and *Ernest Turner Electrical Instruments Ltd.* v. *Performing Right Society Ltd.* (1943 1 All ER 413): 'music while you work' in a factory is a public performance.

1944   2,002 members.
New members include Nicholas Medtner, Priaulx Rainier, and Oscar Strauss.

1945   2,062 members.
Gross income £857,986.

1946   7 June: BBC television transmissions restart.
29 Sept: BBC Third programme begins.
New members include Sydney Torch (Dir. 1958).
William Grice becomes Secretary of the Members' Fund.
Colombian performing right society established.

1947 PRS hosts first Congress of CISAC to be held in Europe since the war.

1948 Brussels revision of the Berne Convention.
New members include Richard Arnell and Malcolm Arnold (Dir. 1964).
Icelandic performing right society established.

1949 New members include Peter Racine Fricker and Steve Race (Dir. 1964).

1950 2,416 members.
Gross income £1,494,611.
New members include Eric Crozier (Dir. 1963), and Ernest Tomlinson (Dir. 1965).
Yugoslav performing right society established.

1951 New members include Adrian Cruft and Graham Whettam.
GDR and Paraguayan performing right societies established.

1952 Gregory Committee Report on Copyright (Cmnd. 8662).
Gerald Hatchman becomes General Manager, and is then succeeded by Leonard Walter.
New members include Charles Chaplin, T. S. Eliot, Alun Hoddinott, Joseph Horovitz (Dir. 1969), and Harry Mortimer.
John Pinfold becomes Secretary of the Members' Fund.
Peruvian performing right society established.

1953 British Joint Copyright Council established.
New members include Donald Swann.
Hungarian performing right society established.

1954 Sir Arthur Bliss becomes President.
New members include Michael Flanders and Tony Hiller (Dir. 1980).

1955 2,835 members.
Gross income £2,443,726.
22 Sept: Independent television begins.
New members include Tristram Cary, Cecil Day Lewis, Thea Musgrave, and Edith Sitwell.
Venezuelan and Chilean performing right societies established.

1956 New members include John Dankworth, Anthony Milner, and Robert Simpson.

1957 3,030 members.
1 June: New Copyright Act comes into operation.
The Performing Right Tribunal set up.
New members include Lionel Bart, Alexander Goehr, Humphrey Lyttelton, Wilfred Josephs (Dir. 1980), George Martin, and Richard Rodney Bennett (Dir. 1975).
Robert Elkin becomes Chairman of the Members' Fund.

1959 In its first decision the newly established Performing Right Tribunal reduces the proposed PRS tariff for commercial dance halls (PRT 1/58).
Egyptian performing right society established.

1960   The Performing Right Tribunal approves the PRS tariff for juke-boxes (PRT 5/60).
3,370 members.
Gross income £3,295,502.
30 May: New Copyright House opened in Berners Street.
New members include Don Black.

1961   New members include Tony Hatch, Benny Hill, and William Mathias.
South African performing right society established.

1962   New members include Nicholas Maw (Dir. 1981).

1963   The Performing Right Tribunal approves the PRS tariff for bingo sessions in cinemas, ballrooms, etc. (PRT 11/62).
New members include John Lennon, Paul McCartney, and Geoff Stephens.

1964   PRS celebrates its fiftieth anniversary, and hosts the twenty-third congress of CISAC.
The Performing Right Tribunal reduces the proposed new PRS tariffs for popular concerts, and for performances at municipal and other local authority premises (PRT 13/63 & 14/63).
Royce Whale becomes General Manager.
Denis de Freitas appointed as Legal Adviser.
28 Mar: Radio Caroline (pirate radio) begins to broadcast.
New members include Ray Davies, Mick Jagger, Bill Martin, (Dir. 1977), Northern Songs Ltd., and Keith Richards.
Bill Ward becomes Chairman of the Members' Fund.

1965   3,715 members.
Gross income £5,611,634.
Lease of Copyright House purchased.
New members include Harrison Birtwistle, Carl Davis, Roger Greenaway (Dir. 1976, Chairman 1983), George Harrison, Dudley Moore, and Ronald Stevenson.

1966   The Performing Right Tribunal rejects the Society's application for an increase in its tariff for popular concerts, and reduces its proposed new tariff for variety shows (PRT 20/66 & 21/66).
Inauguration of first PRS computer.
New members include Howard Blake (Dir. 1978), Derek Bourgeois, Faber Music Ltd., Christopher Logue, Tony Macauley, John McCabe (Dir. 1985), and Ringo Starr.

1967   Stockholm revision of the Berne Convention.
The Performing Right Tribunal's decision in a dispute between the PRS and the BBC leads to representations by the Society for reform of the Tribunal (PRT 22/67).
4,126 members.
Leslie Boosey retires as Chairman of General and Executive Councils, and is succeded by J. G. O. Roberts.

30 Sept: BBC Radio 1 begins.
New members include Barry Gibb, Maurice Gibb, Robin Gibb (The Bee Gees), Edmund Grant, and David Bowie.

1968   Laurence Swinyard becomes Chairman of the General and Executive Councils.
New members include Wayne Bickerton, (Dir. 1978), Chris Gunning (Dir. 1983), Oliver Knussen, Ezra Pound, Pete Townshend, proprietors of Hymns Ancient and Modern, Tim Rice (Dir. 1978), John Tavener, and Andrew Lloyd Webber (Dir. 1975).
Tunisian performing right society established.

1969   Michael Freegard becomes General Manager.
New members include Eric Clapton and Chrysalis Music Ltd.
Indian performing right society established.

1970   5,053 members.
Gross income £9,127,395.
New members include Nicola Lefanu, Elton John, and George Waters.

1971   Paris revision of the Berne Convention.
The Society receives the Queen's Award to Industry for export achievement.
New members include Mike Batt (Dir. 1978), Phil Collins, Trevor Lyttelton, and Yoko Ono.

1972   Deciding a further dispute between the PRS and the BBC, the Performing Right Tribunal approves the Society's proposal for a royalty based on a percentage of the BBC's revenue, but reduces the percentage proposed (PRT 24/71).
6,126 members.
New members include Georgie Fame and Stomu Yamash'ta.
Senegalese performing right society established.   `

1973   7,788 members.
New members include Joan Armatrading, Lotte Klemperer, Gilbert O'Sullivan, David A. Stewart, Virgin Music (Publishers) Ltd., and Trevor Wishart.
Performing Right Society Ltd. v. *Rangers FC Supporters Club* (1975 RPC 626): confirmed that performance by a band at a football supporters' club is a public performance.
USSR and Algerian performing right societies established.

1974   Leslie Britton becomes Secretary of the Members' Fund.
Bulgarian performing right society established.

1975   Sir Lennox Berkeley becomes President.
Alan Frank becomes Chairman of the General and Executive Councils.
8,697 members.
Gross income £17,180,733.
New members include Marc Feld, Freddy Mercury, and Mike Oldfield.

Performing Right Society Ltd. v. *Marlin Communal Aerials Ltd.* (1977 FSR 51 Supreme Court of Ireland): confirmed the Society's right to license the cable retransmission in Ireland of broadcasts from the UK of works in its repertoire.

1976   9,458 members.
CISAC celebrates its fiftieth anniversary, and awards its Gold Medal to Leslie Boosey.
Performing Right News starts publication.
New members include Melvyn Bragg, Terry Britten, Harold Pinter, and Rodney Temperton.

1977   Whitford Committee Report on Copyright (Cmnd. 6732).
10,536 members.
New Dublin offices opened.
First open forum for all members, Extraordinary General Meeting, and constitutional changes.
Establishment of Music Copyright (Overseas) Services Ltd.
New members include Adam Ant, John Betjeman, Kate Bush, Christopher Hogwood, Alan Plater, Paul Weller, and Victoria Wood.
Hong Kong performing right society established.

1978   The High Court upholds an appeal by PRS against a decision of the Performing Right Tribunal that the latter has jurisdiction to hear a reference brought by the suppliers of background music equipment used for public performances (PRT 30/77: *Reditune Ltd., The Ditchburn Organization Ltd. & Planned Music Ltd.* v. *The Performing Right Society Ltd.*)
11,870 members.
The Performing Right Yearbook starts publication.
New members include Mark Knopfler, and Gordon Sumner (Sting).
Mauritian and Zairean performing right societies established.

1979   5 Sept.: Death of Leslie Boosey.
Richard Toeman becomes Chairman of the General and Executive Councils.
Performing Right Society Ltd. v. *Harlequin Record Shops Ltd.* (1979 FSR 233): confirmed the Society's right to license demonstration performances in record and music shops.
Performing right societies established in Cameroun, Congo, and South Korea.

1980   13,462 members.
Gross income £39,341,612.
Performing right societies established in Guinea, Madagascar, and Mali.

1981   Hubert David becomes Chairman of the Members' Fund.
Ivory Coast and Polynesian performing right societies established.

1982   The High Court rejects an appeal by PRS against a ruling of the Performing Right Tribunal (PRT 38/81) that the latter has jurisdiction to hear a reference brought by the television programme contractors appointed by the Independent Broadcasting Authority (*The Independent Television Companies Association Ltd.* v. *The Performing Right Society Ltd.*).

New members include Ann Lennox and Boy George.

16,142 members.

Zimbabwean performing right society established.

1983   The Performing Right Tribunal rules on a dispute between PRS and the Independent Television Companies' Association, rejecting the Society's proposal for a royalty based on a percentage of net advertising revenue, but awarding greatly increased annual lump sums (PRT 38/81).

Vivian Ellis becomes President.

Roger Greenaway becomes Chairman of the General and Executive Councils.

Kenyan performing right society established.

1984   New Scottish offices opened in Edinburgh.

Nigerian and Trinidadian performing right societies established.

1985   20,712 members.

Gross income £74,487,000.

John Logan becomes Secretary of the Members' Fund.

Sri Lankan performing right society established.

1987   Ron White becomes Chairman of the General and Executive Councils.

Geoffrey Bush becomes Chairman of the Members' Fund.

Singapore performing right society established.

New Copyright, Designs, and Patents Bill introduced into Parliament.

INDEX